CORPORATE IDENTITY

CORPORATE IDENTITY

Making business strategy visible through design

WALLY OLINS

With over 350 illustrations

THAMES AND HUDSON

To Edwina, Rufus, Ben and Harriet

Picture Research by Julia Engelhardt
Designed by Wolff Olins/Hall

Printed in Spain by Artes Graficos Toledo SA
D.L.TO:200-1990

Contents

Introduction 7

CHAPTER 1

The Invention of Tradition 11

CHAPTER 2

The Corporate Search for Identity 27

CHAPTER 3

Visual Style 47

CHAPTER 4

Corporate Structure 77

CHAPTER 5

Corporate Strategy 131

CHAPTER 6

Creating an Identity Programme – The First Stage 147

CHAPTER 7

Creating an Identity Programme – Managing Change 165

CHAPTER 8

Launching and Maintaining an Identity Programme 177

CHAPTER 9

Corporate Identity and the Future 201

Select Bibliography 216

Author's Acknowledgments 218

Illustration Acknowledgements 218

Index 221

Identity: What is it?

In order to be effective every organization needs a clear sense of purpose that people within it understand. They also need a strong sense of belonging.

Purpose and belonging are the two facets of identity.

Every organization is unique, and the identity must spring from the organization's own roots, its personality, its strengths and its weaknesses.

This is as true of the modern global corporation as it has been of any other institution in history, from the Christian church to the nation state.

The identity of the corporation must be so clear that it becomes the yardstick against which its products, behaviour and actions are measured.

This means that the identity cannot simply be a slogan, a collection of phrases: it must be visible, tangible and all-embracing.

Everything that the organization does must be an affirmation of its identity.

The *products* that the company makes or sells must project its standards and its values.

The *buildings* in which it makes things and trades, its offices, factories and showpieces – their location, how they are furnished and maintained – are all manifestations of identity.

The corporation's *communication material*, from its advertising to its instruction manuals, must have a consistent quality and character that accurately and honestly reflect the whole organization and its aims.

All these are palpable, they are visible; they are designed – and that is why design is a significant component in the identity mix.

A further component, which is just as significant although it is not visible, is how the organization *behaves*: to its own staff and to everybody with whom it comes into contact, including customers, suppliers and its host communities. This is especially true in service industries that have no tangible products. Here, too, consistency in attitude, action and style underlines the corporation's identity.

In small companies and in young companies the management of identity is intuitive. It is a direct reflection of the founder's obsessions and interests. The company is what he or she makes it.

In the sprawling, complex corporations with which this book is mostly concerned, where innumerable interests – each supported by individuals – conflict and compete for power and influence, the company's long-term purpose, its values, its identity must be managed consciously and clearly, or they will be overwhelmed and disregarded in sectional infighting. The organization will simply become an inert victim of the various factions that seek to control it.

When companies lose sight of their individuality, their real purpose and strengths, they get deflected – often through peer pressure – into making mistakes. They make inappropriate acquisitions, diversify into blind alleys, make inferior copies of other companies' products.

That is why identity management in major corporations must be the job of the Chief Executive or a senior board member, supported by an in-house team and where appropriate by outside consultants.

Identity is expressed in the names, symbols, logos, colours and rites of passage which the organization uses to distinguish itself, its brands and its constituent companies. At one level, these serve the same purpose as religious symbolism, chivalric heraldry or national flags and symbols: they encapsulate and make vivid a collective sense of belonging and purpose. At another level, they represent consistent standards of quality and therefore encourage consumer loyalty.

Sometimes names and symbols need to be created. Traditions and rites of passage have to be invented and re-invented for corporations, in the same way as they have always been for different regimes in different countries.

The main thrust of this book is to examine the commercial operations of the modern multinational from the point of view of its identity.

The book is concerned with how the visual style of an organization affects its positioning in the market; and how the corporate purpose is made visible through design and behaviour.

An integral part of this process is corporate structure, and how acquisitions can be absorbed, how brands are developed, extended, cultivated. The book examines the fields of communication, advertising, public relations, internal communications, audiences; it looks at purchasing, selling, people development and internal politics.

It takes the view that the corporation's actions are indivisible: that how it behaves, what it says, how it treats people, what it makes and sells are part of a single whole; that everything within the corporation has an effect on everything else; that everyone has an effect on everyone else. It also takes the view that the corporation is, whether it likes it or not, becoming more closely integrated into society, and that society is becoming increasingly judgmental about the behaviour and actions of corporations.

We are entering an epoch in which only those corporations making highly competitive products will survive. This means, in the longer term, that products from the major competing companies around the world will become increasingly similar. Inevitably, this means that the whole of the company's personality, its identity, will become the most significant factor in making a choice between one company and its products and another.

Finally, the book shows how consultants from different backgrounds – design, human resources development, advertising research and public relations – are co-operating and competing to develop this new market opportunity.

It therefore lays out in detail how to create and sustain an identity programme for the long-term health and profitability of the corporation.

CHAPTER **1**

The Invention of Tradition

In everything it produced, including its name, the CSA emulated its admired model, the USA. Thus CSA banknotes were approximately the same size, shape and general design as those of the USA.

In December 1860, South Carolina formally announced its secession from the United States of America. Almost immediately Mississippi, Florida, Alabama, Georgia, Louisiana and Texas followed. A few states from the Upper South joined them. Each of these seceding states could have become, had it wanted, an independent country, but it seemed sensible to unite – or, as they put it, to confederate. Thus the Confederate States of America was born. The CSA, or the Confederacy as it came to be called, soon produced a constitution, a flag, even a Declaration of Independence, all of which were remarkably similar to those of the USA.

Within an extraordinarily short time the CSA had a capital city, Richmond; a Senate; a House of Representatives; an army; and a navy. It issued notes and coins, appointed ambassadors and plenipotentiaries – and it even produced a variety of unofficial anthems.

In all of these things, in almost every respect, the CSA was uncannily like the USA. Of course, there was one fundamental difference between the two countries. The Confederacy wanted independence from the Union because it felt that inside it there was no hope of expanding the slave culture on which its society was based, while the Unionists, or Federals, insisted that the Union was indissoluble.

All of this greatly influenced those building up the Confederacy to move fast. After all, a dangerous precedent had been set. If a state could secede from one union, hitherto believed to be sacrosanct, then it could certainly – and perhaps on more friviolous grounds – secede from another. It became vital, therefore, to create a new nation out of the seceding states, a nation complete with the entire panoply of national symbolism.

And the natural model to choose, the admired model, was the USA.

Within months, almost weeks, the whole structure was born. In the classic phrase first used by Eric Hobsbawm and Terence Ranger in their fascinating book with that title, the Confederates engaged in *The Invention of Tradition* (1983).

In a brilliant series of essays Hobsbawm and Ranger, and their contributors show how throughout history rituals, symbols, visual imagery of different kinds have been invented by nations, sometimes unofficially but quite often as a matter of policy, in order to create new loyalties, obliterate old ones, mark out territories, reinforce ideas and initiate new ways of doing things.

The creation of the Confederacy called for just such action. The men behind the scenes did their work superbly. The symbolism they created was so potent and attractive that much still exists. It's all memorialized, commemorated, institutionalized and highly romanticized by the thriving industry which has grown up around that monumental tragedy, the American Civil War.

Confederate military uniforms were similar to those of the Union army. The major difference was that Union troops wore dark blue coats and Confederate troops wore gray. Hence the Blue and the Gray.

The stars and stripes, the traditional American flag, was retained by the Union. It had profound emotional content. It was also unique in design and therefore difficult to imitate, though the Confederates tried more than once.

Two attempts by the CSA to create flags to rival the stars and stripes. Top right: the National flag, introduced March 1861. Bottom right: the Battle flag, introduced at about the same time, which eventually became the prime symbol of the Confederacy and was called – in conscious imitation of the stars and stripes – the stars and bars. It remains a popular piece of symbolism today.

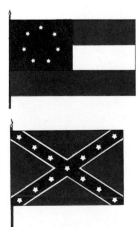

Significantly, much of the language still used about the CSA is to do with the imagery created in those few short months between late 1860 (when the secession took place) and early 1861 (when the war began). The Blue and the Gray, the stars and bars, the tune 'Dixie' all come from around this time.

Today it is impossible to imagine the Confederacy without its symbolism. What is remarkable is that the tools used to create and project the major new or repositioned industrial corporation today are just the same – allowing for changes in technology – as those used to project the new nation a hundred years or so ago.

The Order of the Star of India was created in 1861 as a piece of self-conscious, elitist mock-medievalism. Like most Orders of Chivalry its membership was small – originally only 25 people, both British and Indian, it had expanded to 36 by 1903. Above: the badge. Far right: the star.

The main illustration is of the Maharajah of Indore GCSI (Grand Commander of the Star of India), photographed in 1877, together with a servant and a mass of jewels and decorations – amongst which the chain, badge and star of the Order can be seen.

At about the same time as the American Civil War, in a very different part of the world, and in a wholly separate culture, the same kind of invention of tradition took place. The analogy with the rebirth and rededication of some of our modern corporations is remarkable.

After the Indian Mutiny – that is, the rising of 1857 against British rule in India, which was crushed with a brutal energy not uncharacteristic of the age – a policy was adopted of getting rid of the pitiful remnants of the old Mughal empire around which the rebels had coalesced, and establishing a formal, clear mandate for British rule. This process is described in the most fascinating and, to my mind, comic detail by Bernard S. Cohn in his essay 'Representing Authority in Victorian India', which is part of the invaluable Hobsbawm/Ranger work, *The Invention of Tradition*.

India, in those days, consisted of the parts under direct British rule, and also of territories at least theoretically owned and ruled by native princes. The territories over which these princes presided varied in size from a fair-sized sports stadium to a country rather larger than France. Size had to be taken into account when determining their order of precedence, as did other matters, such as how rich they were, how they related to the British, whose side they were on in the rebellion, and so on.

Gradually, the British introduced a complex set of symbols and a fiendishly complicated hierarchy of ranks into the previously random structure.

A royal order of Indian knighthood was established – the Star of India, complete with glittering robes and baubles, all of European mock-medieval origin.

As part of the process, the Queen became Empress of India, at the pinnacle, as it were, of a diverse country with people of different cultures, races and religions. The native Indian princes, the rajas, maharajas, nawabs, bahadurs and nizams who formerly owed allegiance to the Mughal Emperor, now had to acknowledge the leadership of the British Queen, who had succeeded the Mughals in the imperial role.

These momentous changes were celebrated in an Imperial Assemblage or Durbar, or – as we might say today – in a major launch event. Launching the British Empire in India was for its time an even bigger event than launching Unisys, the brave new computer company.

Each Indian state had its own army and uniforms. These were created in a pecullar idiom which combined traditional Indian-European military clothing in an attractive and entirely impractical fashion.

Baria was one of the smaller states; it had 150,000 inhabitants and 150 troops. Above left: a colonel of the Baria State Forces, 1937.

Hyderabad was one of the largest states. It had 20 million people and 5000 troops. Below left: the Commander of the Cavalry Brigade in full dress, 1937.

The event took place in Delhi in 1877 in the city where the Mughals had ruled for centuries. Every significant element of Indian public opinion attended. It was on an enormous scale and involved about 85,000 people in one way or another. Major-General Roberts, who later became Field Marshal Lord Roberts of Kandahar, was in charge of organizing the show. Lockwood Kipling, father of Rudyard Kipling, was put in charge of design – that is, uniforms, graphics, signage and the rest. The theme for the entire Durbar was especially conceived by him.

It was not generally regarded as highly successful. One commentator said: 'They have stuck pieces of needlework into stone pillars and put shields and battleaxes all over the place.' The Queen-Empress received a new title, 'Kaiser-i-Hind', thought up by a Hungarian professor (they had them even then) on the basis that this name was associated with Caesar, Czar or Kaiser, that it was neither Hindu or Muslim, that it would not be susceptible to mispronunciation and that most Indians would be familiar with the word. This set of assertions was not, however, researched.

In addition, most of the Indian princes were awarded a new coat of arms loosely based on European medieval heraldry. The coats of arms were stuck on to enormous silken banners, which flapped

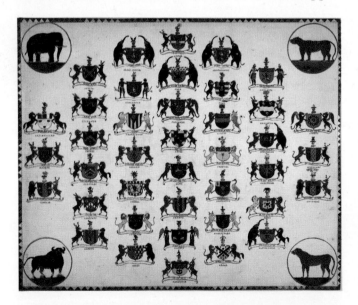

Each Indian prince or princeling was awarded a coat of arms. These were prepared in London by the College of Heralds. Attempts were made to combine European heraldic symbolism with that traditional to the native rulers, often with bizarre results. Sixty-four coats of arms had been created by 1877, the year of the Delhi Durbar.

The gradations of hierarchy within the Indian Empire created by the British were infinite and were the subsequent cause of much jealousy and argument between the princes. For example, each prince was awarded a salute of guns, the number depending on the size of his state and its wealth.

Val Prinsep was commissioned to paint the Imperial Durbar of 1877, which was held in Delhi to celebrate the creation of the British Indian Empire and Queen Victoria's assumption of the title Empress of India. Prinsep was not impressed by what he saw of the Durbar. 'A kind of thing that outdoes the Crystal Palace in "hideousity". It has been designed by an engineer and is all iron, gold, red, blue and white. The dais for the chief[s] is 200 yards across and the Viceroy's dais is right in the middle and is a kind of scarlet temple 80 feet high. Never was there such Brummagem ornament or such atrocious taste!' 'Brummagem', originally an informal name for Birmingham, became synonymous with a cheap imitation.

about uncontrollably during the ceremony and from time to time fell onto people's heads.

Bearing in mind that it was the first one, however, the Durbar seems to have passed off very well. It was repeated from time to time at appropriate moments in Imperial history, such as the accession of George V in 1911.

The whole business was contrived to create new loyalties and supplant old ones in the most spectacular and dramatic way.

Interestingly, although the old British Raj died in 1947, many of the traditions that it created in the last half of the nineteenth century have become embedded into Indian ceremonial life. The closing ceremony of the British Indian Empire, presided over by Lord Mountbatten, had echoes of the opening ceremony seventy years before. And paradoxically, nothing is more redolent of the British Raj than the annual Independence Day celebrations in Lutyens-designed New Delhi. Words like Kaiser-i-Hind no longer seem invented, but simply appear to have been part of the natural fabric of Indian life at a particular time in its past.

No nation and no century has been immune from inventing traditions. France, amongst European nations, has perhaps been the most prolific. It has, after all, had five republics, two empires and about four kingdoms, depending on how you count them. Some of these changes of regime have been initiated with the clearest symbolism.

The creation of the first French Republic was celebrated not just with a change of flag, from fleur-de-lys to tricolour, but also by the introduction of a new anthem – the Marseillaise – a new system of weights and measurements – the metric system – and a new calendar – with new names for the months. Even a new religious ritual, the Worship of the Supreme Being, took place at the Pantheon.

Within a few years of the creation of the Republic, the French found themselves with an Empire and an Emperor: Napoleon Bonaparte. Napoleon, like many autocrats both before and after him, had a passion for symbolism, an instinctive feeling for its power, a real understanding of how it could sway people.

On 18 May 1804 the Senate had confided the government of the Republic to General Bonaparte by proclaiming him Emperor. Within hours Napoleon (as he immediately styled himself) was immersed in the detail of the names, titles, badges that his Empire would use. On 19 May, one day later, Napoleon created the new title, Marshal of the Empire, for fourteen of his better and more loyal generals, each of whom he graciously agreed to address as 'mon cousin'.

Within a few weeks, there were also Grand Almoners, Princes, High Constables and the rest, all with uniforms, symbols, colours and the newly created panoply of office.

Napoleon crowned himself at his own coronation, in imitation of Pepin and Charlemagne, and then had the occasion immortalized by Jacques-Louis David, the great court artist-propagandist.

It is not an accident that many of the major crises in Napoleon's career have been perpetuated in paint. Mostly he or his propaganda machine commissioned such work.

Napoleon's successors, the restored Bourbons and then the Orléanists, were overwhelmed by the weight of the Bonaparte legacy. It was during Louis-Philippe's reign (1830–48) that the Arc de Triomphe, celebrating the Napoleonic victories, was built and that Napoleon's body was brought back from St Helena to be buried at the tomb in the Invalides. The event is described by Corelli Barnett in his book *Bonaparte* as 'one of the most remarkably successful public relations exercises in French history'.

Bonapartism, a carefully cultivated political force based around hero worship amounting to deification, was a major political phenomenon in France for much of the nineteenth century. It played a large part in the propaganda campaign that ultimately enabled Louis-Napoleon, the first Napoleon's nephew, to become the second and last Emperor.

Jacques-Louis David became Napoleon's favourite court artist and propagandist. Main picture: detail of Napoleon crossing the Alps on the way to his victories in Italy. An idealized piece of imagery.

Opposite top: the distribution of the Imperial Standards at the Champs-de-Mars, 5 December 1805.

Opposite bottom: as part of the festivities that celebrated Napoleon's coronation as French Emperor, the famous crossing of the St Bernard Pass into Italy in 1800 was re-created with fireworks, soldiers and an illuminated crown suspended from a balloon. At an appropriate moment an effigy of Napoleon appeared. Finally, a ship – emblem of Paris – came into sight from the river.

As Hungary evolves politically and economically away from a rigid Communist system, national symbols reflect change. In 1988 the Hungarian government began implementing measures to revert to traditional Magyar symbolism.

Top left: Communist symbolism featuring the Red Star. Centre and bottom: proposed 'new' Hungarian state symbols, with and without the Iron Crown of St Stephen. In the 1956 rising the symbol without the crown, used previously in the Kossuth rising of 1848 against Austria, re-emerged.

Plan for a commemorative memorial to mark the centenary of the French Revolution in 1789. The French engineer Gustave Eiffel was commissioned to design a memorial marking the centenary of the Revolution, to be erected for the Paris Exposition of 1889. He prepared this project drawing in 1884, with the Arc de Triomphe and Notre Dame to scale.

Opposite: a popular print produced to celebrate Bastille Day, 1880. The original caption reads: 'The radical Republic with the Phrygian Bonnet. The triumphant Republic presides over the Great Nation's Holiday on the 14 July 1880.' The conical Phrygian cap, originally worn in ancient times, became a symbol of liberty during the French Revolution.

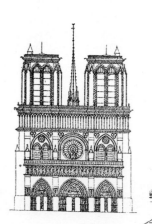

After the debacle of the Franco-Prussian War in 1870, the end of the Second Empire and the collapse of Bonapartism as a significant political force, there emerged the Third Republic, managed at least most of the time by the moderate bourgeoisie.

The Republic faced threats from both right and left, for there was no special tradition of love in France for republicanism, since it was associated with Robespierre, the Terror and instability. So a new tradition had to be invented and instilled, a tradition of love for the republican idea. Bastille Day, which is the primary assertion of the French as a republican people, born in the fires of 1789, was actually invented in 1880, nearly one hundred years after the event, in itself something of a non-event, actually took place.

In addition, the Third Republic, officially, semi-officially, unofficially, but always assiduously, through indoctrination in state education, through public speeches, through exhibitions and such symbolic monuments as the Eiffel Tower, never ceased to express its apparently natural and legitimate heritage.

The same story is true in a slightly different form in Germany, Italy, all the successor states to the Empire of Austria–Hungary and later in Israel, in Pakistan, in Bangladesh and the crazy patchwork of nations that has emerged in the post-colonial era.

Virtually without exception, new countries invent new names, new flags, new rituals, new traditions. They celebrate their reality with pageants and, where they can afford them, national monuments like power stations, steel mills and dams, whose symbolic value is infinitely more significant than their economic value, which is for the most part dubious.

When Rhodesia became Zimbabwe and Salisbury became Harare, the symbolism was clear. Robert Mugabe and his colleagues were inventing new

traditions in order to create a new country. Mugabe, in common with every other leader of every new regime in every new country, knew intuitively what businessmen and industrialists sometimes find hard to accept or to understand: that people need to belong, they need to know where they stand, they need their loyalties underlined and emphasized, and they desperately need – we all desperately need – the magic of symbolism.

The modern multinational is quite as complex as any nation state, in some ways perhaps more so. The issues involved in motivating people are much the same.

How do you get people to understand what an organization is about, to accept its behaviour pattern, to accept new ownership, new management styles, new names?

Although the language used to describe corporate activity is very different from that normally used by historians, all these issues are the same.

A corporation will only work properly if the people inside it have a sense of belonging, if they are proud of their organization and what it does, if they share some kind of common culture, if there is agreement about what is and what is not acceptable behaviour within the organization, if they understand explicitly and implicitly the aims and ambitions of the whole business.

This will not happen in a large organization if things are left to chance. In order to create loyalties, the organization has to manufacture the symbols of loyalty: the flags, the rituals, the names. The organization must celebrate what it is and what it stands for through rituals and ceremonies. Affirmation of faith must be followed by constant re-affirmation.

Museums, company history, buildings in the corporate style, work-clothes, major events based around anniversaries, or product launches have to be a significant part of the rhythm of corporate life. Everything that the company does, everything that it makes or sells, everything that it builds, everywhere that it operates, everything that it says or writes or displays, should build up the corporate spirit, the corporate identity.

If you don't believe in what you do, you can't possibly survive. Empires fall and companies collapse as much because they lack the will to survive and grow, as much because they fail to engage their people in the enterprise, as because they are attacked by predators.

In an age in which corporate affairs are given so much and such detailed professional consideration, in which virtually every aspect of the industrial and business life is analysed in so much detail, I find it remarkable that the power of symbolism should be so little detailed and so little understood.

Even more remarkable is the fact that in organizations whose propaganda machines, or (as they would prefer to call them) communication departments, are so significant, whose budgets are so vast, whose influence is apparently so great, there is such a paucity of imagination displayed in this area of activity.

CHAPTER **2**

The Corporate Search for Identity

Parker, Sheaffer and Lamy all produce writing instruments. Each company's product has a different image, largely conditioned by its appearance and price.

SS Cars changed its name to Jaguar (previously only a model name) in the 1940s in order to avoid disagreeable associations. The name, the appearance and performance of the car, together with the symbol, combine to emphasize the idea of Jaguar as an expensive, fast, luxury product.

Companies are concerned with loyalties, with creating a common culture, shared values and a clear sense of direction. That is why mission statements are so fashionable. Nowadays you can hardly meet a chairman of a large corporation who won't buttonhole you to recite his own version.

Mission statements tend to be about being fast, responsive, energetic and dedicated. They are all too often the corporate version of the old Boy Scout oath, which demanded, as I recall, that thirteen-year-olds should be clean in body and mind. They reflect the wish rather than the reality.

Companies feel the need to tackle the consequences of their own patterns of behaviour. They are diversifying – that is, becoming involved in a large number of different, and sometimes distantly related businesses; they are also globalizing – that is, operating all over the world, in countries with quite different national cultures and behaviour patterns. And, inevitably, because of these two factors, they are decentralizing the management of these operations.

Unless they can find ways of holding these activities together, global companies simply fall apart. So they search desperately for some kind of glue that each part of their business can share. They look for a common identity.

In reality, though, all businesses already have an identity, and if that identity is explicitly controlled, it can be the single most powerful influence on the corporate culture. Corporate identity is concerned with four major areas of activity:

Products/Services – *What you make or sell*
Environments – *Where you make or sell it – the place or physical context*
Information – *How you describe and publicize what you do*
Behaviour – *How people within the organization behave to each other and to outsiders*

All of these communicate ideas about the company. But in fact the entire corporation communicates in everything it does all the time. The fact that the company exists at all is itself a form of communication. The potency of different forms of communication varies, however, together with the degree to which they are modulated.

In a product-based company, it is the product that is the most significant element in the identity mix. The most important single factor in creating the identity of, say, the Jaguar company is the car itself – what it looks like, what it costs, what it feels like inside, what it smells like, how it sounds, how it starts, stops and goes. It is these qualities that influence, to a very large extent, the identity of the whole company.

The same holds true for Parker, Sheaffer or Lamy in the writing-instrument business. How the product feels in your hand, what it looks like, what it costs, how it works – these are the major determinants in the identity mix.

Sony's success largely derives from the sustained brilliance of its product design. Below left: the 1988 Sony Walkman. Although Sony's advertising is often clever and imaginative (left: Japanese poster for the first Walkman), it is the product that largely nourishes and develops the Sony identity.

Test the theory. When you think of Sony, what do you recall first? Not Mr Morita, its peripatetic, outgoing, English-speaking, speech-making, book-writing chief executive. Certainly not its advertising, nor the dreary wasteland of electronic hardware shops through which its products are sold. Not even its symbol and logotype, if you can remember them. No. You think of its apparently endless range of brilliantly innovative products, and most particularly the Walkman. Sony's identity is largely conditioned by its products.

Of course, environments do matter to product-based companies as well. A glamorous new car looks better in a glossy showroom on Park Avenue than in a dusty compound somewhere near Newark, New Jersey. The advertising counts too; so do instruction manuals, brochures, and the manners and style of the salesman. What you expect and what you get from after-sales service also contributes significantly to the overall identity of the organization.

But in the end, in product-dominated companies it is the product itself that is most influential in creating and maintaining the identity idea.

And, most important, even if the products themselves are full of character, it helps if the identity is symbolized and ritualized, with names, graphic devices and other elements. The Jaguar name and symbol, for example, are intended to symbolize all the speed, power and beauty that we associate with the company's products.

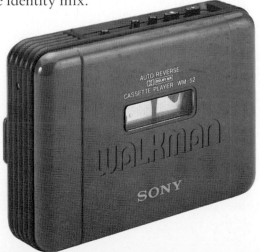

The fresh-fish counter at Harrods. It is decorated with a new display daily. Packaging, carrier bags (opposite, top) and other graphic material help to support the Harrods identity – but they do not create it.

Opposite, bottom: Bloomingdales, like Harrods, is environmentally led. Graphic material, much of it imaginatively designed and executed, plays a subsidiary role.

There are other kinds of business – retailing and leisure, for instance – where the environment dominates, and sets the tone for the identity as a whole.

Take Harrods, or for that matter, Bloomingdales. Their huge size, their vast range of products, the lavishness of the displays, the overwhelming cornucopia of goods are at the heart of their identity. There is hardly anything that you can get at Harrods or Bloomingdales that you can't get somewhere else, often cheaper. It is not so much the products that are available at these two stores that create the identity idea, as the places themselves.

The communications material produced by Harrods and Bloomingdales is, of course, significant and supports the whole idea behind the organizations; the brochures and the advertising also make a contribution; but it is the places themselves that form the heart of the identity of these great department stores.

And the totality of what Harrods represents, the whole idea behind Harrods is encapsulated in that strange combination of green and gold and the Harrods logotype, which is modified so cautiously from time to time. Symbolism is important to Harrods.

In the hotel field this is also true. Holiday Inns have imposed their bland, mid-American style over the whole globe. Once you enter the germ-free, plastic world of Holiday Inn, it's the Holiday Inn environment that takes over. Holiday Inns aim to have total control over the traveller's hotel experience, and in this – for better or worse – they are largely successful.

For the most part the Holiday Inn layout of common spaces varies relatively little. Bedrooms tend to be the same size; they have the same kind of equipment. The food, drink and service are all intended to conform to the common standard. In every Holiday Inn that I've ever visited there's a mugshot, prominently displayed, of a bewildered-looking young person designated as 'employee of the month'. All this is part of the Holiday Inn world. It helps to create the mythology of Holiday Inn life. It contributes to the development of the Holiday Inn culture.

It's hardly surprising, then, that when you wake up in a Holiday Inn bedroom, you have difficulty in knowing whether you're in Wichita, Wolfsburg or Wolverhampton – or even Warsaw.

In the case of Holiday Inn there is no doubt that it is the environment that leads the identity idea; product and communication do count, but they play a subordinate and supportive role.

Holiday Inns have signs and symbols, graphic devices which sum up everything the organization stands for, which say everything that needs to be said about Holiday Inn as an operator.

There are a number of identities that are largely communication-led. Most ordinary household products have no life of their own, no real character. A bar of soap or a soft drink would, without its packaging and advertising, simply be another anonymous commodity. Information techniques of various kinds, especially advertising, influence and even create the identities of certain consumer products.

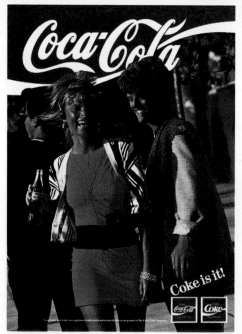

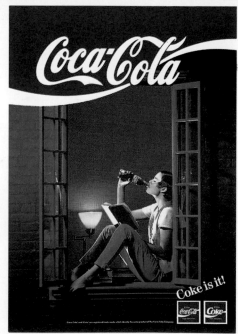

Coca-Cola is probably the world's most famous and ubiquitous brand. McCann Erickson, the Coca-Cola advertising agency, together with other suppliers – like Landor Associates, who redesigned the symbol – have created with the Coca-Cola company a system that allows a single joyful idea to emerge in the widest possible range of cultural contexts. Illustrated below are Coke cans before and after rationalization. Top left: an early can featuring the contour bottle (in use 1963-66). Cans from the United Kingdom, South Africa, Hong Kong, Indonesia, Japan, USA, Holland and Australia. They all look more or less the same.

Coca-Cola is a maroon fizzy liquid of – some would say – no intrinsic interest or merit. It is little different in itself from thousands of other soft drinks made all over the world. The imagery of Coca-Cola, however, is simply stupefying. Its global success is a tribute to the ingenuity, fanatical dedication and immense sums of money devoted to communication. The traditional bottle, the logotype, the colours, and the lavish advertising on a mega scale have combined with obsessive attention to detail and an unequalled global distribution system to create the world's greatest-ever brand.

Through the most sophisticated techniques supported by untold billions of dollars, Coca-Cola has become synonymous more or less throughout the world with all the good things in life; with fun. That is why Coke commercials show young and physically perfect families of subtly differing shades of colour and ethnic origin, cavorting about by the sea or in the mountains displaying acres of pristine lily-white teeth, clutching in their exquisitely manicured hands – guess what? The Real Thing.

In the US nearly as much Coca-Cola is drunk as ordinary water. Can you believe it?

Because communication, more particularly advertising and packaging, gives life and personality to consumer products, advertising especially has become a prism through which many products that we use in everyday life – fizzy drinks, soaps, toothpaste, breakfast cereals – are projected. Almost inevitably, therefore, many people have come to associate advertising with identity, or with image.

This is a misleading and potentially dangerous idea, because it has the effect of devaluing the real power of product, environment and behaviour in the identity mix, at the risk of overvaluing information techniques.

Perhaps even more importantly though, the idea that identity is somehow inextricably associated with conventional communication techniques, and particularly with advertising, inevitably distorts the reality, which is that identity is usually a manifestation of what the organization is all about; and that in the end, identity is the responsibility of the people who run the organization and not only of its designers, public relations people or advertising agencies.

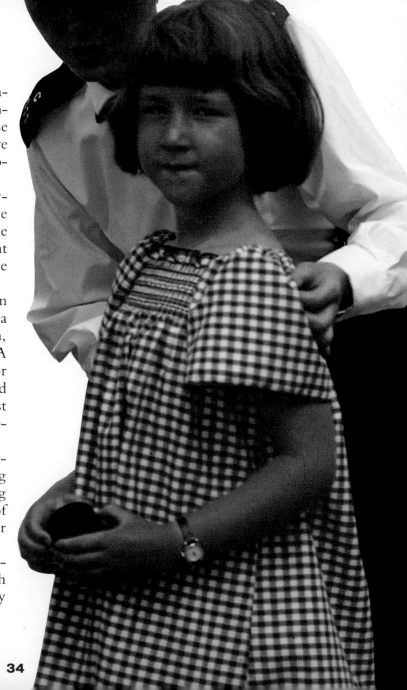

The image of a police force is largely conditioned by how individual police officers are thought to behave. Most police forces want to be perceived as 'caring', like the London policewoman (below).

At the opposite end of the spectrum from Coca-Cola and other products whose identity is manifested largely through communication, are those organizations that are service-based, and therefore depend for success upon the way in which their people behave.

A police force is perhaps the ultimate service activity. Each encounter that we, as consumers, have with Coke is more or less the same as the last; Coke the product remains consistent. But each contact that we have with a police force largely depends on the behaviour of each police officer.

A police force depends for its success largely on how the individuals who belong to it behave in a multitude of individual encounters – many of which, in the nature of things, are likely to be stressful. A police force resembles an airline in the sense that for the most part it is the most junior and inexperienced members of the organization who have the greatest contact with the public, and who are therefore largely responsible for its reputation.

Of course, a police force also has special characteristics. It offers a huge spectrum of services, ranging from giving directions to tourists to controlling riots. It also allows its junior officers a degree of discretion that is probably greater than any other organization.

It is certainly symbolized through its visual identity. The helmets of the British police force, though uncomfortable and impractical, remain because they represent authority.

Very few companies perceive the relationship between the various parts of their identity; very few therefore attempt to control the totality of the impressions that they make upon all the different groups of people with whom they deal, by treating everything they do as a part of a single, seamless whole. The totality of all the impressions that a company makes on all its audiences is often called its image. And this image varies widely between different audiences.

Every company, however big or small, has an identity, whether it recognizes it or not, and the real question that needs to be faced is whether the organization seeks to control that identity, or whether it allows the identity to control it, so that it has entirely different images with all of its different audiences.

There is another issue, too; increasingly, identity is going to make the difference between successful companies and failures.

For the most part the products and services of all big organizations that compete with each other in the marketplace are very similar. One chemical company, one bank and one petrol company provide much the same products and services as another, which they market in about the same way at about the same price.

If any company gains a slight advantage in terms of price, quality or service, its competitors usually catch up quickly – if not, they go bankrupt or they get taken over. It's what Professor Carlo Brumat describes as the Darwinian theory applied to business.

Increasingly therefore, we, the public, are having to make a choice between one company, one product or one service and another on the basis of factors that are very difficult to quantify, such as reputation. It's certain that the companies with good products and powerful, well-coordinated identities, will beat their competitors whose products are just as good, but whose identities are weak.

The world's great chemical companies are an interesting example of this. Superficially, they seem pretty much the same, and they live in a world in which commercial and industrial pressures are apparently making them more and more alike. In terms of what they actually do, the products they make and sell, the prices they charge, their terms of trade and the quality of their service, there isn't much to choose between them, despite the occasional short-term advantage gained from a new composite material, perhaps, or a new pharmaceutical product.

Yet they all have strong individual personalities. In terms of culture and style, the world's great chemical companies are in fact as different from each other as people are. They have different national origins; they have been led by different kinds of people; some of them have rather different structures from others. All of these things have affected the way they behave and look, and this in turn affects how they are perceived and influences their commercial positioning.

More often, because of their uniforms, their vehicles, their equipment, and above all because of their behaviour, they are seen as remote – and sometimes threatening – authority figures, like the New York policeman (opposite, top left), the Italian *carabinieri* (in dress uniform, right) and the Beijing traffic police (top right).

The major chemical companies increasingly seek to emphasize their individual reputations and identities, based upon the realities of their personality, because they perceive the commercial advantages involved.

Take Du Pont. Du Pont was once the largest chemical company in the world. This huge American corporation with a French name is based in Delaware, a small state now known – among other things – almost equally for its fiscal regulations and as the home of Du Pont. Delaware is said to have been chosen by Pierre and Irenee du Pont on the advice of Thomas Jefferson when they arrived in the US as refugees from the French Revolution – even from the beginning, the du Ponts had good connections. Jefferson is said to have suggested the site because in 1801, when the firm was founded, it was at the geographic mid-point of the USA.

Du Pont soon came to dominate the state. Over the last couple of centuries, the family have provided some of its governors and donated fortunes to welfare. Where local facilities haven't been up to standard, they have not hesitated to do things the Du Pont way. The company put up its own hotel in Wilmington to look after its guests, because what was available wasn't good enough.

Du Pont has an interesting, even exciting history as a technologically and commercially lively and aggressive organization. During the nineteenth century, when business manners were rougher than they are today, it tried – and for a time succeeded – in dominating the US explosives business, buying up a rival without anyone knowing. In 1917, Du Pont bought 23 per cent of General Motors which it held onto until forced to abandon its holdings by a federal anti-trust action in 1950.

The du Pont family, who have a tradition of working in the business, are, however, never averse to introducing new blood into the business, provided it does the old firm a bit of good. Irving Shapiro, who was appointed chairman and CEO in 1974, did not – as his name indicates – derive from old Delaware stock. His father was an immigrant Jewish trouser-presser from Minneapolis, but he helped Du Pont along quite a bit. Under Shapiro's guidance, Du Pont renewed its ability to innovate. During the Seventies and Eighties the company that had given the world nylons, squeezy bottles and stick-free pans came up with a lot more innovative products. It also went out and bought a major oil company: Conoco.

Du Pont's long history, its farsighted dedication to research and development in new products, its pioneering of modern management techniques, have – combined with a certain high-handedness – given it a style and personality unique among its peers both in the United States and in the chemical industry worldwide.

Du Pont is one of the oldest of the world's great chemical companies. Akzo is one of the newest. In most ways you can think of Akzo is unlike Du Pont. Where Du Pont has a rich history and a high profile, Akzo until very recently had neither. And it suffered for the lack.

Akzo is a classic case history of a massive organization, formed from numerous parts which initially deliberately chose to start as a federation. Akzo grew up without a shared identity, a shared set of values, a shared mission. For a time it could manage like this, but eventually an Akzo identity had to emerge.

Akzo was founded in 1969 through a series of complex mergers, which were themselves a result of previous mergers. Like most other major chemicals businesses, Akzo is a mixture of umpteen different companies in different places, doing relatively complementary things. Again like many of its competitors, the origins of some of its component parts go back to the eighteenth century.

Akzo, however, has its peculiarities. To start with, it is based in the Netherlands, but not in Amsterdam, the major commercial city, or in Rotterdam, Europe's largest port, or even in The Hague, the Dutch capital; but in Arnhem, a provincial town, deep in the Netherlands countryside, close to the German border – a city made famous as a Second World War battleground. There are a number of major multinationals that operate from a small city base: BASF at Ludwigshaven, Bayer at Leverkusen and, in the Netherlands, Philips at Eindhoven. But each of these dominates the city in which it functions.

Akzo doesn't dominate Arnhem; that is not its quiet, deceptively unassuming way. It sites its headquarters in a modest 1960s building next to one of its works. You certainly wouldn't guess to look at it that this is the home of one of the world's largest chemicals businesses.

It is inconceivable that Akzo should put up its own hotel in Arnhem as Du Pont did in Wilmington. When you visit Akzo in Arnhem you stay at a pleasant country inn, or one of the unpretentious bourgeois hotels in the area.

Akzo is highly decentralized. The head offices of its major operating units are scattered throughout the Netherlands. All are small, modest and unobtrusive. Akzo puts a high value on decentralization and individual achievement.

Opposite: although quite a lot of the printed material produced by different Akzo companies and divisions was of an acceptable standard, it did not form a cohesive whole. Nobody could tell what kind of a company Akzo was by looking at its literature.

Left: some Akzo brands and companies were better known than Akzo itself. Organon pharmaceutical products, Sikkens paints and Enka fibres were well-known names in their respective fields. Each had its own distinctive visual identity. None were related to the Akzo identity.

Although Akzo is very Dutch – that is, pragmatic, stubborn, tough and enterprising – it also happens to have absorbed an influential German element. The fact that Akzo has managed to do this successfully, where many other Dutch-German mergers have failed, is also a significant influence on the personality and identity of the organization.

Until the mid-1980s most of Akzo's operating units had powerful individual identities deriving from their own histories. Organon, Sikkens, Enka and other Akzo companies and brands were far better known than Akzo itself. And for a time this suited everybody. During the 1970s, Akzo went through a financial crisis. While the company's financial strength was suspect, it was in the divisions' interest to sustain their own identities, in which policy they were encouraged by the Akzo management.

The only major central coordinating function was finance. Research and development were almost entirely carried out by the operating companies, with some central participation. Recruitment was shared between the centre and the operating businesses.

For many years – particularly when times were hard for the group as a whole – this worked well. It appeared to be in the group interest to keep a low profile, while the individual operations worked out their own destiny.

Inevitably, though, this degree of decentralization had its disadvantages.

Their high level of independence inhibited divisions from acting together when the opportunity emerged to develop new products.

Over time it became clear that the lack of cohesion was beginning to affect the research and development effort of the group as a whole.

The individual operating units were also unwilling to share in group recruitment and training. The divisions wanted to recruit and retain their own people. But of course, they also wanted the best people that the group could provide. Naturally, none of them wanted to give up their own best people in favour of other parts of the group.

The lack of group presence also began to affect acquisitions. As Akzo's financial strength grew, it needed to make acquisitions. Nobody wants to join an organization it has never heard of – so Akzo began to lose in this direction too.

The one place that Akzo did perform well as a group was in the financial world. Financial audiences knew of Akzo. They knew it was in the chemicals business, although they did not necessarily know exactly what it did.

So Akzo's anonymity – you could have described it as the world's largest unknown company – came to be seen by the management of the organization as a disadvantage.

The idea of a group with a clear identity and focus, and a culture shared by all of the operating businesses needed to take hold. In other words, an identity needed to be made manifest for the whole enterprise to make a new strategy visible.

Strategically, Akzo required more co-ordination to develop effectively. It laid down three objectives: first, strengthening of core business objectives; second, developing new activities; third, developing a global focus. All of this meant that the idea of a group had to emerge.

But what sort of group? What was the personality of Akzo as a whole? How did it stand in relation to other chemical companies, and for that matter in relation to other Dutch companies? What were its strengths and its weaknesses? What was Akzo like?

Akzo investigated itself and it hired consultants to help it. Teams of senior executives discussed their attitude to their own divisions, to other parts of the group and to the group as a whole. Consultants talked to people with whom various parts of Akzo dealt. Competitors, customers, financial analysts, journalists and others world-wide were asked for their views on the organization. As a result of these discussion groups, mission statements were developed and became part of a process of self-discovery.

Gradually a picture emerged. Akzo is not like anyone else in its industry; nor is it like any other major Dutch company. Akzo is unassuming, even provincial, but at the same time extremely ambitious, determined and pragmatic. It has its feet firmly on the ground. Above all, it depends upon the individual and continually encourages him or her to develop. It's a group made of sub-groups, and sub-sub-groups, each of which is run by somebody anxious to accept responsibility. Its clearest characteristic is its willingness to let the individual get on with the job. Akzo is, in other words, very largely about individual achievement.

Once the personality of Akzo became clear to its management, they set about creating a programme that would articulate these ideas to all the people within it, as well as to everyone with whom the organization and its people came into contact: customers, suppliers, recruits, collaborators, the financial world, politicians, trade unions, the local community, and the rest.

Changes were made to the nomenclature system, so that the name Akzo emerged more clearly. Although some of the names collected by the company in a haphazard fashion over the years were retained, they were re-organized into a clear structure, given shape and order, so that the totality of Akzo could be made visible. A policy was laid down in which brands were retained for those businesses close to the customer, while industrial businesses became more Akzo in name and feeling. The highly decentralized structure essential to Akzo's way of doing business was, however, retained. The corporate identity programme was linked both to a management development programme to improve quality and flexibility of management and to a greater commitment to R & D.

Akzo had to consider how it was to encapsulate an idea of itself so that the organization as a whole and its products could be recognized wherever and whenever they appeared.

It became necessary for Akzo to create a tradition for itself, in order to re-dedicate the organization internally and to make its presence felt externally. For Akzo this represented a rite of passage from adolescence – the group was only about twenty years old – to manhood.

The traditions created for Akzo fall into precisely the same category as those created for the Confederacy, for the Indian Empire, for every nineteenth-century nation state.

Akzo considered everything. Its case history is relatively uncommon in the world of building up companies, but highly familiar in the world of building up countries.

Should the name of the group be changed? Should the names of the divisions be changed? Should old symbols be kept? How should the new Akzo idea be communicated to its different parts, to Akzo in different countries, and to the world beyond? All these things were discussed and a plan of action agreed.

The simplest and most powerful way to present an Akzo identity is through graphic symbolism. Graphic symbolism holds the same potency for Akzo as the symbols of nationhood do for a country.

The use of logotypes, symbols and all the other graphic paraphernalia of corporate identity is the subject of Chapter 3. Nevertheless, the development and introduction of the new Akzo identity, its purpose and its success cannot be dealt with effectively without reference to this activity.

It was important to find a symbol that would be beyond class, colour or culture – a symbol that would show the achieving nature of Akzo.

Right: the bas-relief upon which the design of the Akzo symbol is based was originally put outside a place of education in Greece in about 450 BC, and was a source of precise measurement and proportion – it was both a scientific and an artistic symbol. It is now in the Ashmolean Museum, Oxford.

The Akzo symbol was developed to a series of specific criteria. The face and body had to look strong but not threatening, neither old nor young, with no clearly discernible ethnic characteristics. The design had to be easy to reproduce in any material from paper to neon signs, in every conceivable size, by every available reproduction process. The symbol is designed to have a minimum life of 25 years before any substantial modification is required. Shown on these pages is a small proportion of the development work.

AKZO

The Akzo symbol, like so many highly successful and enduring examples of graphic symbolism, has its origins in another culture, in another place, in another time. Akzo man, as the symbol is now called, is derived from a bas-relief created in the Eastern Mediterranean around 450 BC.

The original bas-relief was adapted by the design consultants to suit the multiplicity of purposes that are appropriate for a modern multinational corporation, while still expressing the original idea – of achievement.

Every day Akzo produces millions of products of every kind, in packages and cartons of all shapes and materials. These products emerge from Akzo factories and warehouses; they are loaded on to Akzo pallets and Akzo trucks, and driven by Akzo drivers to Akzo distribution depots, where Akzo people phone or write to their customers. At every hour of the day and night, in practically every country in the world, Akzo people are involved in relationships with their customers, suppliers and competitors. All of these encounters provided opportunities to launch and sustain the new Akzo.

The visible manifestations of Akzo are now presented in a coherent and co-ordinated fashion. Buildings, brochures, packaging and exhibitions have all adopted the new Akzo visual identity.

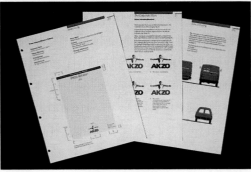

The launch of the new Akzo was celebrated through a series of events, different in technology but similar in intent to those surrounding the Indian Imperial Durbar in 1877. Videos were made. Executives of the various Akzo operations were gathered together in their different countries to watch the videos, which launched the new identity. The group chief executive patiently explained again and again and again the reasons behind the Akzo identity. An advertising programme was directed at the outside world, and eventually the new Akzo was on its way. All this was integral to the way in which the new identity was communicated both to insiders and the world at large.

Some applications of the new Akzo identity to vehicles, buildings and literature.

What the world sees today is an Akzo company that it had previously scarcely heard of, based around a human symbol of achievement.

Identity is the focal point for Akzo's global reputation. But all that is new. It was a conscious development of the late 1980s.

For Akzo the identity programme represented a major step in the group's development and growth. Identity was the principal instrument used to position the company and to introduce and manage change.

The corporate strategy and the corporate structure of Akzo have been made visible for all the world to see. Akzo is a model for the identity process.

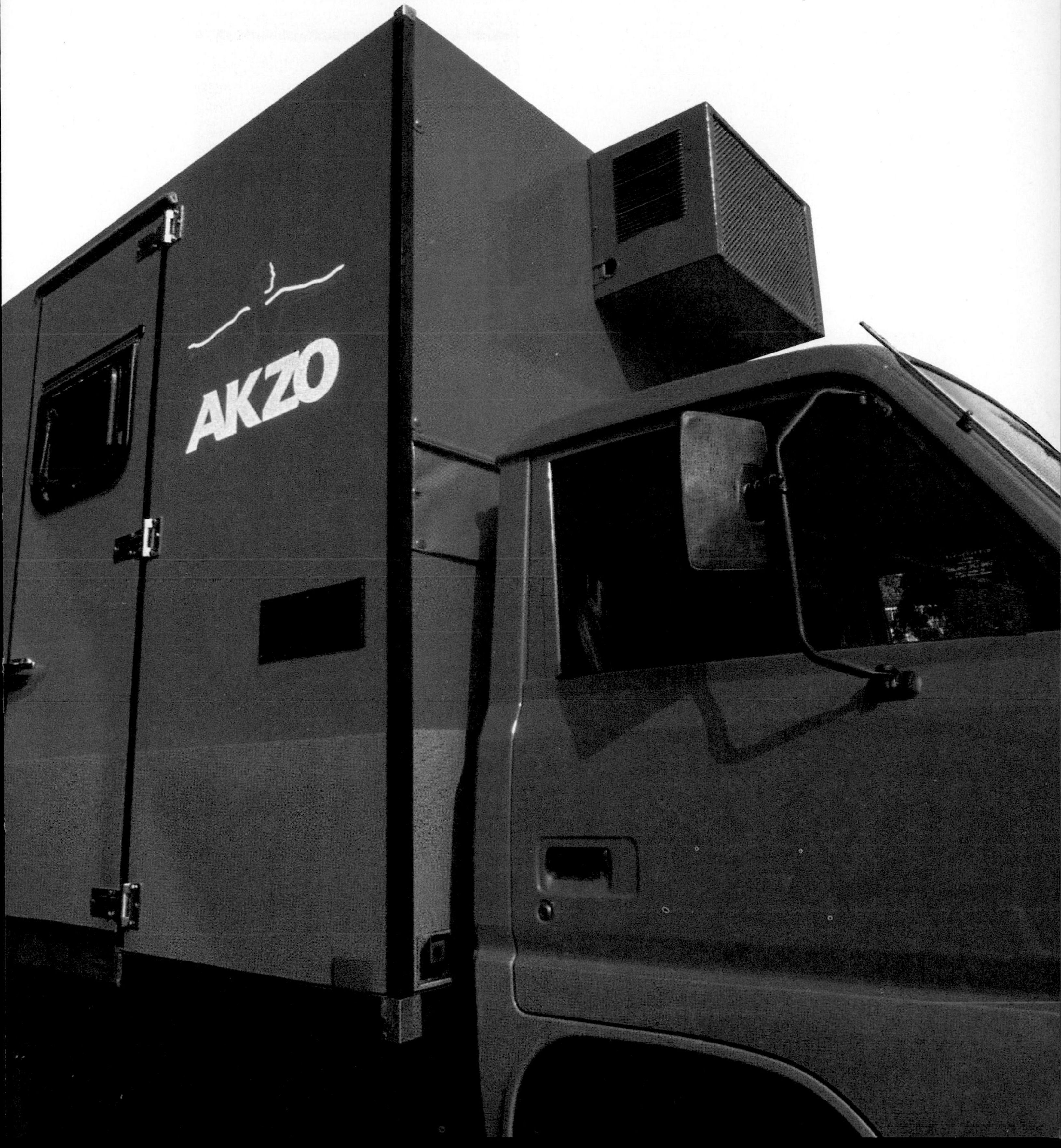
AKZO

New techniques in information technology, market research and production are increasingly driving successful manufacturers into making products that are alike in all tangible and quantifiable characteristics – price, quality and service, and even to a certain extent appearance. Here is a selection of products taken from the shelves of UK supermarkets in the spring of 1989, which demonstrates this rapidly growing trend.

Identity programmes that clearly demonstrate the intangible and not so readily quantifiable characteristics of an organization or product will play an increasing part in customers' purchase decisions.

M.Bibendum has been the prime symbol of Michelin since 1898. He is said to have been inspired by a pile of rubber tyres, and is unique amongst symbols for industrial companies in being both memorable and friendly.

CHAPTER **3**
Visual Style

On 1 October 1907 Peter Behrens, architect and designer, took up the post of 'artistic adviser' to the giant AEG company in Berlin. He became responsible for the design of buildings, products and publicity material. Over the next few years, he and his talented team – which included Gropius, Mies van der Rohe and Meyer – displayed a prodigious output.

Between them these people influenced virtually every aspect of visual expression of the great AEG company, from workers' housing to factories, to such consumer products as electric kettles, to letterheads, to catalogues and exhibitions. For a few years AEG was a corporate identity paradise.

The design work produced by Behrens and his associates was both prolific and startling. For the first time ideas that later became the norm by which twentieth-century design was judged, were employed on a large scale. The designers employed by Behrens were in the vanguard of the modern movement and were just entering their most creative period. Cookers, kettles and light fittings emerged from behind masses of metallic foliage; catalogues and exhibition stands disgorged large curvaceous females, revealingly draped in what appeared to be ample white sheeting; factories and offices were no longer built as castellated moated granges, but to look like what they were.

The modern style espoused by the Deutsche Werkbund, which was to find a pure form of expression fifteen years later in that superb propaganda machine, the Bauhaus, was suddenly taken up by Germany's greatest company – one of the largest, most modern, most productive companies in the world.

Imagine a combination of Sony, IBM and GE and you will have some idea of AEG's power and presence on the world scene in the first decade of the 20th century. It employed 70,000 people worldwide, huge numbers for the day. Its achievements in electric power were at the forefront of technology. It built everything electrical, from turbines for power stations to domestic consumer products. AEG was also the symbol of the industrial might and ambitions of Germany, much the greatest military power in the world at that time and vying with America for the world's industrial leadership.

In a detailed and fascinating account, one of the very few really thorough, academically respectable case histories about a corporate identity programme so far published, much of the story of the relationship between Behrens and the AEG company emerges.

This book, *Industrial Culture* by Tilmann Buddensieg and Henning Rogge (1979), shows the relationship between Behrens and both Emil and Walter Rathenau, and Paul Jordan. The Rathenaus, father and son, had built up AEG. They had a dedicated sense of mission, not just commercial mission; they believed, like many people of their kind who came later, that 'socially orientated art' could make people's lives easier. In addition to this, they were fierce German patriots; they wanted to emphasize the quality of German products in world markets. The Rathenaus believed, like the Japanese seventy years later, that good design would imply higher quality.

Paul Jordan, works director of AEG, appears to have been more pragmatic. He believed that good design improved sales. In

a remarkably prescient observation made in 1909, he said: 'Don't believe that even an engineer takes an engine apart for inspection before buying it. Even as an expert, he also buys according to the external impression. A motor must look like a birthday present.'

So the programme was undertaken with a broad set of commercial and cultural objectives in mind.

There can be no doubt that AEG knew what it was doing; enough archive material remains to make that quite clear.

In a lecture that he gave in 1909, Behrens concluded: 'The example of the French is proof enough. For centuries and right up to the present day, they have been able to derive benefit from their aesthetic and cultural domination. Particularly as Germany's situation makes it dependent on the world market, the AEG's commendable decision to give full attention to the question of taste is something of far-reaching and symptomatic importance to our age.' The implication was that products which looked good and were associated with high technology and high performance would enable the nation that produced them to gain a competitive edge.

The AEG corporate identity enterprise went down with the commencement of the First World War – and it was never revived. But the idea behind it occurs again and again in the history of the twentieth century.

Metalldraht-Lampe.

Hochkerzen-Lampe.

When Peter Behrens, the German architect, was appointed Künstlerischer Beirat (artistic adviser) to the AEG company in 1907, he and his colleagues – including Mies van der Rohe and Gropius – developed an identity programme embracing products, architecture and publicity material of a uniquely modern style for the period. Far left: domestic, portable fan. Above: the redesigned, simplified AEG logo. A recognizably similar version still exists. Left: publicity material for lamps. Below: an AEG factory for transformers, resistors and high voltage equipment, designed by Behrens and Bernhard, Berlin, 1909-10.

The launching and sustaining of identity programmes is a characteristic feature of a number of major, much celebrated, highly publicized organizations in the twentieth-century industrial scene. AEG was the first and in many ways the most ambitious and influential, but Italy's Olivetti, Britain's London Transport, the USA's IBM and Container Corporation of America, to name just a few outstanding examples of the type, all have a similar story to tell. Each has been associated with one or two great industrialists or administrators possessing a patrician will who launched identity programmes to associate commerce and industry with art and design, both for public instruction and corporate profit.

Less well publicized, but also of great significance, is the work carried out in this field by some of the great shipping companies, especially on their prestige transatlantic service.

Top right: Cunard White Star produced two magnificent ships in the 1930s – the three-funnelled *Queen Mary* (maiden voyage 1936, 81,235 tons) shown here and the twin-funnelled *Queen Elizabeth* (maiden voyage 1940). The *Queen Mary* was not as glamorous as the *Normandie* – although it was a shade faster.

The Norddeutscher Lloyd Company of Bremen introduced the *Bremen* (1928, 55,000 tons) and the *Europa* on their North Atlantic Service. Illustrated above is a poster advertising 1st class on the *Bremen*.

Here, each major nation, through its appropriate shipping company, created a shop window for the finest of its creative output: in Germany, Norddeutscher Lloyd and Hamburg-Amerika; in France, the Compagnie Générale Transatlantique, whose *Normandie* was perhaps the most fantastical piece of product and interior design the world has ever seen; and in Britain, Sir Colin Anderson's Orient Line, operating on the Eastern Services. All deserve great respect.

Many of the books written on the subject of design and identity focus on these organizations and those like them. There is no doubt that they are highly significant in their influence on industry as a whole, but they are nevertheless untypical. While it is important to recognize their importance, we should not over-emphasize it.

The fact is that for a variety of reasons most organizations do not tend to use either their identity or their potential for design in the full-blooded, overtly missionary fashion of Rathenau/Behrens at AEG, Watson/Noyes at IBM or Pick/Barman at London Transport. They are, on the contrary, tactical rather than strategic, and selective rather than holistic. They are usually concerned with immediate commercial benefit rather than longer-term economic and cultural impact within which commercial considerations play a part.

All the major maritime nations competed for passenger traffic on the prestige North Atlantic service. In the 1930s the French won. The *Normandie* (maiden voyage 1935, 83,102 tons) was perhaps the most spectacular liner ever built. Right: a Cassandre poster for the *Normandie*. Below: drawing of the Grand Salon – said to be larger than the Hall of Mirrors at Versailles – by Roger-Henri Expert. Below centre: cabin 65. Bottom: the Winter Garden in the *Normandie*.

Generally speaking, when companies use identity expressed through design, they use it as a commercial tool; their purpose is to make greater profit out of what they do in the short term. In the quaint jargon of our day this is sometimes called 'adding value'.

To underline the point, contrast the activities of Vidal Sassoon in revolutionizing hairdressing both in the UK and the US with those of AEG in the days of Behrens. Both used visual tools to make a series of statements. But Vidal Sassoon's ambitions were more tightly focused, short-term and modest. And of course, the canvas on which he worked was infinitely smaller. Nevertheless the fact of the matter is that Vidal Sassoon, starting in the 1960s, carried out a minor revolution using design in various ways. He changed hair fashion with the famous five-point cut, but there were plenty of young hair stylists who had innovated at different times. Sassoon added something else. He introduced a new, livelier, younger, more informal environment into what had been a rather chocolate-boxy sort of world: a world hitherto exemplified by Raymond, familiarly known as Mr Teazy-Weazy. Vidal Sassoon may not have been the first with music, open interiors, unisex salons, young gossipy stylists and a wide and expensive range of hair-care products ingeniously packaged and heavily promoted; but he was certainly the most thorough and the most successful.

Vidal Sassoon introduced a minor revolution in hairdressing, starting in the 1960s. He used all the techniques of corporate identity. In product design he created the famous five-point cut (left). He also pioneered well-designed salons (bottom right, London), with open interiors, music and well-trained, motivated stylists. To complement these, a wide range of carefully designed, well-promoted Vidal Sassoon hair-care products became available (top right).

Sassoon saw a commercial opportunity in the hair-dressing world of the 1960s and he exploited it with great flair and energy. Of course, he used all the classic identity tools: products – the styling of hair and the hair-care products that went with maintaining the appropriate appearance; environments – the layout and interior design of his salons; information – publicity, advertising and PR, at which he was remarkably successful; and behaviour – the relaxed, informal atmosphere created by his own staff inside his salons.

Through all this activity Sassoon managed to create a new market in the hairdressing and hair-care business, aimed largely at increasingly affluent younger people. In marketing jargon, he created a new niche positioning.

In retrospect it is easy to make the connection between the business of caring for hair and visual style. Yet judging by how the traditional hairdresser's salon looked and frequently smelt, this connection had previously eluded many people in the hairdressing trade itself.

In a sense we can consider Sassoon an earlier version of all those fashionable retailers who found and subsequently developed niches in the marketplace: Benetton, Esprit, Next and the rest, all owe something to Sassoon.

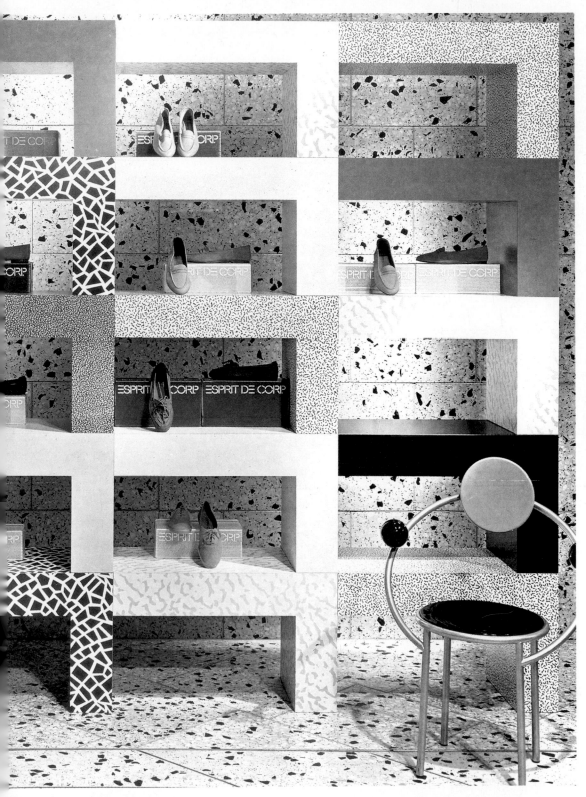

During the 1970s and 1980s there has been a revolution in the design and presentation of fashion-related shops with products, environments and packaging all complementing each other. In this niche the demands from the market sector are so universal that national character plays little part in identity. Far left: Next, the British fashion retailer, designed by Din Associates, London 1988. Main picture: the Esprit store in Cologne by Esprit of San Francisco. Below: The Benetton of Italy store in Brompton Road, London.

One way or another, whether they are conscious of it or not, most commercial organizations use design to delineate their relationship with their customers.

Banks, which are not generally regarded as visually sophisticated, let alone visually aware institutions, have over many years deliberately and consciously used design to emphasize their idea of themselves, and to define their relationships with customers and staff.

In 1924, when the UK's Midland was the largest and richest bank in the world and Sir Edwin Lutyens was busying himself with creating the new capital of the Indian Empire at New Delhi, he found time to work, in association with other architects, on the proposed new Midland Bank headquarters in the heart of the City of London, practically opposite Mansion House, the official residence of the Lord Mayor of London, and just across the road from the Bank of England.

Lutyens and his colleagues were encouraged to produce a building in keeping with Midland's far from humble opinion of itself, and which would also keep up the tone of the neighbourhood. In his respectful and monumental biography of Lutyens, A.G. Butler writes, 'It is obvious that a bank should choose to look strong. It should also, up to a point, look rich.' There can be no doubt at all that the Lutyens head office for the Midland Bank looks both strong and rich.

Today, although they still look magnificent, the offices also project an idea of the bank that some

judge to be no longer appropriate. Banking has changed since the first half of the century. The Midland Group, like every banking organization, now looks for a more participative culture; but the formal, grand style of the Lutyens building remains.

Here is a major problem of architecture designed to be permanent, in a commercial and industrial environment where the tempo of change continually increases.

In the Twenties and Thirties of this century, when many major banking institutions went through massive building programmes, it wasn't just head offices that were intended to look 'strong' and 'up to a point . . . rich'. Virtually every branch of virtually every bank was designed to look strong and rich – and to encourage the well off people to come in and the poorer to keep out.

This observation may sound less bald if we put it in today's marketing jargon, when we would probably talk about niche markets, socio-economic groups, As, Bs and perhaps C1s – but in order to make the point without saying it, banks were designed to look respectable, rich and conservative. In both city and small town they cultivated an air of respectable reticent opulence.

Top left: during the 1960s banking – worldwide – lost its way visually and within each country banks began to look similar. A street in Leeds, Yorkshire (1965), with branches of (left to right) National Provincial Bank, Westminster Bank, Lloyds Bank, Yorkshire Bank, Barclays Bank and Midland Bank.

Right: Midland Bank headquarters designed by Sir Edwin Lutyens – 'strong' and 'up to a point rich'. Above: the Banking Hall.

It wasn't just buildings that followed the style. It also emerged in graphics and related material. Most financial institutions went in for the kind of bogus heraldry so dear to the hearts of nineteenth-century institutions and they plastered this invented tradition about the place: on letterheads, cheque books, even on crockery and table linen. Charles Dickens' 'bran-new' family, the Veneerings, of *Our Mutual Friend*, in their 'bran-new' house, had such 'bran-new' heraldry: 'The great looking glass above the side-board reflects the table and the company. Reflects the new Veneering crest, in gold and in silver, frosted and also thawed, a marvel of all work. The Heralds college found a crusading ancestor for Veneering who bore a camel on his shield (or might have done if he had thought of it) and a caravan of camels take charge of the fruit and flowers and kneel down to be loaded with salt.'

Clearly, the banks and the Veneerings bought their traditions from the same place.

Naturally, the behaviour of the servants of the bank – hierarchical, bureaucratic, efficient, unobtrusive, reliable – was in line with all the characteristics that I have described. The bank, pretty well any bank of any size or reputation, was a magnificent example of style used pervasively to make a commercial statement.

Left: letterheads and stationery from banks in an era in which they were still trying to look powerful and prosperous – and not cool and trendy.

There was a cosy oligopoly, a world in which a few banks competed with each other over a limited range of products and services. At branch level it was regarded as inappropriate, even disreputable behaviour to try to take business from a rival. After all, he might retaliate.

Times changed.

The range of products began to broaden, different kinds of financial institutions began to compete with each other in the financial world. Banks began to offer mortgages and insurance; building societies – that is, savings and loans institutions – lent money; insurance companies became estate agents (realtors). At the same time technology began to change the way people dealt with money. Plastic cards became currency. Automatic machines built into a wall meant people no longer had to deal with a human being behind a counter to get money.

This process of change has so far taken about a generation – say twenty-five years. And it's still going on. In a relatively short period banks have become more ordinary, less holy, less precious, more like every other commercial enterprise.

And as they have changed, so has their style.

For a while the banks lost their massive sense of certainty. They were not sure whether they wanted to be exclusive any more. They did not quite know how to tackle potential new customers.

The visual style of banks evolved in the same uncertain way as their marketing attitudes – it was, indeed, a direct reflection of them. At first, as the evolution began, banks were hesitant. They knew in the early 1960s that their buildings should no longer be wholly traditional, but was it right to discard completely qualities like stability, and displays of wealth and dignity? Was the old Midland dictum to Lutyens appropriate any more?

The truth is that the banks didn't know what their style should be, and the buildings that they put up at the time reflect this uncertainty. Some bank branches of the 1960s look like giant transistor radios of the period, others like monstrous nuclear fall out shelters; few of them look like traditional banks.

The graphics visualized through the new heraldry produced by big banks and other financial institutions at about this time was also quite different from

what had gone before. In the United States, major banking institutions were advised by their design consultants to discard eagles, lions, tigers and similar ferocious fauna in favour of simplified versions of currently fashionable and expensive works of art. Bridget Riley, Victor Vasarély, Max Escher and others became the inspiration for much of the US banking symbolism that emerged in the 1960s. Much of the resulting work was just as pompous, empty and self-regarding as what it replaced – but the idiom was brought up to date a bit.

In Europe a similar pattern was pursued. The Deutsche Bank symbol became a simple green stripe: the ultimate in simplification, one might say. The Royal Bank of Scotland, on the other hand, went in for a modernized quasi-heraldic mark, with arrows apparently symbolizing the giving and receiving of money. The National Westminster Bank, formed in 1968 from a merger between National Provincial, Westminster and District Banks, commissioned an emblem that was presumably intended to celebrate the merger of three institutions, since it is formed from three identical shapes following each other to make a circle. The significance of the symbol was, of course, only temporary, as few people now remember the provenance of the bank. Unhappily, perhaps, it bears a strong resemblance to the Isle of Man symbol.

In the 1960s many banks changed their heraldry from complex, mock-medieval coats of arms to more simple and abstract – but for the most part equally empty – devices.

In the UK in 1968 the National Provincial, Westminster and District Banks combined to form the National Westminster Bank. The old heraldry was rejected in favour of three arrows (presumably symbolizing the three merged banks) following each other (left). To many people, the NatWest symbol looks like a chunky modernized version of the Isle of Man coat of arms.

Above: Midland Bank advertising in 1926. The banks tended to be both pompous and patronizing in their buildings, their literature and also in their relationships with staff.

As the evolution of banking continued, not everyone in the financial world was comfortable with the way the banking visual style was developing. There began to be a few bolder, more restless spirits. In the UK the Industrial and Commercial Finance Corporation, sometimes called Finance for Industry but more usually known through its various sets of initials, was one such. ICFC or FFI was a niche player in the British financial world. Its main activities were associated with investing in smaller businesses, often privately owned. The real success of ICFC was in using money more imaginatively, ingeniously and inventively than its equivalents. It had been carrying out these and associated activities with great success since its foundation in 1946. The shareholders were the major British clearing banks and the Bank of England. Because ICFC had pioneered an activity which had grown to a quite substantial size, it attracted other institutions as competitors; amongst these, curiously, were ICFC's own shareholders. Jon Foulds, chief executive of ICFC, saw the threat and thought it important to underline the unique position of his organization in a business which it had effectively created.

In a move of some boldness he called in design consultants and, working with them, abandoned the different names in favour of Investors in Industry, familiar known as 3i, and created a dramatic new pastel-coloured identity programme around a symbol originated by the artist Phil Sutton. The 3i programme, like all the best programmes of its kind, has been extended to offices, advertising, sponsorship – to the totality of the organization's business. In visual terms it has had a considerable impact in helping the financial world to see itself in a different, more open way.

Far left: fine artists and designers work together only very rarely. When they do, they can occasionally produce remarkable results. In 1984 designer Michael Wolff commissioned fine artist Phil Sutton to produce a watercolour on which the 3i symbol was based.

Left and above: advertising, brochures, neon sign – for 3i. Corporate identity by Wolff Olins.

In another part of Europe at about the same time, another financial institution made a similar commitment to a new identity. Caja de Pensiones is the biggest Spanish savings bank. The key to the change in 'La Caixa' is that it is based in Barcelona, capital of Catalonia, Spain's most dynamic and rapidly growing region. Catalonia has its own language – 'La Caixa' is Catalan for strong box – its own great commercial and industrial traditions, its own brilliant artistic heritage. Gaudí, architect of the Sagrada Familia, was a Catalan; so was Dali; so was Joan Miró. Catalonia has its own sense of identity, of which it is intensely aware and proud. Catalonian-registered cars normally carry a 'C' on a yellow background with red stripes, to demonstrate their independence from the rest of 'España', which of course uses a black 'E' on a white ground.

In a mixture of artistic piety, commercial shrewdness and regional loyalty characteristic of its origins, 'La Caixa' created a new visual style for the bank derived from the most flamboyant but disciplined Miró traditions. Devised by the US-based design consultants Landor Associates, it is based on part of a tapestry cartoon that Miró created for the bank, which used the star and two-dot symbol.

It is a fascinating, original and brilliantly successful example of a visual style originating in deep regional feeling, modified by a creative, probably intuitive grasp of what younger people will be prepared to respond to in the financial world.

By a strange coincidence, at about the same time (early 1980s) that 3i was developing a new way of presenting a financial services institution in London, 'La Caixa' was doing exactly the same in Barcelona, using Miró as artistic inspiration and Landor Associates as design consultants. Right: 'La Caixa' logo. Bottom left: a sketch for the tapestry by Joan Miró, from which the symbol derives, in the entrance hall of the corporate head office in Barcelona. Above: 'La Caixa' promotional material.

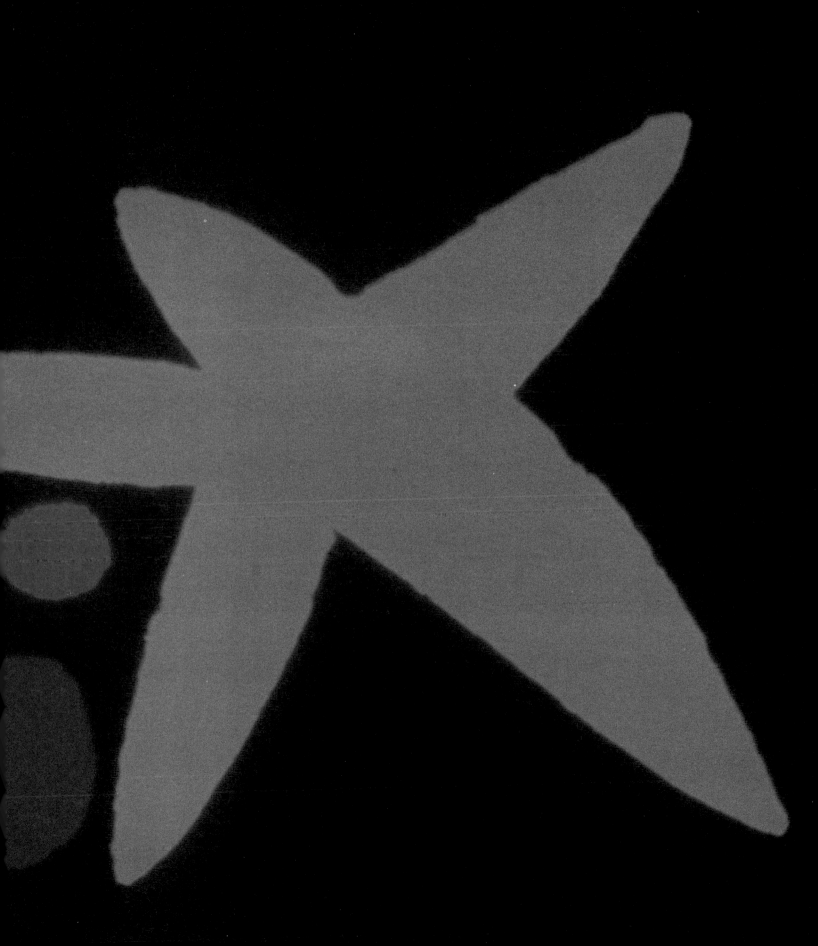

The new kinds of visual style that are emerging in various parts of the financial world have, of course, also affected architecture. Financial institutions have always been great patrons of architects, and this tradition continues. Lloyd's of London, the unique group of insurance underwriters, commissioned a new building in the 1970s from Richard Rogers, architect (with Renzo Piano) of the Paris Pompidou Centre.

The result is quite as controversial as Lloyd's itself. It has all of the Rogers visual trademarks; for example, it makes an apparent virtue of displaying its own underwear. The outside of the building is festooned with piping and ducts. It couldn't be described as a building in the mainstream of financial tradition. Whether it works properly, whether the people who work in it like it, whether it does anything for Lloyd's, are all matters that remain, as I write, unresolved. Certainly it is as unlike a traditional City of London building as it is possible to be.

At the same time, more or less, Norman Foster, Rogers' great rival and contemporary, received a commission from the Hongkong and Shanghai Bank to design their new head office in Hong Kong. The new Hongkong Bank head office building is a spectacularly modern, beautiful and expensive structure. It is, moreover, patently designed to impress, to show that the bank is rich and strong in a quite traditional sense. In fact, I very much doubt if the brief from the Hongkong and Shanghai Banking Corporation to Norman Foster was substantially different from the brief from Midland Bank to Lutyens about 50 years earlier. So, although the building is modern in its appearance and, to my mind, a masterpiece of contemporary architecture, it remains – paradoxically – a traditional piece of symbolism.

The financial world now moves so fast, with players coming in from every angle at very different speeds, that banks, however large or apparently stable, can no longer afford to build monuments to themselves – it's too much like tempting providence. The Bank of America building, put up in the heyday of its power, aimed to emphasize its position in San Francisco as the world's number one bank; now it has been sold by the corporation, which has moved to a building that meets its current needs. The volatility of banking today means that several different visual styles compete in different corporations.

The financial world was dominated for a very long time by one visual style – or generic. And the same situation is characteristic of most industries. A generic is usually created by chance, by what the leader in the industry happened to choose to do at a certain point in its development because it seemed right for the circumstances. Then peer-group pressure takes over. Everybody wants to look like the most successful business in the industry – regardless of whether or not it's appropriate – so everybody starts to emulate the visual style of the industry leader. And then, hey presto, you've got an industry visual generic, practically carved in stone.

Large financial institutions have always felt a need to display their wealth and strength through expensive and sometimes ostentatious buildings. Sometimes they get more than they bargained for. Bottom left: Bank of America building, San Francisco (designed by Skidmore, Owings & Merrill in 1970, since sold). Above: Hongkong and Shanghai Bank headquarters in Hong Kong (designed by Norman Foster, completed in 1986); the new Bank of China building will be taller. Right: Richard Rogers' Lloyd's Building in London (1986).

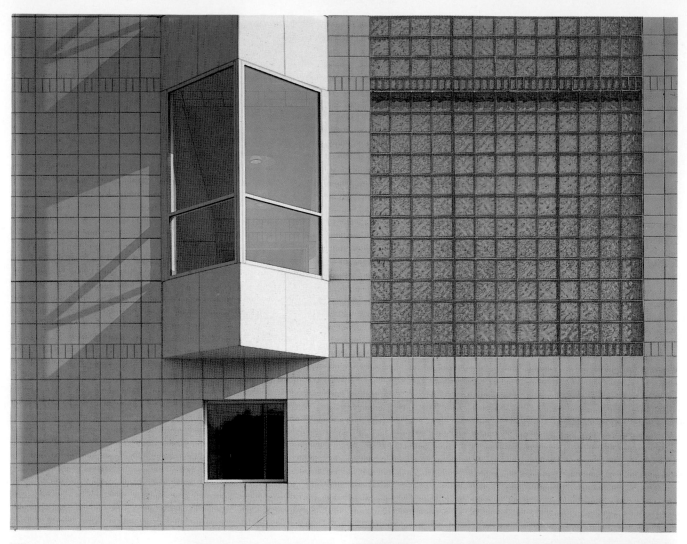

IBM set the visual style that the entire information technology industry followed – spare, modern and muted. It looked superb when IBM did it, but anonymous and boring when emulated mindlessly and on the cheap by the competition.

At this point it becomes almost impossible to imagine the industry looking any different. This is what this industry looks like, because this is what it has always looked like. We are too timid, too unimaginative, too locked into the convention of the moment, to imagine that things could be otherwise.

When an organization within the industry has a strong personality and wants to demonstrate its individuality to those with whom it deals, there is no clearer, more powerful statement than that demonstrated by a strong, individual visual style. But this means breaking the generic (like 3i or 'La Caixa' in financial services) and it demands a level of imagination, courage and self-confidence way beyond that of the average large organization. That's why most companies in the same industry look like each other, regardless of whether they actually behave like each other.

The speed at which a visual generic can take root, dominate an industry and virtually throttle individuality, never ceases to amaze me. The information technology world is a classic example. It only began, in a real sense, in the 1950s; before that there were only calculating machines and office equipment companies. And yet today, with very few exceptions, it seems as though there is only one way for computers to look, and that is the way IBM has chosen to look. IBM, or Big Blue as it is appositely nicknamed, seems to have dominated the world of information technology for ever. And Big Blue takes its visual style very seriously. It is an integral part of the way the company wants to be seen to be.

Ever since Thomas Watson Jnr and Eliot Noyes began working together, there has been a specific IBM style. It is applied to architecture, to factories, offices, showrooms; it is also applied to communications material, to advertising, brochures, films and the like, and of course, it is applied to the products designed for and made by the IBM organization.

Like the other companies in the finest tradition of corporate identity, like the old AEG or Container Corporation of America, IBM has used the world's best architects and designers to make a series of statements about itself, all of which add up to 'We are the most thoughtful, thorough company in our field. We are the best.'

The impact of IBM's visual style on the competition was that it simply obliterated all consideration of other options. To be in computers you had to look like IBM. The nearer to IBM you looked, the more like a real computer company you would feel yourself to be. Most computer companies – in their architecture, their showrooms, their products, their information material – emulated IBM. The point is made perhaps most clearly in the communications area: IBM used the slogan 'Think'; ICL said 'Think ICL'; Honeywell, for its part, for a time actually called itself 'The other Computer Company'.

It didn't occur to other companies in the business to question whether what was right for IBM was necessarily right for them – that indeed, it might be very wrong for them; that by emulating IBM they may have been demonstrating a feeling of inferiority and lack of worth, denying their own individuality, or making negative feelings manifest to their staff and customers. Although they aped IBM, they didn't use the IBM style with the same commitment and originality. They ended up looking like, and sometimes being perceived to be, imitations, would-be IBMs.

If Thomas Watson Jnr had not been persuaded by Noyes to commit IBM wholeheartedly to the cause of modern design, IBM would probably have looked very different. And so presumably would the rest of the industry.

Breaking the visual generic demands courage and imagination. It also probably helps to be a bit ignor-

Apple was the first company in the computer industry to break the visual generic created by IBM.

The new name and symbol were quite unlike anything else in the industry. Apple, like IBM, uses design with imagination and vigour in product, environment and communications, but applies it more humanistically, with equally successful results. Top: the Apple symbol. Below and right: Apple literature and on-screen software applications.

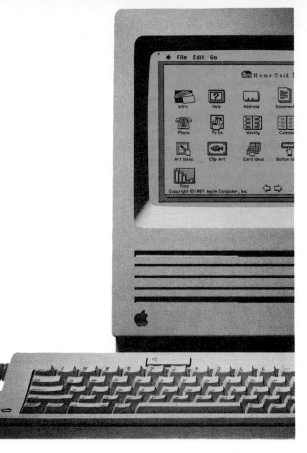

few close colleagues, influenced no doubt by the heady combination of informality in social life and high technology in industrial life that is so characteristic of their part of the world, invented the micro all over again and decided that they could sell computers like transistor radios. So they called the company after a fruit and got on with it. And of course, as we all now know, despite various vicissitudes, it is a huge success.

Imagine the reaction if this had happened in a conventional information technology company. All the marketing men, all the corporate courtiers would have attended meetings, had brainstorming sessions, wrung their hands and ended with a weak compromise. 'Call the company after a fruit and sell the products like a transistor radio? You must be crazy.'

Eventually, Apple became a victim of its own success. As it has grown, the company has become more conventional, and the revolution in style and content has now created a new kind of orthodoxy. Apple's success suddenly made fruit acceptable in the computer world. Peach Tree, Apricot and the others have now followed Apple into the orchard. Machines don't just have numbers any more. They have cutesy little names like Macintosh (an American variety of apple – not a raincoat).

The achievement of Apple in breaking a generic that had a pulverizing hold on the industry, and creating something original and successful, is greatly to be admired.

Much of the originality of Apple can be attributed, I am inclined to believe, to the youth, courage and market flair of its founders. Just as some, at least, of the originality of 'La Caixa', lies in the powerful regional roots of the company. Being locally based and having strong regional roots sometimes helps.

ant, too. After all, if you don't really know, or follow closely, what everybody else is doing, it's inevitable that it won't influence you all that much.

Perhaps that's what happened with Apple – the company that first broke the IBM visual stranglehold. Like all romantic tales the Apple story has been told so many times that nobody seems to know the whole truth any more.

What seems to have happened is this. The microcomputer had been well known within the industry for quite a long time – at least conceptually. IBM and Xerox certainly knew of it, so did a number of other companies. The problem was that nobody thought there was much use for the product.

Computers were sold to offices, factories and shops in a business-to-business environment. They were the equivalent in product design terms of white shirts with button-down collars and grey flannel suits. Computers had nothing to do with people's ordinary day-to-day lives.

Then a couple of very young northern Californian computer buffs had a different idea. Steve Jobs and a

This photo gives a very inadequate representation of the real thing.

It gives no idea of the comfort.

It does not tell you that the radiator is of stainless steel, that safety glass is all round, that there is a four-speed gear box with easy change.

That there is 12 volt equipment rear tank, clock speedometer, large tyres, etc., etc.

All these things are, however, set forth in our Catalogue, which we will post off to you on receipt of a p.c.

Better still, perhaps, we have an Agent in your town who will demonstrate a Jowett without obligation.

Prices from £150.   Tax £7.

JOWETT CARS LTD., IDLE, BRADFORD

In the doldrums

To our extreme disappointment we are compelled to announce that so far at the Show we have not signed any contracts running into millions of pounds.

Other firms seem able to do it, but we can't. Cars it be that our Sales Manager is always off our Stand when these anxious buyers are floating round?

Never mind.

We're working night and day and our "Kestrels" are winning golden opinions wherever they go, and 1933 is going to be a good one for Jowett owners and for Jowett Cars Ltd.

Get our catalogue. You'll like it!

Prices from £135.   Tax £7.

JOWETT CARS LTD., IDLE, BRADFORD

Regional manufacturers in many countries have become successful through self-caricature. The Jowett brothers began building cars in the first decade of the twentieth century, at Idle, Bradford, Yorkshire. The two-cylinder engine on which most of their designs were based sputtered on until the 1950s.

The appearance and construction of many Jowetts, especially in the 1920s and 1930s, was rustic. For a time, Jowett self-consciously and cleverly exploited its own uncouth and gutsy Yorkshire character in its advertising.

Above and right: London Motor Show advertising of the early 1930s.

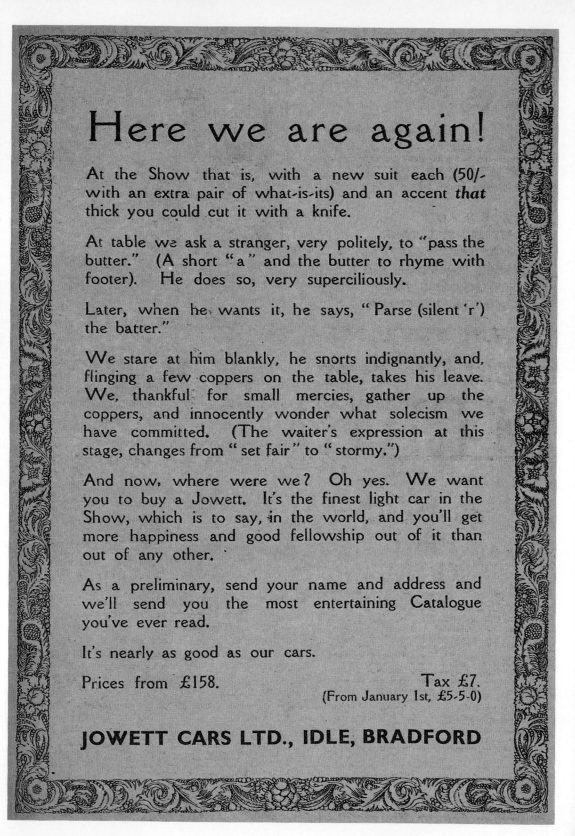

Here we are again!

At the Show that is, with a new suit each (50/- with an extra pair of what-is-its) and an accent *that* thick you could cut it with a knife.

At table we ask a stranger, very politely, to "pass the butter." (A short "a" and the butter to rhyme with footer). He does so, very superciliously.

Later, when he wants it, he says, " Parse (silent 'r') the batter."

We stare at him blankly, he snorts indignantly, and, flinging a few coppers on the table, takes his leave. We, thankful for small mercies, gather up the coppers, and innocently wonder what solecism we have committed. (The waiter's expression at this stage, changes from " set fair" to "stormy.")

And now, where were we? Oh yes. We want you to buy a Jowett. It's the finest light car in the Show, which is to say, in the world, and you'll get more happiness and good fellowship out of it than out of any other.

As a preliminary, send your name and address and we'll send you the most entertaining Catalogue you've ever read.

It's nearly as good as our cars.

Prices from £158.   Tax £7.
(From January 1st, £5-5-0)

JOWETT CARS LTD., IDLE, BRADFORD

There was once a small, little-known example of just such a regional manufacturer. For some decades the Jowett brothers made small, cheap, ugly, two-cylinder cars in Bradford, Yorkshire. Their products had a rustic simplicity and charm of which they seem to have been well aware; indeed, their publicity actually underlined it. The personality of the company and its products emerged in a quaint but powerful way, and it was all clowned up a bit, just to bring the point home. For a few years Jowett was a great success; then it expanded, and eventually disappeared, a victim of its own growth. But it was great fun while it lasted – and very different from the industry norm.

Jowett was so folksy it didn't really use a symbol, or if it did you wouldn't have known it. On the other hand, both 'La Caixa' and Apple use visual symbols which depart dramatically from what is usual in their industry and which embody almost magically the essence of what they are and what they are attempting to communicate. They use these symbols in a vivid, dramatic and exciting way, because they know that symbols have power to affect the way people feel.

The Cross is the most significant and enduring Christian symbol. Far right: statue of Christ with outstretched arms, Rio de Janeiro, Brazil. Right: statue of St Peter, Rome. Above, top: priest with cross, Ethiopia. Above, centre and above: processions, Greece.

The power of the symbol to influence should never be under-estimated. Amongst the most intricate, complex and ritualized uses of symbolism are those which occur within Christianity. The cross is an integral part of the process of worship. It also appears in various places within Christian buildings, in paintings, in books, on vestments, and at different stages in the service, as part of the ritual. The sign of the cross is even made by individuals, both priests and worshippers, an intimate and all-embracing hand movement.

Symbols have the same power as music to play upon the emotions, memories and sensitivities. Symbols can evoke fear or horror, as in, say, the Nazi symbol; they can also, and with equal immediacy, evoke pleasure, a smile. Mickey Mouse in the entertainment world, or the Michelin Man, Mr Bibendum, in the business world provoke pleasurable ideas.

Symbols also, in a remarkable way, have the power to encapsulate the senses; just to look at the woolmark is almost to feel the wool.

Design consultants involved in building identities for organizations usually and very properly put the symbol at the heart of the creative process. If you get it right, the symbol can in a magical way summarize the idea of an entire corporation.

But if it is important to understand that symbols can be brilliantly and memorably right, it is also worth remembering that they can occasionally go hideously wrong.

The Procter & Gamble symbol was registered in 1882 but was in use well before then. It has never been widely used on packaging. In 1982 a smear campaign emerged, purporting to link the company with Satanism – supposed 'evidence' of this was provided by the symbol!

Procter & Gamble of Cincinatti, Ohio, the world's most research-conscious company, the organization that never puts its left foot in front of its right without feeling what the ground is like first, found itself the unlikely and extremely unhappy victim of such a problem. The company's trademark, registered as early as 1882, is a circular design featuring the man-in-the-moon looking out over a field of thirteen stars. In 1982 a monstrous rumour began to circulate, through leaflets originating in the US, linking Procter & Gamble with satanism. A properly outraged company press release describes how the leaflets 'falsely claim that the President of Procter & Gamble recently appeared on a US chat show saying that he was a satanist, that the company gives financial support to satanism, and that following this appearance the company was required to print a satanic symbol on all its products. *None of this is true.*'

Eventually, Procter & Gamble, which had always placed a high value on the quality of its products and the integrity of its behaviour in the marketplace, was able to overcome this piece of unpleasantness. Its sales and reputation have now completely recovered.

The problems in developing symbols are complex. In addition to avoiding negative connotations, technical, creative, fashion and cost requirements all have to be considered. Creating something that is unique to the organization for which it is devised, that will encapsulate the idea behind the organization, that won't go out of date, that is flexible and cheap in use, and that will evoke strong, positive emotional feelings in all those who come into contact with it, is actually a very difficult thing to do.

Most organizations naturally look for a symbol to inspire feelings of confidence, comfort and empathy. They like to play safe, but of course, they want to be distinctive. They want to be modern, but of course, they want to be timeless. They want to be strong and memorable, but of course, they don't want to be offensive.

With this kind of compromising, contradictory brief it is hard to produce an effective solution.

The very best and most appropriate symbols often come from within the organization itself. P & O has had its house flag, an amalgamation of the personal standards of the royal houses of Bourbon in Spain and Braganza in Portugal, ever since the company was founded to trade with the Iberian peninsula in 1837.

Early in the 1970s, when a new corporate identity was being developed for the organization, the flag was removed from the obscurity in which it had been hidden for so long, and it became the heart of a flexible visual system which the organization currently uses with some ingenuity.

Another company that has evolved using its traditional symbolism is Renault. This great manufacturing enterprise uses its traditional lozenge, but fashionably modified by Victor Vasarély in the 1970s, linked with an elaborate visual programme created by Wolff Olins based on a system of typographic rules and a colour code for different Renault activities.

Renault has, however, failed to imbue its lozenge with any real emotional content. Instead of being used with panache and purpose, it largely remains a static device on the Renault vehicles.

Daimler-Benz, on the other hand, has succeeded triumphantly with the three-pointed star. Said to

WHY SAIL ACROSS THE CHANNEL WHI

represent the old Gottlieb Daimler engine manufacturing activity on air, land and water, it has become a symbol, perhaps *the* symbol of engineering excellence. Daimler-Benz treasures its symbol and sometimes uses it with surprising elan. The symbol is at its most effective as it stands above the car radiator directly in the driver's line of vision. It moves up and down with the motion of the vehicle, imparting an air of impressive invincibility. When the three-pointed star is there, one feels nothing can go wrong.

It is, of course, perfectly possible to sustain a significant commitment to design without using a symbol at all. Among the great names committed to design and identity in the twentieth century, Olivetti, for example, eschews symbols.

There isn't any general rule or agreement on whether symbols are appropriate for one industry and not for another. In the chemical world, for example, while Akzo uses a symbol, BASF and Du Pont use logotypes – that is to say, a special way of writing a name, a kind of signature.

YOU CAN CRUISE ACROSS? P&O European Ferries

WHY SAIL ACROSS THE CHANNEL WHEN YOU CAN CRUISE ACROSS? P&O European Ferries
A MEMBER OF THE P&O GROUP

The Peninsular & Oriental Steam Navigation Company was formed in 1837 to sail between Britain, Spain and Portugal. In 1975, the company's house flag became the corporate symbol, heart of the corporate identity created by Wolff Olins. The symbol is used in an active and imaginative way by McCann Erickson in advertising.

All of these great organizations place a financial value on their visual style. The name and visual style of an organization are sometimes the most important factors in making it appear unique. To this extent a visual style can be an immense financial asset. It is very difficult to place a value on such an intangible, emotional, kaleidoscopic, but nevertheless ubiquitous asset; but people try. Bayer, one of the three great German chemical companies, sensibly thought it was worthwhile to buy back its name and symbol in the US, for all activities except those in the pharmaceutical field, for 25 million dollars.

A trade has grown up amongst lawyers and patent agents in the protection of marks and symbols, and attempts are being made by some of the more imaginative legal people to extend this protection to a much wider area. A view is beginning to develop amongst some legal experts that it is the whole of what some of them call the 'intellectual property' that increasingly gives the company its individuality and therefore its strength in the marketplace.

All of which seems to indicate that most organizations that dedicate adequate resources, in terms of people, time and money, to presenting the totality of what they do effectively, are going to be worth a lot more money than those that don't, all other things being equal.

Which brings us right back to AEG and the Deutscher Werkbund. At the inaugural meeting of the Deutscher Werkbund on 5-6 October 1907, one of the delegates said: 'Art is not only an aesthetic, but a moral force; the two together lead to the most important power of all: economic power.'

How right he was.

CHAPTER **4**

Corporate Structure

Prologue

Most people think that corporate identity is about symbols, logotypes, colours, typography, even about buildings, products, furniture, about visual appearance, design.

And it is.

But identity can clarify how a company is organized, indicate whether it is centralized, or decentralized, and to what extent; it can also show whether it has divisions, subsidiaries or brands, and how these relate to the whole.

The organization has an infinite number of ways of expressing its structure.

Take an example. If a company has, say, five divisions and it uses one name, one set of colours, one symbol and typestyle in all of them, it will convey a simple, centralized idea of itself. If the same company gives each division a separate colour, it will inevitably project a more decentralized identity. And if it uses different names, symbols and logotypes for each division, it will give an even more disparate impression. The identity resource can clarify an organization's structure – and enable its purpose and its shape to emerge clearly.

Broadly speaking, the structure of identities can be divided into three separate categories.

Monolithic – Where the organization uses one name and visual style throughout. Examples: BMW, Tesco, IBM

Endorsed – Where an organization has a group of activities/companies which it endorses with the group name and identity. Examples: General Motors, United Technologies; P & O

Branded – Where the company operates through a series of brands which may be unrelated either to each other or to the corporation. Examples: Procter & Gamble, Unilever

Although this division sounds neat and tidy, in real life the edges between different kinds of identity are often blurred. For instance, it's sometimes difficult to know where an endorsed identity ends and a branded identity begins. Without necessarily realizing it companies may evolve from one of these categories into another, frequently in an uneven and uncontrolled fashion. Nevertheless, as a general guide this overall definition serves.

The decision to clarify an identity and make it work effectively should not be taken rashly. There are in any company inconsistencies that need careful consideration. Companies that move very fast without thinking things through sometimes look foolish.

The spur to change from an anonymous branded identity structure to an endorsed structure may come from an outside threat. In Britain, Allied Lyons – previously stumbling quietly along under umpteen brand names and for the most part unknown as a company – suddenly decided to endorse itself using the slogan 'Allied Lyons – A Great British Company', because it was being threatened by takeover. Since some of its products, like Castlemaine lager, are conspicuously not British, it has wisely allowed this qualifying phrase to fall into disuse.

It's worth remembering that none of the three identity categories is intrinsically superior to any other. Each category has its own advantages and disadvantages; one that is appropriate for one company may be wrong for another. However, each category is, or has traditionally been associated with specific kinds of business. The monolithic identity is associated with banking, airlines and oil companies, for example.

Tradition exercises so compulsive a grip that it is sometimes difficult to get a company that needs to review its identity structure even to consider evolving from one category to another. Organizations almost always demonstrate a ferocious tenacity in staying where they are. Try telling Procter & Gamble, a firm believer in brands, that with the growth of own-branding in supermarkets, their traditional branded activities need to be modified; that they should even consider developing an endorsed identity policy.

Harder still, talk to oil companies about introducing branding on a major scale at their retail outlets and reducing the power of their monolithic identities. They don't like it; they show every sign of feeling threatened.

And the reason for this defensive behaviour is comprehensible. All companies are traditionalist. No companies like change. But more importantly, the identity structure is not superficial, it is built deep into the management system.

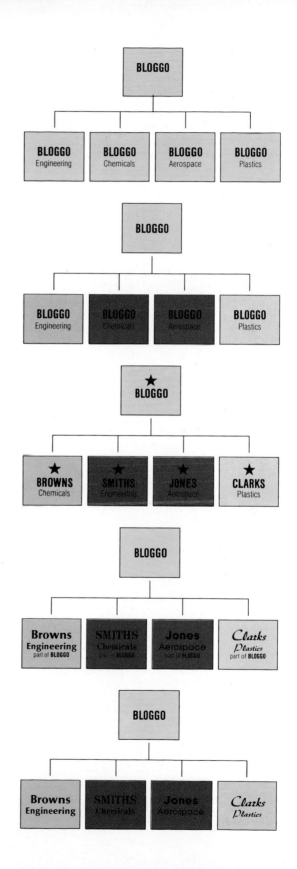

In principle there are three ways of creating an identity structure, but in reality many permutations are possible within each category.

It is more than just a way of naming things; it's a deep commitment to a particular way of doing business.

In a company like Shell, where one name dominates, if part of the business doesn't use the name, it's by implication a second-class citizen. The idea of diluting Shell, of adding other names, challenges the roots of Shell citizenship. Who has heard of Billiton, Shell's metals division? It's a huge company, one of the largest in its field in the world, but it doesn't seem like Shell at all, simply because it doesn't carry the Shell name. On the other hand, in an organization with an endorsed structure, using several names and identities, each part of the organization needs to feel its own power and strength, to find its own place in the sun in relation to the whole. To people who work at Pratt and Whitney, what they are and what they have is more important than UTC itself. Nobody at Otis Elevators, another UTC division, would seriously consider calling their activity United Technologies Elevators. And in the branded system, the brand managers and their partners in the advertising agency need the brand because that is what their fortunes are built around. So inevitably, in each of these different kinds of organization there is massive, built-in resistance to changing the current orthodoxy.

Changing identities isn't easy. The next few sections show where the strengths and weaknesses of each type of identity lie.

A Shell retail petrol sign from *c.* 1960.

Section 1 — Monolithic Identity

When the organization uses one
name and visual style throughout.

More than 90 per cent of Shell's business throughout the world bears the Shell name. Can you imagine Shell without its symbol, its colours or its name? Suppose it used different names for each of its activities. Suppose its petrol were called, let's say, Supol; its industrial lubricants, for example, Bloggan; its chemicals, Jarvi, and its exploration business, Diagon. Suppose different parts of Shell had different names in different countries; suppose that in France it was called Mollux, in Germany, Marschel, in Sweden, Swedoil. Suppose these activities not only had different names, but that they also looked different from each other. Suppose they even had different symbols and colours and different typefaces . . . Where would the power of Shell be then? How could Shell operate successfully in different countries, in different activities? How would it get its cohesion? How would people within the organization relate to each other?

Above all, who would know what Shell was and what it did?

The reputation of Shell is symbolized to a quite extraordinary extent by its name and visual imagery. If there were no single name, no symbol, no colours, there would be no single, simple idea of Shell. That's why Shell, and for that matter all the other major oil companies – BP, Elf, Agip, Arco, Mobil, Exxon, and the rest – have spent millions over many decades in creating, and then sustaining their identities. It's true that from time to time they come across a problem or two, like Exxon and Esso, and BP's Sohio. It's also the case that occasionally even the magic name of Shell is thought inappropriate for peripheral parts of the business, such as mayonnaise or metals. But with the odd exception here and there, the oil companies pursue their monolithic identity policies with vigour.

In the old days, when they first began, many of the oil companies did use a multiplicity of names and identities for their products in different countries.

Gradually, though, they came to realize that the most effective way to create loyalties amongst their employees was to develop a clear, cohesive single identity for the corporation as a whole. That is why the oil companies have tended to concentrate on just one name. The company could introduce one set of common standards, one way of doing things, which people working throughout the group could understand. A single name and visual identity became significant as a rallying point for the staff. In this way, employees, wherever they lived and worked, whatever their social, cultural or religious background, could identify with the whole enterprise.

There were other factors influencing them, too. Shell and the other majors were, in their heyday, much more than just large international companies. They became almost separate geo-political powers, negotiating on equal and sometimes superior terms with countries whose lands were fortunate enough to bear oil. Like nineteenth-century nation states, they needed to invent symbols in order to display their power in the outside world. Symbolism became important for diplomacy.

They used these symbols of power as negotiating weapons to bully and sometimes to override their unsophisticated partners.

In today's political climate, where OPEC power has become an important and often subtle negotiating instrument, that thought may make us smile, but it was once so, none the less.

The visual identity of Shell and the other oil majors also has a strong influence among customers. The identity purports to give customers a clear idea of what they can expect – in terms of product, service and price – in the belief that people will stay loyal to the organization that respects their needs and with which they are familiar. In this context one has to say that most oil companies fail to exploit the advantage that a single name and identity could give them largely because their corporate interests lie in what they call 'upstream' activities, exploration, distribution, and so on – and not in their 'downstream' businesses like marketing and retailing. That's why, generally speaking, oil companies are poor retailers. Compared with other retailers, oil companies often fail to offer consistency. That's why they have been known to court customers by offering free gifts of drinking glasses.

It isn't only customers who rally to a single idea, clearly expressed visually. Suppliers, competitors, potential recruits and influential people, from journalists to members of local and national government, are also powerfully influenced by it. So are shareholders and the financial community. Creating a single identity involves a vast and complex programme. It demands obsessive single-mindedness. But if you get it right, it converts anonymity to fame, respect and profit.

Opposite, and bottom left and right: using the Shell name in early promotional material. Below: some Shell products. Each is clearly labelled Shell, although in some cases brand identities are quite strong.

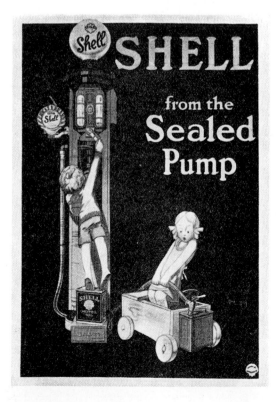

1948

1955

1930

1904

1961

1900

1971

Marcus Samuel Junior

The typeface used for the name and symbol varied considerably in the past. Above: the development of the Shell symbol over the years, surrounding Marcus Samuel, principal contributor to the foundation of the company.

Right: an unmistakably Shell station.

A characteristic of the monolithic identity is longevity. Most companies in the oil business have had versions of their identities for a very long time, in many cases for nearly a century. Although these identities are regularly monitored and modified where this seems appropriate, fundamentally they don't change much.

Shell has regularly revised its identity – altered the shape of its symbol to keep it up to date, and modified its typography and colours – but the basic elements of which the identity consists, the name, the colours, the typeface, have been around in one form or another for almost a century. Shell has applied this identity to service stations and shops (though standards of service may not have been consistent throughout the period), to its vehicles, buildings and advertisements around the world.

Within the oil business, the pattern set by the majors is clear. They try to have one simple name and one visual look wherever they go. They are powerful adherents of the monolithic approach.

Between the world wars, when the monitoring system was not so well developed, the occasional error got through the system. Above: a Shell-owned Fiat truck of the 1920s, carrying Shell products. Neither truck nor products bear the correct identity.

Although the oil industry is perhaps the outstanding example of organizations dedicating themselves to a single name and idea there are other major business areas in which this concept also finds favour, among them airlines. All the world's airlines, from the simplest third-level commuter company to global companies like Air France and British Airways, tend to use monolithic identity structures. It wouldn't do to call SAS Scandiwegian Airlines in the US; wherever they go, major airlines have to look consistent and perform in a coherent fashion.

Like oil companies, they operate globally, employing people of differing ethnic, religious and cultural backgrounds. If these people cannot work together, the airline simply will not operate smoothly. Employee commitment must emerge through appearance and behaviour.

Since all the major airlines tend to use the same aircraft, fly to the same places, charge the same prices and offer more or less identical services, they can only be distinguished from each other by minutiae that are expanded in the public mind by rumour and first-hand experience – and of course by advertising.

In an effort to bind together its three participating nationalities and compete effectively with its international rivals, SAS introduced a radical way of making its employees understand the concept of service. A new visual identity formed a substantial part of that package.

SAS – the Scandinavian airline redesigned by Landor Associates in 1983 on the monolithic model.

Within the information technology industry, IBM projects its omniscient, yet perennially youthful countenance to the whole world. Regardless of whether you are in Japan or Cameroon, IBM's buildings, products and communication materials gleam out at you. They are the corporate equivalent of 'Have a nice day!' From time to time, in order to keep that grin firmly fixed in place, one has the feeling that Big Blue goes off for a quiet facelift. But for the most part you won't see even the hint of a wrinkle on IBM's face.

And that, of course, is precisely the reason why IBM does it. The corporation wants to be seen to be offering the same product, to the same kind of customers, with the same kind of service, wherever it goes.

IBM's idea of itself is projected through its devastatingly precise control of its buildings – offices, factories, showrooms – its products, its communication material – letterheads, brochures, instruction manuals and advertising.

IBM tells us a lot about the kind of companies that adopt and then sustain a single idea of themselves, and consistently project that idea through everything they do.

They are companies that have grown largely organically.

They are proud of their achievement.

They usually have a reputation for quality.

They often operate in a coherent but relatively narrow band of activity.

They believe that their name and reputation are essential elements in the growth of their business, and they use them precisely and powerfully to distinguish themselves from their competitors and to attract customers.

Therefore, almost inevitably, like IBM, they are fanatical about the degree of detail they exercise over all manifestations of their identity.

Very often, although their products and services may be different from those of their competitors, they aren't necessarily *that* different; and it might be the case that the apparent differences between themselves and others in the market resides principally in the way they use their identities.

They often share one other characteristic, too.

Companies that go in for monolithic identity programmes are usually very easily characterized. Everybody knows what they stand for.

Amongst retail chains, Marks & Spencer (even though it continues perversely to use the St Michael brand mark) was a classic example of the genre until it began to make American acquisitions, starting with Brooks Brothers in 1988. Marks & Spencer is and has always been rather special.

The company has associations with a few remarkable and remarkably intertwined dynasties, whose paternalistic care for their staff has been quite as consistent as their interest in building up the business for the customer. The company has pursued a policy of enlightened self-interest in virtually every sphere that it has entered. It looks after its staff, openly educates its customers, especially with newer, more unusual foods, and it never underestimates their ambition or attraction to innovation.

Marks & Spencer offers a mixture of cleanliness, high quality, clarity, intelligence and acumen, without waste or unnecessary luxury, which adds up to uniqueness.

Main picture: Marks & Spencer use the name St Michael on all their brands, thereby creating unnecessary duplication, confusion and expense. St Michael, however, has been used as the Marks & Spencer brand name for many years and although the management cannot justify it rationally, they prefer it that way. All this confirms the irrational and emotional nature of the human condition, revealed in business as in personal life. Above: St Michael packaging is elaborate, expensive and seductive – and it works well.

Opposite: Brooks Bros – owned by Marks & Spencer, but with its own distinctive, exclusive, 'preppy' style.

In another sphere, BMW also has a monolithic identity. Like Marks & Spencer, BMW has for the most part expanded organically. Although at various times in its past the company has taken over the walking wounded of the German motor industry, in the main its expansion has been self-fuelled.

BMW cars and motorcycles have a unique reputation. They are classy, expensive, well made, reliable and somewhat sporting in their overall feel.

So what's the difference between BMW and its major national rival Mercedes-Benz?

In reality probably not a lot. In image terms, though, there is a wide gulf between them. Within Germany BMW is perceived to be Bavarian, while Mercedes is perceived to be German! Which effectively means that a technical shortcoming might be overlooked in BMW, but not forgiven in Mercedes. In the world as a whole, however, BMW is perceived to be lighter, less Teutonic, more exciting, younger, more fashionable.

BMW has deliberately set out to cultivate this idea of itself.

Of all the world's car producers it may be that BMW is the most image-conscious. Everything BMW does seems to project a BMW idea. Its head offices and museum in Munich, its advertising, its dealer showrooms, its catalogues and manuals are all sleek, prosperous, clean-cut and in good trim. There isn't anything podgy or overweight about BMW. Even its 12-cylinder 7-series flagship, a vehicle created for leaders in industry and commerce, looks as though it seats tall, silver-haired, clear-thinking, decision-makers in great physical shape, rather than overweight, balding, stress-ridden company directors waiting for their next coronary.

Bayerische Motoren Werke's head offices and main factories are located in Munich, capital city of Bavaria. BMW's symbol (above) incorporates the Bavarian colours, blue and white. Its head offices (right) with museum below are showpieces of Bavarian industry and demonstrate BMW's own progress.

Bottom left: the 7 series – flagship of the BMW model range.

The test for those companies with monolithic identities is simple but clear. If they went into another business, made something quite different, would you still recognize what it was as deriving from them? Put another way, how far can you effectively stretch the single idea?

Just for the sake of argument, could IBM, Marks & Spencer and BMW successfully expand into competing activities, and if so would their products differ much?

It's perfectly conceivable – although perhaps somewhat unlikely – that all three companies could move into, say, white goods – domestic consumer durables.

All three companies would be credible marketing washing machines, dishwashers, cookers, fridges, microwaves and similar domestic paraphernalia under their own brand names. What's more, each company would produce equipment which would be individual and subtly different from the others. They would each be competitive in their own different ways at the upper end of this difficult and overcrowded marketplace.

Going on from there, BMW could quite easily move into men's and women's clothing (they already produce a range of so-called motorsport accessories). BMW could so easily link with that other prestige manufacturer Hugo Boss to continue to widen the range; BMW leather goods, BMW perfumes for men, are all perfectly credible conceptually, simply because of their strength of the BMW idea.

Through single-minded devotion to the product, to the environment in which it appears and through the way in which it communicates, BMW has created a tangible idea of itself, and so have all other successful companies using the monolithic concept.

There are some businesses that have deliberately set out to give their name so special an aura that they can sell practically anything under it, providing that it seems to meet some kind of quality requirement.

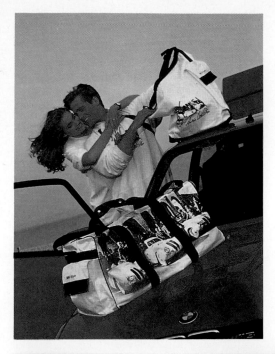

BMW's M (for Motorsport) range of accessories (left and right).

Bottom left: part of the BMW Museum at Munich.

Below: brochures for BMW 5 and 6 series cars.

Alfred Dunhill, after a foray into motoring equipment, set up in 1907 as a maker of pipes, tobaccos and smoking accessories. Between the Wars, Dunhill had a limited but affluent clientele, largely made up of British middle- and upper-class tweedy males. Today Dunhill has become the ultimate name in expensive gentlemen's baubles, frequently called gifts – which is paradoxically the last thing they are. Watches, belts, blazers, scent and similar items are sold in Dunhill shops all over the world. Located in duty free sections of airports and on expensive real estate in smart cities, these shops are temples devoted to 'Dunhill-ness'. The only, absolutely the only reason for buying the products in them is that they bear the Dunhill name and symbol, which in turn says that they are expensive. And that is apparently enough to guarantee their success with a certain kind of customer.

Dunhill (which is partly owned by Rothmans) is not alone in having moved away from its origins into a range of associated products. Many companies with very strong images, or reputations, if you like, have done it, including Yves Saint-Laurent and Dior starting from a base in clothing, and Davidoff from cigars.

What happens in this case is that the manufacturer's name is franchised to any company that thinks it has a product that fits the image. Sometimes, when a company like Dunhill polices its activities carefully and doesn't get too greedy too quickly, it all works well. Sometimes, though, through over-ambition, incompetence, short-sightedness, or even over-exposure, or through trying to stretch the idea too far too fast, the name degenerates into meaningless nothingness.

There are, however, a few companies that have used a single name over a

Dunhill markets expensive luxury products in temples dedicated to the Dunhill idea. Dunhill developed from motoring accessories into pipes and pipe tobacco and then into cigarettes, lighters, watches, clothes and women's products.

Section 1 – Monolithic Identity

Davidoff began life as cigar traders. Now there are Davidoff branded Havana cigars – and Davidoff cognac, men's toiletries and similar items.

vast range of activities with complete success. These companies are usually Japanese.

Yamaha build musical instruments. They also build motorcycles. It didn't occur to Yamaha that their reputation in one field might not be transferable to another.

Mitsubishi go much further. This venerable institution is one of the largest companies in Japan, which makes it one of the largest in the world. There isn't much that Mitsubishi hasn't done. In manufacturing, it makes, amongst many other things, cars and aircraft; both are called Mitsubishi. It owns a bank called Mitsubishi. It also operates in the consumer goods field; you will find Mitsubishi tinned salmon, crab and tuna in your main street store. To appreciate the full size and scope of the Mitsubishi phenomenon you have to look for a parallel. Suppose there was a Ford bank, Ford canned salmon and a Ford funeral parlour.

Mitsubishi, the name and the visual identity, the sign, represents a series of qualities to Japanese customers, and increasingly to consumers around the world, which remain constant, regardless of the field of activity in which the company operates.

Conceptually, the monolithic identity has immense advantages for Mitsubishi, for Shell, for IBM, for BMW, for Dunhill and for everyone else who operates it. It is the clearest and most economical way of declaring what your standards are, what you offer to customers, suppliers and staff, and in return what you expect from them.

It underlines the point that one simple message is far clearer than four or five different messages.

But in return the monolithic identity demands consistency of performance and quality, minute attention to detail, and endless self-criticism.

Mitsubishi is one of Japan's oldest and largest corporations. Various Mitsubishi enterprises operate in a wide variety of industries, using the three red diamonds symbol.

Yamaha make a wide variety of products, including musical instruments and motorcycles, all under the Yamaha name. Like very many Japanese companies – and unlike most Western companies – Yamaha believes that using one name on all products lends credibility and strength to the entire enterprise.

Section 2 — Endorsed Identity

Where an organization has a group
of activities or companies which it
endorses with the group name and
identity.

Armies have the most complex, sophisticated, flexible identity structures of any large organizations. Military identity structures are continually being adapted to suit different sets of circumstances; they expand monstrously in size in war and shrink in peacetime. They are carefully orchestrated so as to exact a fierce loyalty from those who belong to the various parts, and to demonstrate exactly who and what each part is in relation to every other part and to the organization as a whole.

In the British army all this is done through the thoughtful and ingenious use of names and visual symbols, and thorough-going and continuing indoctrination.

The detail of it is constructed out of that typical mixture of tradition and overt social snobbery that appeals so strongly to the British people. The infantry is not just the infantry. At the top of the infantry hierarchy there is the Brigade of Guards. Within the Brigade are the Grenadier Guards (single buttons on dress tunics), the Coldstream Guards (buttons grouped in twos), the Scots Guards (buttons grouped in threes), the Irish Guards (buttons grouped in fours) and the Welsh Guards (buttons grouped in fives – so God help a clumsy Welsh Guardsman!). Below the Guards regiments, though not far behind in status, come the Royal Green Jackets, who are also part of the Light Infantry. They march fast, and on ceremonial occasions wear a kind of hunting green uniform, thereby revealing their direct (and irrelevant) descent from Hessian Jaeger mercenary units which fought with the British army in the late eighteenth century.

Then, in hierarchical terms, comes the rest of the infantry of the line, which somehow or other has survived dramatic expansion, contraction, role change, merger and amalgamation, and through symbols, names and geographical associations continues to use identity as a powerful focus for loyalty.

Another major fighting arm has also adapted remarkably to its present circumstances. The Royal Armoured Corps consists of five tank regiments and many more cavalry regiments – Hussars, Lancers, Dragoons and Dragoon Guards – who use much the same equipment. While all armoured regiments do the same job, however, the cavalry regiments are much more fashionable than the tank regiments. Their plumes are gaudier, their officers richer, their names and badges are swankier. In fact all round they remain what they always were: 'quite the thing'.

For the purposes of forming a significant fighting unit that can operate on some scale, it is necessary to combine elements of the various arms into larger formations. The most significant of these is a division. In some armies (the German, for instance) the division is the major focus of loyalty, and traditionally divisions also have nicknames and visual symbolism, usually of a crude and macho, but forceful nature. The British 7th Armoured Division was called Desert Rats, because its symbol was a gerbil and it spent much of the Second World War in the desert.

Although the military identity appears to be unique, in reality this is not so. The identity structure used by an army is simply a more sophisticated version of the endorsed identity structure used by many large organizations, both industrial and commercial, and even academic, in very many parts of the world.

An endorsed identity structure is based around the concept that the individual parts of an organization can be readily identified but are also seen as part of a larger whole.

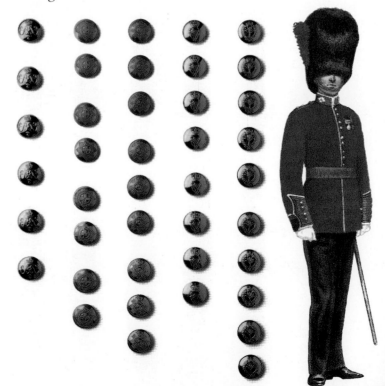

PLAYER'S CIGARETTES.
19TH REGIMENT OF FOOT;
Grenadier's cap, 1750.

PLAYER'S CIGARETTES.
18TH (THE KING'S) LIGHT DRAGOONS;
Officer's full dress helmet, 1768.

PLAYER'S CIGARETTES.
HIGHLAND REGIMENTS;
Full dress bonnet, 1790.

PLAYER'S CIGARETTES.
7TH (QUEEN'S OWN) HUSSARS;
Officer's full dress shako, 1807.

PLAYER'S CIGARETTES.
HIGHLAND REGIMENTS;
Feather bonnet, 1810.

PLAYER'S CIGARETTES.
LIFE GUARDS;
Officer's full dress helmet, 1815.

PLAYER'S CIGARETTES.
91ST REGIMENT OF FOOT;
Officer's full dress shako, 1816.

PLAYER'S CIGARETTES.
2ND DRAGOON GUARDS;
Officer's full dress helmet, 1822-31.

PLAYER'S CIGARETTES.
THE RIFLE BRIGADE;
Officer's full dress shako, 1829-44.

PLAYER'S CIGARETTES.
9TH (QUEEN'S ROYAL) LANCERS;
Officer's full dress cap, 1830-40.

PLAYER'S CIGARETTES.
15TH THE KING'S HUSSARS;
Officer's full dress shako, 1834.

PLAYER'S CIGARETTES.
4TH (ROYAL IRISH) DRAGOON GUARDS;
Officer's full dress helmet, 1834-43.

PLAYER'S CIGARETTES.
6TH DRAGOON GUARDS;
Officer's full dress helmet, 1843-47.

PLAYER'S CIGARETTES.
21ST FUSILIERS REGT. OF FOOT;
Officer's full dress shako, 1844.

PLAYER'S CIGARETTES.
3RD (KING'S OWN) LIGHT DRAGOONS;
Officer's full dress shako, 1846-55.

PLAYER'S CIGARETTES.
93RD REGIMENT OF FOOT;
Bandsman's forage cap, 1849.

PLAYER'S CIGARETTES.
1ST LIFE GUARDS;
Officer's full dress helmet, 1860.

PLAYER'S CIGARETTES.
25TH REGIMENT OF FOOT;
Officer's full dress shako, 1869-78.

PLAYER'S CIGARETTES.
5TH REGIMENT OF FOOT;
Officer's full dress fur cap, 1874.

PLAYER'S CIGARETTES.
THE ROYAL SCOTS;
Officer's full dress Kilmarnock, 1904.

Most of the world's armies, especially perhaps the British, enthusiastically embrace bizarre distinctions of name and dress.

Opposite: dress uniforms of the different regiments of the British Brigade of Guards have minor distinguishing characteristics. From left to right: Grenadier Guards (single button), Coldstream Guards (grouped in twos), Scots Guards (grouped in threes), Irish Guards (grouped in fours), Welsh Guards (grouped in fives).

Above and left: military headgear – a set of cards issued by Players Cigarettes in 1931, illustrating the diversity of British military uniforms through a history of military headgear.

The two ancient universities of Oxford and Cambridge use an endorsed identity structure, although the officials of these two organizations would, I suspect, be surprised and perhaps even alarmed to be told so.

There has grown up over hundreds of years a collection of separate colleges, each of which competes against the others in sporting and scholarly attainments. Each of the colleges has its own heraldry, coats of arms, college colours, much of it no doubt devised by those busy inventors of tradition, the Victorians.

Quite separate from these institutions, in which students live and are taught by academics, are the university faculties of sciences, languages, philosophy and so on. These are shared by the whole institution, so the colleges are part of, and also endorsed by the university.

It is quite common for venerable institutions that have adapted themselves over time to changing circumstances to develop endorsed identity structures in this way.

In Britain, P & O began life as the Peninsular & Oriental Steam Navigation Company in 1837. In France it was the great Colbert who established Saint Gobain as a state glass works in the seventeenth century. Daimler-Benz, now Germany's largest company, is a centenarian; even upstart Volkswagen is more than fifty.

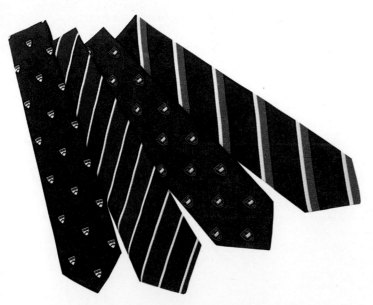

Companies such as these have grown both organically and by acquisition. Sometimes in growing they have discarded their original activities. Companies that began as small, local affairs have become vast international enterprises with global activities.

Companies projecting an endorsed identity normally have the following characteristics:

They have usually grown largely by acquisition. Often they have acquired competitors, suppliers and customers, each with its own name, culture, traditions and reputation amongst its own network of audiences.

They tend to be multi-sector businesses, often operating in a very wide band of activities – manufacturing, wholesaling, retailing, selling components to competitive manufacturers, making finished products themselves, and so on.

They are generally anxious to retain the goodwill associated with the brands and companies they have acquired, but at the same time they want to superimpose their own management style, reward systems, attitudes and sometimes name upon their subsidiaries.

They have certain audiences, e.g. the financial community, certain suppliers and so on, whom they want to impress with their total size and strength. Amongst these groups, they will want to emphasize uniformity and consistency as opposed to diversity.

Often they have acquired competitive ranges of products. They therefore have problems of competition, even confusion, among suppliers, customers, and often, their own employees.

Finally, they frequently operate in a large number of countries in which their products and their reputations vary.

Companies that seek to create a corporate identity covering a wide range of activities, with subsidiaries of differing and frequently competing backgrounds, face a complicated task. On the one hand, certainly at the corporate level and for corporate audiences, they want to create the clear idea of a single, but multi-faceted organization with a sense of purpose. On the other hand, they want to allow the identities of the numerous companies and brands they have acquired to continue to flourish in order to retain goodwill, both in the marketplace and amongst employees.

 All Souls

Balliol

Brasenose

Campion Hall

Corpus Christi

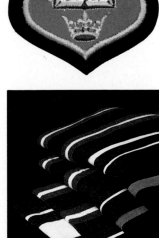

Christ Church

Exeter

Green College

Greyfriars

Hertford

Jesus

Keble

L.M.H.

Lincoln

Linacre

Magdalen

Merton

Manchester

Mansfield

Nuffield

New

Oriel

Pembroke

Queen's

Regent's Park

St. Hilda's

St. Catherine's

St. Antony's

St. Ed. Hall

St. Hugh's

St. John's

Somerville

St. Peter's

St. Anne's

Trinity

University

Wadham

Westminster

Wolfson

Worcester

The different colleges of Oxford University have their own colours and heraldry. Shown above and left are scarves, ties and wall plaques supplied by Shepherd & Woodward, the Oxford outfitters.

Oxford's traditional colour is dark blue, while Cambridge's is light blue. An athlete who is picked to represent either university is awarded a 'blue'.

General Motors, once the world's largest industrial enterprise, was the first modern corporation to recognize and hence to solve the problem. Unhappily, it also provides a case study of what happens when things are allowed to slip.

Round about 1918 Alfred Sloan, the commercial genius who managed the growth of General Motors, was alarmed by the overwhelming dominance of Ford in the market place. Ford had one car – the Model T – which until VW's Beetle was the world's most ubiquitous automobile. General Motors, on the other hand, had a multiplicity of makes and models which defied description or analysis. It had grown simply by acquiring every automobile manufacturing and component company in sight. So, although General Motors was a vast company, it was – in the words of Sloan – a ramshackle business. It produced competing makes and models, and owned a plethora of component makers. Companies did their own purchasing, designed their own products, competed with each other in the marketplace, had their own names, badges, visual symbolism and a complex, and sometimes romantic history – just like the regiments in an army. Companies recruited their staff separately; there was no central research and development, nothing.

'The product policy we proposed', says Sloan in his classic book *My Years with General Motors* (1963), 'is the one for which General Motors has now long been known. We said first that the corporation should produce a line of cars in each price area, from the lowest price up to one for strictly high-grade quality production.'

A key element in this system was to take existing motor-car companies and position them all the way up the range, from Chevrolet, which was intended to compete with Ford, at the bottom; through Oakland (replaced by Pontiac), Oldsmobile and Buick to Cadillac at the top. Each company retained its elaborate visual symbolism, and although each knew its place, each was encouraged to be proud of what it was.

As Sloan put it in his dry way: 'The core of the product policy lies in its concept of mass-producing a full line of cars graded upward in quality and price.'

From our perspective in the last years of the twentieth century, this looks a simple – even obvious – strategy. But as Sloan said: 'It certainly didn't seem simple at the time, when Ford had more than half the market with two grades . . . and others had substantial positions in the industry and were making or preparing bids with other product policies. For all we knew our policy might not have worked best.'

At the time Sloan introduced the policy in 1919/1920, Ford had 60 per cent of the market and Chevrolet had 4 per cent. Within ten years, Chevrolet alone had a higher market share than Ford, and General Motors had become the world's largest manufacturing enterprise.

The General Motors endorsed structure introduced by Sloan was the first, most complete and most successful example of its kind. It lasted from the 1920s to the 1970s, and set the pattern for the entire industry. It was emulated by Walter Chrysler, with Chrysler, de Soto, Dodge and Plymouth, and eventually by Ford itself, who in the 1930s belatedly introduced Ford, Mercury and Lincoln on exactly the same lines. Later, BMC and its successors in the UK were to apply the General Motors system with disastrous results.

Since the late 1970s General Motors has lost its identification with Sloan's principles. It has gradually reverted to an unshaped mass, similar to the one Sloan found when he moved into the company. Its major manufacturing units all compete with each other and resemble each other, forming a complicated web of international relationships. Yet it also has large chunks of business, like Hughes and EDS, which have no relationship with anything else it does. And it seems to be on the receiving end of one blow after another from its competitors. Sloan's description of General Motors as he saw it in the second decade of the twentieth century seems to contain a good lesson for today: 'In the great expansion in General Motors between 1918 and 1920, I had been struck by the disparity between substance and form; plenty of substance and little form. I became convinced that the corporation could not continue to grow and survive unless it was better organized, and it was apparent that no-one was giving that subject the attention it needed.'

A selection of US-built General Motors automobiles at the height of their predominance in the mid-1950s. Top to bottom: Chevrolet, Pontiac, Oldsmobile, Buick and Cadillac; hardtops and softops. All these cars share a common look, but each has its own individuality. Engines and components were frequently shared across divisions.

Although each division had elaborate graphic symbolism, it was continually modified. Top to bottom: Chevrolet symbol; Pontiac symbol of the 1930s; Oldsmobile symbol of the 1920s; Buick symbol of the 1920s; Cadillac symbol of the 1950s.

Another great American manager did a very similar thing in another great American company two generations later. Harry Gray created United Technologies out of a mass of squabbling, directionless engineering companies, some of which had important reputations in their own right.

Gray decided what should be centralized, what should be left to the divisions, how the divisions should relate to each other, what the corporate contribution to the whole should be. He capitalized on the reputation of each of the divisions and used their names and contacts both for their own benefit and for that of the whole enterprise.

In identity terms, Harry Gray enabled each of the major operating units of United Technologies to develop its own identity and to share in the identity of the group as a whole. All of this was worked out visually by his identity consultants Lippincott & Margulies, and introduced in 1981.

Sloan of General Motors and Gray of United Technologies reorganized their huge structures, with their multiplicity of names and identities, in such a way as to achieve coherence. Where the group strength was required – in purchasing, senior recruitment, research and development, government relations or relationships with the financial community – they presented the whole; but when individual companies needed to express their own identities – in relation to their customers, their collaborators, the local community – they could do that too. Without necessarily being aware of it, Sloan and Gray used the military as a model for the identity structure that they set up.

The reason why Alfred Sloan of General Motors and Harry Gray of United Technologies are important in the history of identity is that they took a complex and difficult system and imposed it upon their organizations. They rightly saw identity as an instrument of management. They saw that it defines relationships within the organization and makes the corporate purpose visible.

A LIFT FOR THE CITY Skyscrapers wouldn't make sense without elevators; and in elevators, Otis is the name that means most. Otis is a United Technologies company. So are Pratt & Whitney Aircraft, Carrier, Sikorsky, to name a few. All great names. All

Most companies that have grown by acquisition do not recognize that identity is a way in which the organization can clearly articulate what it is; the way in which the acquiring company can clearly stake out its purpose. The majority of companies, however, allow the individual units they have acquired to retain their existing names and visual style unaltered.

There are many ways of practising the endorsed identity system, from the full-blooded approach used by Alfred Sloan at General Motors and Harry Gray at United Technologies, right across the spectrum to the more usual base-line acknowledgment.

There is a level, however, beneath which the token acknowledgment simply ceases to serve any purpose. It is so inconspicuous that it might as well not be there. Management that does not effectively endorse often does not effectively manage.

The whole point about an endorsed identity programme is that it must actually do what it is supposed to do – it must be seen and acknowledged by those inside and outside the corporation who deal with it.

...part of United Technologies Corporation. Now, *that's* a name that may not mean much to you. But it will, it will. We're one of the top 10 U.S. manufacturing corporations and, as they say at Otis, going up. Remember United Technologies, Hartford, Connecticut 06101.

United Technologies Corporation, under the leadership of Harry Gray, became sophisticated exponents of the endorsed identity system. Within UTC there were a number of divisions that were important in their own industry sectors, such as Sikorsky, and Pratt & Whitney. A complex and subtle identity system created by US consultants Lippincott & Margulies, together with ingenious corporate advertising, enabled each division to contribute to the strength of the whole, while reinforcing its own position.

Section 3 — Branded Identity

Where the company operates
through a series of brands which
may be unrelated either to each
other or to the corporation.

In 1884 William Hesketh Lever, the commercial genius who founded the Lever part of what became the Unilever empire, gave thought to launching onto the market a distinctive sort of soap. Soap was normally sold in anonymous greyish bars, whose quality varied between consignments. Lever had in mind a soap of distinctive and consistent quality.

Lever called on W.S. Thompson, a Liverpool trademark and patent agent, to ask for a suitable mark, '. . . one which could be upheld in the law courts if an imitation came along'. Thompson gave him a list of names; individually none of them appealed to him. Three or four days later it flashed across him that on the list was the name he was looking for. The name was 'Sunlight'. 'When that occurred to me I had to go straight off to Liverpool and ask Thompson to register it at once', said Lever some years later.

Charles Wilson, historian of Unilever, explains: 'Lever had to consider the market which his soap was to serve. Here the changing social situation was his paramount concern. The working-class housewife had to be convinced that soap – Lever's soap – was not a luxury or a semi-necessity but an indispensable necessity for her home.'

Until Lever turned up with his revolutionary ideas, British soap-makers had, for the most part, taken the apparently reasonable view that one soap was much like another, and that you couldn't control the quality between boilings. One manufacturer, Christopher Thomas of Bristol, summed up the traditional view rather neatly: 'There is little or no difference in quality between different makes of Bar Soaps – there is a Thomas's Primrose, a Knight's Primrose, a Cook's Primrose – all the same soap. It is impossible, therefore, by the nature of the case to [attempt] through advertising to create a demand in favour of any one particular make.'

Lever, who realized what he had got with the 'Sunlight' name and 'was all in a tremble to have it registered', thought otherwise.

After a little experimentation with quality – some of Lever's original versions of Sunlight, made for him under contract by third parties, went rancid and stank – Lever got the product right.

He packaged Sunlight in imitation parchment and then in a carton, and he started to advertise it heavily. He later said, in a characteristic mixture of bombast and shrewdness, 'In the very first handbook we issued with Sunlight soap, which was got up by myself, entitled Sunlight Soap and How to Use It, everything was brought down to the level of a working man's needs.'

From then on, Lever promoted Sunlight with vigour. He appears to have acquired a quantity of American advertising material – even a century ago, the United States had established its primacy in such matters – including a slogan, of which he was particularly fond, 'Why does a woman look old sooner than a man?', and which he adapted for the British market.

Saves **LABOUR**
Saves **MONEY**

EQUATION—
LABOUR LIGHT, CLOTHES WHITE = SUNLIGHT

Sunlight was Lever's first branded product. It is over a hundred years old and is still manufactured and sold in many markets. When it was launched it embraced all the ingredients of a good brand – a name that summed up the qualities of the product; bold, clear, well-focused packaging; consistent quality; and imaginative, highly visible promotion. Far left: advertisement, *c*. 1930, featuring early-1900s pack design. Left: poster, 1890s. Above: advertisements, *c*. 1905 and (top) *c*. 1900.

Early promotion material for three Lever products: each cleverly aimed at creating or exploiting market niches. Opposite: with continuing pressure from retailers' own label brands, the increasing cost of advertising and promotions and escalating competition, Unilever – the pioneer of branding – is moving some way towards the endorsed identity model through its Lever range of detergent products. Right: a full-colour advertisement featured in the UK Sunday press for Lever, 1988.

In 1894 Sunlight, by then a roaring success, was followed by Lever's second major brand: Lifebuoy. It was promoted as a disinfectant soap, the enemy of epidemics and microbes. Then came Monkey Brand, Vim and Plantol.

Plantol was a product derived from vegetable oils. Lever's colleague Sydney Gross, apparently some kind of prototypical David Ogilvy, described it as 'fruit and flowers'. He expressed disappointment with a Plantol brochure: 'A pamphlet on Toilet Soap needs picturesque handling, something about the tropic climates in which the materials are produced, the care that is exercised in refining the oils, the flowers that are picked by the women of the South in fields full of colour and beauty. That is rather the line that should have been taken, not a treatise on perspiration, sweat and pores.'

In 1899 Lever introduced Lux Flakes. The name Lux also seems to have been the brainchild of the fertile Mr Thompson.

By the turn of the twentieth century, Lever had established himself in Britain, in the British Empire, Europe and even the United States as an aggressive, effective salesman of household products using the branding system.

Kellogg's cornflakes packs, 1989
(right) and *c*. 1956 (above).
    Opposite: Quaker Oats packs,
1989 (left) and *c*. 1900 (right).

The idea of branding emerged in the middle of the nineteenth century, when technology combined with literacy and rising standards of living to create the first mass market. The thinking that lay behind branding was very simple, but highly original. It was to take a household product, a commodity, no different fundamentally from any other made by another manufacturer, and to endow it with special characteristics through imaginative use of name, packaging and advertising.

The companies, mainly American, that originated the branded idea all began in more or less the same way. They took ordinary standard products, such as soap or tea, coffee or fats, and they gave them a distinctive name and packaging. They advertised them very heavily and then they distributed them widely. The achievement of these companies was prodigious. They took advantage of the latest technologies available at the time: rapid, regular and widespread transport, refrigeration, cheap newspapers, mass advertising to reach a public with improved living standards.

But in addition they had another thought: that you could separate the idea of the company from the products which it made; and therefore, that each product could be aimed at a specific group of people – or as we would put it, in the unlovely jargon of our own day, at a target market.

Once the idea of separate target audiences grew up, the permutations were endless. You could produce a whole range of products aimed at different groups; it didn't really matter if the intrinsic difference between the products was negligible, providing they all had individual names and packaging, and were promoted separately in ways appropriate to each target audience.

With cheap newspapers, rising literacy and the growth of chains of provision stores, the development of consumer marketing as we know it today became possible. Branding soon became the magic ingredient that enabled companies to sell variations of a single product to the greatest possible variety of people.

Within a very few years, brands were accepted as the orthodox way in which to launch, market and promote consumer products.

Branding never totally eliminated the older, more traditional patterns by which companies promoted their own products in their own name. In the chocolate field, for example, Cadbury in the UK, Hershey in the US and Nestlé in Switzerland all promoted through their company name as well as through brands.

Even new and innovative products like breakfast cereal didn't always use a brand name. In the early years of this century, when branding was the norm, the Kellogg's Toasted Corn Flakes Company of Battle Creek, Michigan, was so firmly convinced that its founder's name sold the product, that its packs bore a facsimile signature of W.K. Kellogg. The Quaker company, on the other hand, whose products were in the same field, used the branded system.

Branding is one of the most powerful ways of promoting a product. The greatest single strength of the brand is that, because it is created carefully and deliberately to appeal to a particular group of people at a particular point in time, it can be imbued with powerful, complex, highly charged and immediate symbolism aimed at a specific marketplace.

Betty Crocker was created in 1921 by Washington Crosby Inc. – a flour miller later absorbed into General Mills. In 1924 she acquired a voice. By 1940 Betty was known to 9 out of 10 American homemakers. Left: Her portrait has been painted seven times, on each occasion to suit the American mood. In 1961 Betty Crocker's *New Picture Cookbook* offered encouragement attuned to that era with: 'Think pleasant thoughts while working and a chore will become a labour of love.' The 1986 version, by contrast, helps cooks save time in the kitchen and produce lively meals.

Betty Crocker's portrait appeared first in 1936. In 1941 she became a brand name on packaging; and by 1986 the name appeared on more than 130 products.

Brands can develop strong personalities in the mind of the consumer. Betty Crocker, that indomitably sprightly middle-western housewife, has been producing her homespun recipes for General Mills and its predecessors since 1921 or thereabouts. Betty Crocker not only writes recipes, she also signs her name. She has had her portrait painted on several occasions (like Dorian Gray, she doesn't age) and she has even appeared on radio programmes. And of course, Betty doesn't really exist. She is made up, a figment of the imagination of all the people, within the company and its advertising agencies, who have worked on the Betty Crocker concept for most of this century.

Betty Crocker is typical of a certain kind of brand. This brand has clear values, some of which are based on particular physical properties, but far more of which are rooted in the psychological, sociological, emotional and even spiritual ideas that the brand is deemed to encompass.

In well-ordered manufacturing companies and their advertising agencies, these brand properties are continually examined and, where appropriate, modulated to keep them in line with consumer expectations.

If it is to be successful the brand has to have a life of its own quite separate from that of the company.

Persil is an interesting, and perhaps extreme example of this. Persil has so powerful an identity, has been treated for so long with such loving care and attention, that it doesn't seem to matter much who it belongs to. Through a bizarre quirk of history, Persil is actually the child of two competing companies. The brand was originally created by Henkel, the German chemicals group. After the First World War, the name Persil was appropriated by Lever in Britain and France as reparations for war damage caused to Lever factories.

Since 1918 Persil has belonged to Unilever in Britain and France, and to the German Henkel company elsewhere. And yet the values which the brand projects seem to be almost identical wherever it appears.

But unfortunately the brand system, once so brilliant, simple and original, is in danger of becoming decadent through its institutionalization into the management structure. Many companies which operate through brands have built up a massive, self-perpetuating framework through brand managers and advertising agencies, dedicated to defending the brand systems. In today's devitalized system, the brand manager – frequently a young marketing person on the way up the commercial ladder – sometimes uses temporary occupation of the brand in order to demonstrate flair and originality at the expense of brand consistency. All of which no doubt accounts for the dramatic and often destructive changes of direction which some poor old brands are currently forced to make. A far cry from William Hesketh Lever.

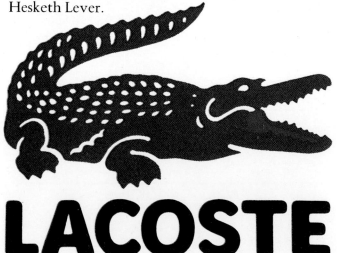

But then, the world in which the brand operates today is infinitely more complex than it was 100 years ago. Until recently, target audiences were thought to be relatively uncomplicated. Even today, some companies still deal in the comically naive social shorthand in which the rich are described as socio-economic group A, followed by the ABs, the C1s, C2s, and ending at the bottom of the scale with Ds, and even the Es. Most companies, however, realize that today things are a bit more complicated than that. Consumers are more sophisticated; they are a lot richer; there are many more of them, and they have unpredictable patterns of purchasing behaviour.

Some young people have a lot of money; some rather old people have a lot of money. Some people with not a lot of money nevertheless spend a high proportion of what they have on hobbies – photography or what have you. Quite a lot of rich people want to look expensively classless, which is why they wear costly jeans. Brand names have become an obsession for some of us. All of which makes branding a happy hunting ground for many manufacturers.

Some examples of sophisticated, thoughtful and imaginative branding from different countries. Left to right: Lacoste – France; Nike – US; Rolex – Switzerland; Burberry – UK; Missoni – Italy.

In addition, the ways in which markets can be approached have become much more complex.

There is a bewildering choice of media: broadcasting in all its forms – radio, television, local, regional, national, international; newspapers of every conceivable type; magazines catering for even the most recondite tastes.

And all this has an effect on the brand. The brand proliferates. Nowadays there is a brand designed for virtually everything and everybody – even animals. That is the reason why Brut is for men, Poison is for women, and Bonio is for dogs. There is now an infinity of choice, or apparent choice, in almost every product – not just in scent and soap, but even in mustard, bread and milk.

While there are a lot of favourable signs for branding, there are some unfavourable indications, too.

People are much better educated than they were; they have much more choice, and they ask far more questions, and sometimes – not always – can spot when a brand is phoney.

On top of that, the distribution channels – the shops, stores, retail outlets, or whatever the current jargon is – are no longer passive purveyors of manufacturers' brands.

Over the last generation the change that has been taking place in the retail stores in many countries has been revolutionary – almost as revolutionary as the growth of the manufacturer's brand itself at an earlier period. Where the branded products were king for over a century, while the retailer was for the most part supine, the monolithic identity has now been 'discovered' by the retailer. In a sense we could say that the retailer has found his strengths and suddenly emerged from nowhere to take a vast slice of the market. In certain countries and in some kinds of market, retailers with monolithic identities in environment (shops), information systems (packaging and advertising) and products are busily knocking the traditional branded manufacturers cock-eyed. All this is still relatively new and somewhat surprising.

Today in Britain, for example, some of the most exciting and innovative packaging and branding in the foods sector comes from the best and the biggest of the retail store groups.

There are niche markets in branding for everyone and everything – Brut is for men, Poison is for women, and Bonio is for dogs.

There are, however, no clear signs as yet that many consumer goods manufacturers have realized what this implies for them: that they too will have to modify their identity strategies so as to strengthen their corporate endorsement. In the traditional war between manufacturer and retailer, all the signs are that after 80 years of manufacturer dominance, the retailer is starting to win.

What *is* becoming clear, is that a lot of rethinking is going on in the world of foods and household products. The century-old legacy of the brand is being challenged, and some time very soon changes will come.

For the most part the retailer revolution has taken place in Europe – especially in the UK where Tesco, Sainsbury and others are challenging the manufacturer's branding. In the US there are also developments. Grand Union, the East Coast supermarket group formerly controlled by Sir James Goldsmith, used Milton Glaser to carry out interior and packaging design.

Meanwhile, in another part of the forest there is a huge amount of excitement. In the financial world it looks as though branding is about to emerge in its full glory.

The old distinctions between banks, insurance companies, building societies (savings and loans institutions), are breaking down.

Over the past few years, the financial services industry has generated a mass of products, most of which are indistinguishable from each other. Everybody is selling everything to everyone.

The consumers for whom these products are designed are for the most part financially semi-educated. They are bemused by the apparently identical offerings with which they are bombarded by competing companies. They cannot tell one company and one product from another. To compound the issue, the number of products in the marketplace is so vast that even the people selling the products are confused. In other words, financial services are becoming a commodity. This, as any simpleton could conclude, is a classic opportunity for branding.

However, the traditional resistance that always emerges to any kind of identity change is also characteristic in the financial marketing field. Financial service companies are frightened of branding because they think it may dilute the power of their corporate reputation.

Despite this, there are clear signs that in the financial services world branding will emerge as a powerful marketing tool.

In the UK, Midland Group has created a series of brands around different groups of products; they are clearly targeted at specific target markets, and they use all the trappings of branding – name, packaging and advertising – to give them life. Midland's original and pioneering initiatives at branding are already being followed by others.

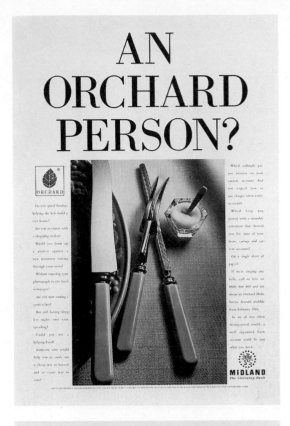

ARE YOU A VECTOR PERSON?

VECTOR

Can you programme a VCR machine without getting four solid hours of Ceefax?

Do you leave clear and confident messages on answerphones?

Could you march into your boss's office to ask for a rise without your voice turning falsetto?

Or open a brown envelope from the tax man without the aid of a stiff drink?

Would you take out an overdraft to go to a friend's surprise party in San Francisco?

And maybe live without carpets to buy a CD player?

Do you believe that if a bank charges you for being in the red, they should pay you when you're in the black?

Is the amount of plastic in your wallet spoiling the cut of your designer suit?

If you've nodded to yourself while reading this, call us free on 0800 400 469 and ask about our Vector Multi Service Account, available from February 20th.

It'll give you interest on your current account, a three-in-one card that will guarantee your cheques up to £100, a guaranteed overdraft, and a lot more besides.

Hear us out. It's a new kind of bank account that we've tailored for a new kind of customer.

MIDLAND
The Listening Bank

The financial services business is becoming more competitive; the product offer is complex and the consumer is semi-literate in financial matters. All this represents an ideal opportunity for branding.

The Midland Group in the UK is pioneering this field with brands aimed at specific market segments. Left and below: advertising and brochures for three Midland brands.

There is another kind of brand, which does not derive from pure invention. Companies sometimes turn organizations they have acquired into brands. Pears soap, for example, now a relatively minor Unilever brand, was once an independent company. The idea behind this strategy is simple and easy to follow. A corporation buys a competitor. It makes economies, closes down plants, modifies the organization, gets rid of unnecessary staff; but it seeks to retain the goodwill that already exists towards the name or names it has acquired. What easier than to keep on making the same products? Or – and this happens often – to keep on using the name while subtly changing the quality of the product, so that it fits in more easily with production requirements? The danger is that a brand treated in this way can deteriorate rapidly because nobody really cares about it any more.

This long-term modification of a company into a brand happens all the time, and can be seen at its clearest – and often, most disastrous – within the motor industry.

There once was a separate make of car called MG. Now MG has become a neglected brand.

In the old days, although it belonged to a big group the MG company had a factory. It built its own products, though largely, it must be admitted, out of the group's spare parts bin. Nevertheless, MG created a world-wide reputation for English sporty style. It won some records, and even, for a short period in the Thirties, gained a reputation in racing – then, slowly, the rot set in. After the creation of the British Motor Corporation and the departure of John Thornley, MG's great champion, nobody was suc-

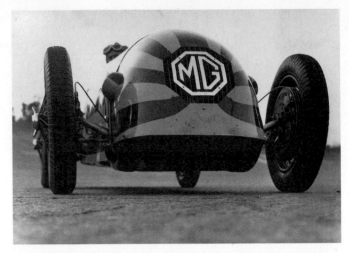

cessful in defending the MG idea; it became a minor name in a huge, sprawling, empire. MG models gradually grew more like others in the group. Its factory at Abingdon in the Thames valley, previously dedicated only to MG, was shared with other companies. MG's individuality was gradually whittled away. Eventually, simple badge engineering took over; the name and badge were subsequently exploited so that today there is virtually nothing left.

Nowadays there is no MG factory and there are no separate MG products. MG is simply a self-styled, prestige model of a standard Rover product range. Nobody can really believe in an MG Montego, Maestro or Metro, and it seems evident from the way in which the brand is promoted that the company doesn't believe in its brand either.

The MG name has been distorted, trivialized, plundered; a name that was once worth many millions in annual profits is now quietly rotting away. This is a story that has been repeated time and again

MG, once a great name in the car world, built a reputation in record breaking (far left: Captain George Eyston's Magic Magnette, 1934) and in small sports cars (below left: TA 1938; opposite, bottom: MGA 1955).

Now MG is simply a Rover Group brand name (left: MG Maestro) of no interest or distinction.

in the motor industry. And it appears to be a lesson that manufacturers simply never learn.

Here is how a typical contemporary road test of an MG begins. It is from the *Independent* newspaper of 10 February 1988:

It has not been a good decade for the MG enthusiast. The then Leyland closed the factory at Abingdon, Oxfordshire, which made MGs, and disbanded one of the most skilled, loyal and strike-free workforces in the group. That loathsome crowd, the market-makers, pasted the proud MG badge on a variety of indifferent machinery – cars such as the MG 1300, the MG Metro and the MG Maestro. (Thank goodness they never made an MG Allegro.)

'*The label MG generated strong imagery of sports cars snarling up gravel-strewn hillsides, or parked under the wing of the Spitfire, waiting to run Johnny in the Sky and his popsy down to the pub with the rest of the chaps from the Squadron. The MG Owners' Club is one of the strongest in the country. There is real feeling for the MG octagonal badge all over the world.*

'*But is it strong enough to generate the same sort of imagery when it is placed in the centre of the front grille, on the centre of the steering wheel and on the rear panel of . . . a Maestro?*

'*The enthusiast curls the lips. The cognoscenti* sneer. *The badge, the name, the proud sporting history have apparently been besmirched by what is seen by some as a cheap marketing ploy.*

How are the mighty fallen. Let that be a lesson to us all. If the brand's integrity is not protected, it just withers away and dies. Perhaps the despoliation of the brand will stop now that there are moves to give brands additional respect through a balance sheet valuation.

Military equipment has always tended to have brand names. Pershing, Trident, Crusader, Hawkeye, Roland, all weapon systems used by the US and its Nato allies, are not for the most part associated with the names of the big defence contractors who design and build them. This is partly, though not entirely, because so many different suppliers are involved. Another reason why these fearsome products are given brand names is to make them comprehensible, even lovable, to us, the poor saps who in the long run pay for them. Branding a piece of weaponry turns it from an inanimate piece of lethal equipment into, in theory at any rate, a trusted friend; so the emotional element in branding pops up yet again, in however unlikely a place. Hence Tiger and Panther tanks, and Big Bertha, the massive German gun from the First World War.

More germane to the emerging global industrial businesses of the next 50 years or so and a new phenomenon in branding are brand names associated with products that are simply too big and expensive for one company to make. We might call these, perhaps, quasi-brands. Although these share some of the characteristics of traditional brands, in other ways they are unique.

Britain's Black Knight missile, Farnborough Air Show, 1959. The project was cancelled – but is remembered for its evocative brand name. Below left: the Iveco brand of truck – built by a company with Italian, German, French and British elements. A truly European product, even though Fiat interests dominate.

Airbus has a number of shareholders from different European countries. Each has come together to sink its individual interests and to create a new brand – Airbus.

Illustrated right: which European aerospace company builds what in various Airbus products.

Airbus is an interesting example of a quasi-brand in the business-to-business field. Boeing had virtually wiped the floor with all its rivals, both domestic and international, in the large commercial aircraft field. With the greatest reluctance, and because they saw no real alternative, teams of ancient and hereditary enemies in Europe came together to fight off Boeing. French, German, Dutch, Belgian, British and Spanish aircraft companies joined together to build a civil aircraft to compete with Boeing, and they called their product Airbus. The consortium, which began as a temporary affair, now seems to have solidified into permanence, and Airbus appears to be emerging as a brand. But in a sense, Airbus is becoming more than a brand. The original single aircraft type has now spawned a family, and the tentative temporary combination of companies has become a legal entity. True, it's a very funny kind of legal entity – called by the French a 'Groupement d'Intérêt Economique (GIE) – which doesn't have to disclose its financial results; but it is a company nevertheless. And Boeing, not surprisingly, doesn't like it very much.

A300-600 production sharing

- Aérospatiale
- Messerschmitt-Bölkow-Blohm
- British Aerospace
- CASA
- Fokker
- General Electric
- Pratt & Whitney
- Messier

A310 production sharing

- Aérospatiale
- Messerschmitt-Bölkow-Blohm
- British Aerospace
- CASA
- Belairbus
- Fokker
- General Electric
- Pratt & Whitney
- Messier

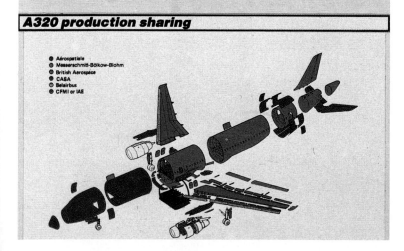

A320 production sharing

- Aérospatiale
- Messerschmitt-Bölkow-Blohm
- British Aerospace
- CASA
- Belairbus
- CFMI or IAE

Airbus parts are built all over Europe – wings in one place, sections of the frame in another – and the whole thing is assembled at Toulouse in France, which is the home of the brand – or is it a company? Characteristically for a brand, Airbus itself does not have a factory. Even in Toulouse, Airbus is assembled by Aerospatiale, the French partner in the project, at the Aerospatiale factory by Aerospatiale employees.

And of course, every participating company and country claims Airbus as its own. The Germans think of it as German; the French, as French.

It's sold just like a brand to certain target markets. For example, Turkey traditionally admires Germany and German engineering; so in Turkey Airbus is sold largely as a product of German engineering prowess. In other countries different Airbus 'faces' emerge.

If Airbus develops into a permanent business, it will be an example of an organization that started as a brand and gradually mutated into a kind of monolith.

In fact, Airbus is probably a model for the future. The increasing complexity of industrial products means that companies in different countries, who may in many respects be competitors, will increasingly come together and form alliances in order to produce ranges of products that they could not manage if they continued to operate separately. This will not, however, prevent them from continuing to compete with each other in other fields. We can see this starting to happen already in chemicals, heavy engineering, nuclear energy, biotech and automobiles, as well as in aerospace and defence.

Branding, in its new form, will ideally suit these new commercial structures.

The industrial quasi-brand, of which Airbus is the most famous current example, even has the one characteristic that most brands share – emotion.

Airbus above all represents the European challenge to American dominance in civil aviation. There can be no doubt that its European origins play a significant part in the marketing process. Emotion is part of the brand tradition. In this sense, if in no other, Airbus is a classic brand.

The branding idea has always been full of emotional content, which has traditionally encouraged its use as a tool of a national propaganda. The symbolism of branding, powerful, subtle, naive, sophisticated, makes it an ideal weapon in any propaganda war.

Nineteenth-century manufacturing companies often used imperial symbolism in their branding. Food companies found it expedient and profitable to associate themselves with popular causes. Today this appears both crude and comic, but it isn't all that different in its own context from some of the ways in which brands are promoted today.

Branding is not the sole property of capitalist nations, nor is it used only by those dedicated to the profit motive. The Chinese and the Russians are keen on branding in the service of the state. In the Twenties the Soviets used every product they could lay their hands on, from soap and cigarettes to candles, to propagate messages of frendship, achievement and hard work. Branding was a major vehicle for state propaganda.

So branding, despite its abuse and misuse over the past 100 years or so, remains alive and hearty.

In its curious, direct way, branding is extraordinarily potent. It reaches beyond immediate commercial objectives and touches the soul – and don't its practitioners know it!

Branding is often used to propagandize. It can have heavy emotional content. Left: after the Civil War between the Whites and the Communists, the 'Red Army Star' celebrates the Red victory and the return of Soviet heroes on a toffee wrapper (1924).

Below: 'Ira'; a Soviet cigarette pack without political implications.

Top right: Murray's 'Varsity' mixture exploits the British weakness for class distinctions.

Right: Regina toilet soap. Clearly fit for a queen.

CHAPTER **5**

Corporate Strategy

Take a selection of annual reports from the world's greatest companies. It doesn't really matter which country you choose; allowing for a few national idiosyncracies, they tend to be pretty much the same. The American ones might be a bit livelier, the German a bit greyer, but it's really just a question of degree.

For the most part, with a few striking and honourable exceptions, they all say much the same thing in much the same way: 'We know exactly what we are doing. Everything is just fine, or is about to be just fine, so don't you worry because we have it all in hand.'

In the pictures that illustrate the report, groups of wise and benevolent folk sit about, apparently engaged in planning the sunlit future of mankind.

The company is presented as smooth and fragrant, omnipotent, omniscient, and above all rational.

But behind the façade all is not as it seems.

In the world of the annual report there are many similarities with Lewis Carroll's *Alice in Wonderland*. Big things can look small, and small things can look big. The world is neatly parcelled up into sections that suit the company's organization. Brazil, for example, disappears with most of South America and all of Africa into a place called 'Rest of the World'. And it seems as though people's lives largely revolve around cement or rubber ducks, or whatever other group of products the company deals in.

All the people who work for the corporation have, of course, made major contributions to the business. They all unreservedly welcome innovation and change – 'Finally, we would like to thank all our employees for the dedication and conscientiousness with which they have worked during the year. Their contribution has been greatly appreciated.' Nobody has been lazy, incompetent, pig-headed or uncomprehending. The unions have been models of co-operation. There are no divisions, no splits, no rifts. Everything in the garden is just lovely. It's all for one and one for all.

The corporate head offices and the annual reports, the corporate environments and the corporate officers, conspire to present the organization as calm, controlled, confident and responsible, as knowing exactly what it is doing and where it is going.

But of course real life is simply not like this. It's full of random opportunities and spillages from human emotions which profoundly affect the way businesses are managed and grow.

To understand how companies really work – what is planning, what is luck, what is good judgment, what is original thinking, what is emulation – it is salutary to examine their corporate strategy. Corporate strategy is fundamentally about growth – and of course profit. And both are vital for any business.

All companies operate and grow, or at any rate purport to do so, with a business plan, which incorporates a growth strategy. This plan is at the heart of corporate development. It is the blueprint for the company's expansion, usually covering a three- to five-year period.

The business plan takes into account the product areas in which the business wants to grow, diversification, location, pricing, cost of manufacture, information technology, equipment, capital resources, competitors' likely behaviour: all those aspects of the business that are increasingly called 'hard issues'.

Inevitably the hard issues drag with them a whole series of soft issues, which growth plans have a habit of ignoring, but which are vital in determining the company personality and often its direction.

It is this multitude of soft issues which so often changes the company's personality and culture as it grows and which should be reflected in the company's visual identity. The hard issues and the soft issues are usually so closely interwoven that it's difficult to separate them. And that is why business plans encompass a far broader area than is apparent at first sight.

In expanding, for example, does the acquiring company try to retain the essence of its original proposition or to modify it? Does it look for a niche position, or try to cover the entire marketplace? Does it try to create or sustain an idea of consistent quality, or one of low price, or both? Do its various activities remain separate from each other, sharing only ownership, or do they also share a similar culture and style – even the same name? These are all issues with both hard and soft aspects.

As soon as a company begins to expand by acquisition its original personality changes. Marks & Spencer grew organically for about a century. It developed a powerful culture and personality based around the single Marks & Spencer idea. Then it decided to have a significant presence on the North American market. It had to grow by acquisition. All good hard issue stuff. In 1988 it bought Brooks Brothers, the preppy clothes company, and then King, the gourmet food chain. Inevitably this means that Marks & Spencer will change. Marks & Spencer plus Brooks Brothers is not the same as Marks & Spencer by itself. Brooks Brothers has its own culture and its own traditions which are different from those of Marks & Spencer. How closely linked should the two companies appear to be? Will Brooks Brothers quality standards be adjusted so that the two companies have identical products? What effect will the Brooks Brothers identity have on Marks & Spencer as a whole? Will Marks & Spencer products be sold in Brooks Brothers stores in the US? Will Brooks Brothers products be sold in Marks & Spencer stores in the UK and France? Will both companies begin to use the same suppliers? Should Brooks Brothers show that it is related to Marks & Spencer? Or should both organizations continue to operate independently of each other?

So much for marketing issues. But what about management development?

Who does the Brooks Brothers executive work for? Where do his ultimate loyalties lie? Where is his career path? Will progressing through the Brooks Brothers route turn him into a second-class citizen in terms of group board material? These are some of a multiplicity of questions asked by employees not just of Brooks Brothers, but of any company that has just been taken over.

So the development and execution of a corporate strategy involves both hard and soft issues. There is in effect a complex interchange between strategy, structure, culture and identity.

How are all these decisions about strategic growth, with their complex network of inter-related factors, arrived at?

On the basis of the Gospel according to the Annual Report, we are led to assume that the whole planning process is carried out in an objective, cool, almost clinical fashion. The various strategic options are considered dispassionately. Geographical options, financial options, resource options: all the strategic opportunities are balanced against the corporate personality as it now exists, against the company's strength and weaknesses in the marketplace, the potential impact of change on the various activities of the organization, and so on. Naturally competitors' activities and potential strategies are examined, and then a decision is taken – to acquire, to divest, to move.

In most companies, some of the time, no doubt this process, or something like it, does take place. However, while this cool, formalized ritual goes on at the surface of the organization, another more frantic, violent and emotional battle is usually taking place between more or less the same protagonists subterraneously.

Behind the closed board-room doors, behind the high-sounding phrases, behind the icons of power there is a seething mass of conflict, doubt, suspicion, rivalry and intrigue.

Different interests, roughly divided into gangs called marketing, sales, production, R and D, struggle for power and for financial support. All curry favour with the chief executive and his henchmen to secure their own place in the sun. The true analogy with the corporation, as Anthony Jay pointed out in *Management and Machiavelli* (1967), is a medieval court. That's why in so many companies the divisional heads are called 'chieftains' and 'barons'. These terms are not colourful and picturesque; on the contrary, they are precise. All the barons look to extend their own fiefdoms, at the expense of their colleagues. They believe that the interests of their own division and those of the corporation as a whole coincide. As far as they can therefore they bend the corporate purpose to their own ends. And this means civil war.

The internecine strife, though grim and deadly, is usually conducted in semi-silence. Mostly, the shouting is very quiet. Only occasionally does news of a battle emerge from corporate headquarters. Only now and again is blood seen to run in the directors' suites.

As for corporate omniscience and omnipotence, so assiduously presented in brochures and reports, that is also a carefully fostered illusion.

It is always tempting to explain a corporate success as part of a carefully planned strategy for growth, even though it may have happened because of fortuitous timing or an independent initiative at a lower level of the organization. And it's equally tempting to keep absolutely silent about a project for growth that failed.

Peer-group pressure, which is an immensely powerful force, is rarely cited as a basis by which corporate growth is determined. But in real life it often is. A few years ago some of the major British banks raced each other into the US. They were so busy copying each other, they didn't notice what they were buying. It wasn't long, just a few years after, that they were racing each other out again, a few billion dollars lighter.

The personal fantasies of a few powerful individuals can also lock a company into a particular direction (another factor you won't find mentioned in the annual report!). If you were chairman of a vast empire, wouldn't you fancy owning the Savoy Hotel or Harrods? The more glamorous and internationally famous the names involved, the greater the prestige attached to their possession. This sort of growth strategy is on a level with two children at a party trying to steal another child's toy; but there's plenty of it about. It's what you might describe as a highly personal approach to corporate strategy.

Some organizations run by a dominating figure display a clear sense of corporate purpose, which encapsulates a vision. Signor de Benedetti in Italy and Lord Hanson in Britain have a highly personal approach to corporate strategy, but they still buy companies for a clear corporate purpose. De Benedetti is attempting to create a major European enterprise through strategic investment, while Hanson largely operates on the basis of a financial return. If a company performs well financially, more or less regardless of its activity, it's in; if it performs less well, it's out – and fast.

Sir James Goldsmith is another well-known proponent of this view of business. It would be not uncharitable to say that he takes an unemotional view of his investments. If the market circumstances are propitious and his companies operate effectively according to the criteria he lays down, which are principally financial, he keeps them; when anything occurs to make his investments less immediately productive, he sells the business.

The Hanson/Goldsmith attitude is unambiguous, straightforward and unemotional. Everybody – shareholders, managers, employers – knows exactly where they are. Inevitably, though, as in so many situations where a board tries to concern itself exclusively with the hard issues like financial performance, soft issues, such as company culture, inevitably crop up. Even in the most macho of managements, like those of Hanson or Goldsmith, there is no escape.

It is hardly possible to overestimate the importance of opportunity in corporate growth. In our personal lives we are dominated by the flux of events – and so is the corporation. In real life if an opportunity turns up, we have to decide whether to grasp it. Quite often it doesn't exactly fit the plans; it may even contradict them. But if the opportunity feels right, many companies will say: 'The hell with strategy, let's take the opportunity.' Look at how Alfred Sloan bought tiny Vauxhall for General Motors when he wanted big Austin or bigger Morris.

So if you take all these factors into account – a board that tries to be genuinely thoughtful, analytical, rational; the various influences brought to bear by different lobbies acting in their own interests; the nature of the hard issues/soft issues relationship; the influence of peer-group pressure; the fantasies and manias displayed by powerful individuals; and, finally, most important of all, the part played by opportunity – then you've probably got the combination of factors on which most organizations base their corporate strategy, as opposed to what they claim in their publicity. No wonder some companies' corporate strategies in a given field seem to be so similar.

Look at the so-called symbiotic relationship between the aerospace and motor industries. Over the first eighty years of their lives, the two industries could take or leave each other. There were a few examples of successful relationships, more of failure. The general pattern seems to be that one side dominated, while the other languished.

Consider a few instances: Rolls-Royce, originally a car company, developed an aero-engine side to the business so important that cars eventually became a loss-making symbol. When the company went broke, the cars went to Vickers, and the aero-engines stayed by themselves. Now both businesses are successful; they share nothing but the name.

Armstrong Siddeley, which built both aero-engines and cars between the World Wars, was never strong enough in either field to be truly successful. Its motor cars, which purported to derive from its aero-engine technology, were heavy, slow and, even by the standards of the day, old-fashioned.

Bristol, the great aircraft company now part of BAe, built cars to aircraft standards for a few years. They were so expensive nobody wanted them.

Fiat's aircraft division has never had the national or international impact of its cars. Despite the achievements of its great designer Celestino Rosatelli in the Thirties it has always been a neglected child and remains so today.

Renault built aero-engines for many years. But they weren't very competitive. As with Fiat, most of its engineers and investment went into the larger and more glamorous car side.

Today Saab builds both cars and aircraft. It also builds heavy vehicles and electronic equipment. Saab has publicly confessed that as things stand in the late Eighties its car and aircraft divisions have relatively little to do with each other, that aircraft manufacturing techniques and materials are a decade ahead of those used in cars, and that because of the higher numbers involved in motor car production, the manufacturing techniques are quite different. In fact, the chief advantage to Saab cars of the presence of an aircraft division seems to be that its advertising agencies can use lots of pictures of aeroplanes in commercials. So much for synergy there.

Despite this long history of high hopes and unfulfilled promise, the love affair between cars and aerospace rumbles on.

The current orthodoxy in the car/aerospace debate runs more or less as follows. As the vehicle building business becomes more complex, it will need an increasing proportion of new materials and electronic components; these will largely be derived from the aerospace and electronic business. That is General Motors' explanation for its expansion into Hughes and EDS, of which the visible outcome appears so far to be zero.

Top right: Saab automobile advertising (by KHBB) makes ample use of aircraft associations, but in real life the divisions do not have close contact.

That is why British Aerospace says it took over the Rover Group.

British Aerospace, one of Britain's largest manufacturing companies, suddenly discovered that it needed Rover desperately because of the close relationship between the two businesses. But will it actually be able to make Airbus wings more cheaply by finding out how Rover make their cars? Will its business relationship with Japanese aerospace companies be improved because Rover has links with Honda? Or is the truth behind this alliance somewhat different?

Even the mighty Daimler-Benz has announced that it has fallen in love with the new technologies.

Over a period of two or three years, from the mid-Eighties, the great Daimler-Benz motor company, ultimate symbol of Germany's technical and commercial prowess, has announced a programme of acquisitions and investments.

It has a major shareholding in three German companies: MTU, Dornier and AEG, and is also intent on taking over MBB.

Motoren und Turbinen Union is a medium-sized company in which Daimler-Benz already has an interest. It is a second-division engine-builder mainly concerned with picking up the crusts left by GE, Snecma, Rolls-Royce, and Pratt and Whitney –

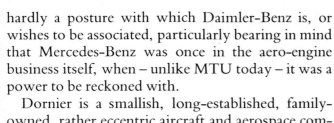

hardly a posture with which Daimler-Benz is, or wishes to be associated, particularly bearing in mind that Mercedes-Benz was once in the aero-engine business itself, when – unlike MTU today – it was a power to be reckoned with.

Dornier is a smallish, long-established, family-owned, rather eccentric aircraft and aerospace company. It has a bizarre mixture of projects. Some are mundane and of no technological significance, like the design and construction of third-level commuter aircraft; others are simply a bit odd, like the revival of the flying boat, an obsession of the Dornier family for the last seventy years; and some, while technologically sophisticated, such as space activity and medical equipment, may or may not be relevant to the long-term thrust of the Daimler-Benz business.

To add spice to this mixture, various members of the Dornier family have indulged in much-publicized acrimony, largely related to the disposition of their not inconsiderable financial resources. All of which must have sent shivers down the spines of the great respectable company which has made an alliance with them. The family's representative has appeared to have been so partisan that in June 1988 Daimler-Benz actually issued a magisterial rebuke: 'One cannot help feeling that the selfish considerations of the family shareholders . . . have been given priority and they have not taken into account either the interests of the company or the workers.' (*Financial Times*)

We last glimpsed AEG on these pages at its apogee, at the beginning of the twentieth century. It has had mixed fortunes since then and at the beginning of the 1980s it found itself bankrupt. Its position is now improving rapidly and it is going through something of a renaissance both technically and from a marketing point of view.

The largest proposed acquisition of all, the one that, it is suggested, even Daimler-Benz will find hard to digest, is MBB. MBB, or Messerschmitt as it is sometimes called, is like British Aerospace or Aerospatiale of France in that it represents an agglomeration of virtually the whole of Germany's aircraft industry. It contains most of Germany's greatest aerospace names – Focke-Wulf, Heinkel and the rest – and as it has grown, it has accumulated all kinds of strange barnacles, from companies that manufacture weapons to others that make mobile homes. Certainly, MBB is a virtually indigestible mass of companies and activities. It is best known – in so far as it is known at all – for making parts of Europe's Airbus, probably at a loss. Daimler-Benz want financial guarantees to save it from trouble in that particular arena.

Daimler-Benz, like most big companies, is eager to explain the logic behind its advance into these ill-assorted organizations in terms of corporate strategy – what else? In language similar to that used by General Motors and by British Aerospace, it rambles on about new materials, electronics, technology and synergy. Daimler-Benz explains what it is doing in terms of hard issues.

Let's assume that Daimler-Benz actually means what it says; that it is not making these acquisitions simply in order to keep up with the pack; or because it can't think of anything else to do with its money; or just because they are available; or because one of the board members is fulfilling a childhood ambition; but because it sincerely believes in what it says in its own press statements. Let's assume it really believes that the organizations in which it has an interest will provide it with new materials, technologies and markets, with far greater technical and commercial opportunity.

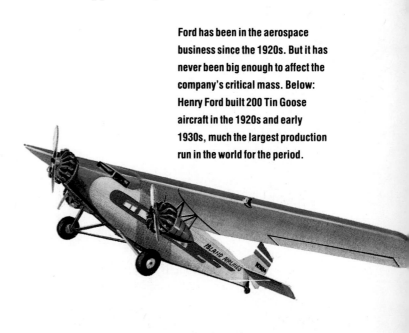

Ford has been in the aerospace business since the 1920s. But it has never been big enough to affect the company's critical mass. Below: Henry Ford built 200 Tin Goose aircraft in the 1920s and early 1930s, much the largest production run in the world for the period.

With the acquisition of significant businesses outside its traditional activities, Daimler-Benz will inevitably change. And what's more, if that is not enough, it has announced that it proposes to change even more in the future.

Edzard Reuter, architect of expansion within Daimler-Benz, has in mind further acquisitions of as yet un-named companies in the United States.

All this means – if everything goes through – that by the turn of the twenty-first century Daimler-Benz will be very different in terms of size, product mix and organization from what it was until the Eighties. It will no longer be a German-based vehicle-maker; it will have become an international technologies business. How can it best take advantage of the resources that lie within each company and within the whole? The strategy, structure and personality of the new, enlarged Daimler-Benz will be projected publicly through its corporate identity. The problem will be to create an identity that effectively enables the organization to demonstrate its spread of activities, and that makes the new role clear, without losing the strength, values and character of the core business.

Above: Dornier's greatest claim to fame is the DoX flying boat, the largest aircraft in the world when it was built in 1929. Like Howard Hughes' Spruce Goose fifteen years later, it was over-ambitious in relation to the technology of the period.

Left: Daimler typewriter! When times were hard in the mid-1920s Daimler Motoren Gesellschaft (a predecessor of Daimler-Benz) turned its hand to typewriters. Note the three-pointed star (1924-27).

Bottom left: AEG's most familiar products are household appliances. But it also makes a complex range of electrical and electronic equipment. In 1989 AEG completed Europe's largest solar power station.

In strategic terms Daimler-Benz has three options. No doubt an infinity of refinements is possible on each of these, but in the end this is what it boils down to.

First, it can integrate – the monolithic route.

Second, it can act as a holding company – the brand route.

Third, it can co-ordinate – the endorsed route.

The first option. If Daimler-Benz wants to introduce real Mercedes standards of behaviour, performance measurements and quality into its acquisitions, if it wants the world, and its own people, to see that Mercedes standards now apply in AEG, MTU, Dornier, and for the future in MBB too, the simplest, most direct action it can take is to create a new, enlarged Mercedes-Benz. This means that it will have to replace or modify existing financial reporting systems, quality control methods, production processes and marketing techniques in all companies, and bring them up to what it regards as Daimler-Benz standards.

Above: MTU builds engines. Although it is a substantial manufacturer, it does not have the prestige associated with Daimler-Benz.

Above right: MBB is a partner in a number of major aerospace projects. This is the Tornado, built by a European consortium.

It can signal that it proposes to introduce Mercedes quality into its new acquisitions through a single action of great boldness and courage. It can replace all existing names and identities with the Mercedes name and star – thereby creating a monolithic identity structure.

If Daimler-Benz were to take such action it would have to take into account a whole series of commercial, marketing, quality and behavioural factors, most of which are not susceptible to objective judgment. The change of identity would have a huge impact on every aspect of the new organization, both internal and external.

We can assume that such a move, however diplomatically proposed – and it's rather difficult to be diplomatic about this kind of thing – would meet with violent opposition from each of the companies whose names were threatened, despite the fact that they themselves have in the past done exactly the same. The once mighty Telefunken, for instance, was taken over and then obliterated by AEG! Each of the subsidiaries, especially AEG, would no doubt claim that a name change would mean instant commercial ruin. Market research, hastily commissioned, would confirm the priceless value of the existing names (although it's difficult to believe that the names of Dornier, MTU and MBB can really be worth that much).

And this would lead to speculation about whether a washing machine, a cooker or a commuter aircraft called Mercedes-Benz and bearing the Mercedes star would be worth more, or less, or the same to its marketplace as the same piece of equipment with the existing name and identity.

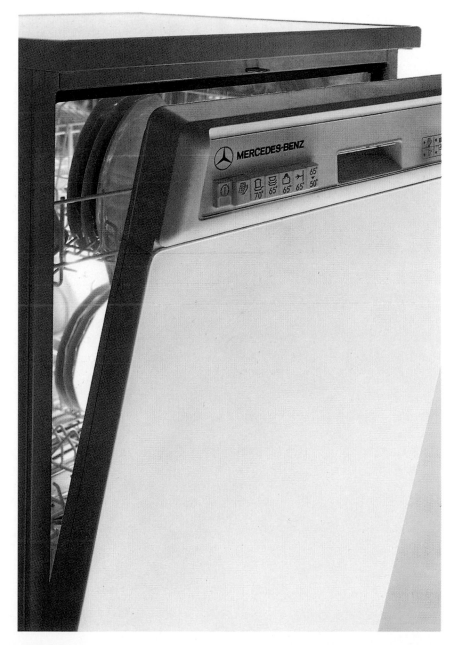

Far left: an AEG dishwasher. Centre: if it was endorsed by Daimler-Benz. Left: if it became a Mercedes-Benz dishwasher.

Well, the problem is that nobody really knows, although some research would help. In the longer term Mercedes-Benz might well prove a more credible, more attractive name than the current names provided, that is, that the quality of the products is sufficiently high to warrant the use of the Mercedes name and star.

Are MBB's and Dornier's projects the aerospace equivalent of Mercedes? Does MTU's technical and commercial performance match up to the standards that are expected of Mercedes? Are AEG fridges, cookers and turbines of Mercedes quality? Do all these products look and feel as though they emerge through the doors of the Daimler-Benz factories? If not, then before any name or identity changes are made it is imperative that appropriate product improvements be made.

What about personal and commercial relationships within and between the various units? Essentially, the issues here relate to pride and self-confidence. If the acquiring company pursues a monolithic identity policy, it will eventually obliterate most traces of the companies which it has acquired, just as they did with the companies they took over. It will introduce its own standards in finance, quality control, marketing, management development and in every other sphere. Even when this hawkish policy is handled in the most subtle and sophisticated fashion it is regarded by those who have been taken over, at least initially, as brutal and oppressive.

There are, however, ways in which such a policy can be softened. When Renault took over Berliet, the faded star of the French heavy-vehicle industry, though it changed the name of the product to Renault, it continued to honour Marius Berliet, founder of the company.

Some of the founding fathers of the German electrical, automobile, and aircraft industries, all of whom contributed to the enlarged Daimler-Benz of the 1990s. Clockwise from bottom left: Claude Dornier, Emil Rathenau, Wilhelm Maybach, Carl Benz, Gottlieb Daimler, Willi Messerschmitt and Ernst Heinkel. In 1989 Daimler-Benz carried out a major advertising programme underlining its association with some of these worthies.

Emotional gestures are very important at times of crisis. There are many ways of assuaging wounded pride. Daimler-Benz could decide to incorporate into its historical framework an appropriate respect for the people and the achievements of the companies it had acquired. Claude Dornier, creator of the great DoX Dornier flying boat, the world's biggest when it was built in 1929, could be seen alongside Emil Rathenau, AEG's great founder, Wilhelm Maybach, Carl Benz, Gottlieb Daimler, Willi Messerschmitt, Ernst Heinkel and others as equal partners in the new enlarged Daimler-Benz pantheon of founding fathers.

Gestures like these could be multiplied a thousand times.

However, whichever way you look at it, this radical option involves turmoil; some in the marketplace and a lot more internally. And that is why brave words like strategy, synergy and symbiosis, so rarely emerge in their most complete form in reality.

If Daimler-Benz were Mitsubishi, there is little doubt about what it would do. The monolithic route would be the relevant one to follow. Within the group as it now exists there are precedents. Even Mercedes-Benz has in its day summarily disposed of both Krupp and Hanomag-Henschel trucks. And it's also worth remembering that Daimler-Benz itself was formed from a merger of two former companies, Daimler and Benz. One of the Benz directors said in the 1920s, when the merger took place, that he thought it might take fifty years to consummate the union effectively, because the Mercedes and Benz cultures were so different.

Which brings us to the second strategic option. Here, each of the businesses would carry on as though nothing much had happened. A few committees would be set up to explore technology of mutual interest, financial planning, resource management, group research and development. There would be a few exchanges of board members at the top of the various companies, and regular meetings of senior executives would be held at agreeable venues such as Monte Carlo or Bermuda, at which there would be a lot of talk, much expression of generalized goodwill, and not much action.

And all this is beautifully easy to justify:

'We didn't acquire these immensely valuable names at great cost in order to destroy them.'

'They know more about their business than we will ever know.'

'The strength of our group derives from the diversity of its activities and from its specialist knowledge and expertise in a number of related key areas.'

'Our relationships with our key customers throughout the world are vital. It would be irresponsible to put them at risk.'

And so on.

There is always some truth in such observations, occasionally even a lot of truth. Usually, though, this type of inaction represents a reluctance to face the realities that getting the best out of the purchase demands. One suspects that General Motors has been successfully fought off both by Hughes and EDS using this kind of argument.

Advertisement announcing the alliance of Daimler and Benz, *c*. 1925.

MERCEDES
-BENZ-

In following this option, there would be few changes in identity. Daimler-Benz would be the name of both the holding and the core company, and where the subsidiaries thought it appropriate, which would certainly not be often, they would identify themselves as members of the Daimler-Benz group.

Finally there is the third option: co-ordination. This involves a much more radical, thoughtful and serious integration process than is implied in the second option, without necessarily going as far as option one.

Naturally, the group would share common resources (finance, investment, R and D, technology, management of people), but it would also need to consider the extent to which each part of the business should retain its own identity and attitudes. If we are talking about common standards in other areas, how can we interpret this in identity terms? Probably through some form of endorsed identity system.

In this model, cars and trucks might retain the name Mercedes, for example, while the group as a whole might be called, say, Daimler, or Daimler-Benz. Each division would be endorsed by the group identity. The company has moved some way towards this model by creating a division called Deutsche Aerospace, into which it has already thrown bits and pieces from its various acquisitions.

Whichever way you look at it, though, Daimler-Benz faces an identity crisis which directly derives from its growth strategy. This strategy must be interpreted structurally, and then the structure must be presented through a clear identity programme.

As one engineering company agonizes, in another the strategy has emerged quickly and with clarity, and the company's identity clearly demonstrates what the strategy is.

Two huge electro-engineering companies, Asea of Sweden and Brown Boveri of Switzerland, came together in 1987, in what they swore with hands on hearts was a merger. To informed people on the outside looking in, it seemed as though Asea's policies had won the day. In any event, it soon became clear that a strategy had been agreed. A new organization was to emerge, in which neither of the old companies would dominate. All this was symbolized in identity terms. A new name, ABB, and a new identity, intended over time to replace the historic names and loyalties, were created. All this was achieved at lightning speed and with admirable clarity.

Even if you can't give ABB many marks for imagination, you can certainly applaud the energy and determination with which they moved. The ABB strategy is quite clear – it is to dominate the global scene in power and electro-engineering products.

No petty wrangling, no internal manoeuvrings, no peer-group pressures were allowed to shatter the Nordic intensity of this vision.

You could argue that because the two companies involved are so complementary, in size, product type, and geographic mix, there are no real problems; the result is virtually a foregone conclusion. That judgment underrates the complexities of the situation. There are issues here of national pride, involving traditional national company names, of product overlap, of branding and so on, just as there are in many other companies. Jealousies and friction, both on the technical and marketing side, of course exist between the different partners; but for the most part these difficulties have been swept to one side, to be dealt with later.

In the case of ABB the corporate strategy is clear, and it is emerging fast through identity. ABB managers know that identity is simply the corporate strategy made visible.

In real life the corporation has many choices. It makes many mistakes, it is thrown off course by emotion, by change, by the fallibility of the human condition.

Naturally the corporation underlines its victories and minimizes its disasters and presents its growth as inevitable. Don't we all?

So all these wise and benevolent folk that we see sitting about in annual reports hide their twitching fingers under the tables, and hope that we won't guess that business planning, like life, is hazardous, that opportunities don't just pop up when you want them to, and that most people behave unpredictably anyway.

Corporate strategy is the best that most corporations can do to harmonize their long-term goals with all the more immediate issues – whether large or small – that keep on cropping up in their day-to-day lives. Perhaps a lesson to learn is that corporate strategy must not be kept in a cupboard and brought out for an airing when the sun comes out. It isn't dead; it lives and breathes. It affects every action the company takes.

It affects not only what products the company makes and how much profit it makes on them, but how those products affect what customers feel about the company. It affects not only where the company builds a new plant, how big the plant should be and how much it should cost, but what people inside and outside the company feel about the choice of location, and what the workforce feel as they hang up their coats in the washroom.

Corporate strategy affects corporate structure and corporate culture – and, inevitably, corporate identity.

Corporate identity tells the world – whether actively or by default – just what the corporate strategy is.

ABB was formed in 1987 from Asea of Sweden and Brown Boveri of Switzerland. This new company is called ABB – logotype by Pentagram.

CHAPTER **6**

Creating an Identity Programme— The First Stage

Corporate identity programmes are emerging as major agents of change. Because of their high visibility and impact they mark out turning points in a corporation's life.

Increasingly, they are concerned with expressing three separate but interrelated themes.

First, the organization wants to present itself as clear and comprehensible. It wants its different parts to relate to each other so that people can find their way around its divisions, companies and brands.

Second, the organization wants to symbolize its ethos, its attitudes, so that everyone who works for it can share the same spirit and then communicate it to all the people who deal with the organization.

Third, the organization wants to differentiate itself and its products from those of its competitors in the marketplace.

These three themes – *coherence, symbolism* and *positioning* – go to the very core of a corporation.

A properly conducted corporate identity programme enables these matters to be considered both separately and collectively. It is the means by which the issues that lie behind them can be resolved and the base from which their resolution can be publicly expressed.

Paradoxically, however, corporate identity practitioners and their clients are only beginning to acknowledge the power that the resource possesses.

Although corporate identity is in a number of ways complementary to other forms of consultancy, it presents itself differently from them. It is not surrounded with the trappings of traditional consultancy practice. It does not yet have a substantial body of support in the world's major business schools. Some designers still have an aversion to wearing suits and are uncomfortable with corporate jargon, even though they are pretty good at inventing their own, and the literature on corporate identity consists for the most part of little more than illustrations of logotypes with examples of their application.

Until relatively recently many designers seemed frightened to emerge from their own cosy little world, to learn new skills and broaden their horizons by developing non-design disciplines. They wanted to keep as near as possible to their drawing boards.

Although things are changing fast, and corporate identity consultancies are now beginning to embrace the commercial world with gusto, this uncertainty has inhibited growth and understanding. Client organizations have been unclear about how to handle corporate identity. They haven't known where to pigeonhole it. Is it another form of management consultancy dealing with the same kind of issues from a rather special point of view? In other words, is it 'proper' management consultancy that justifies high fees and a high level of top management time and energy; or is it a less significant, more subordinate activity altogether, lying somewhere between marketing and communication departments in its focus? Is it just an extension of advertising and public relations – what advertising agencies disparagingly call collateral, or below-the-line material by a grander name? Or is it a new kind of consultancy concerned with soft issues, a development of the hard-edged traditional consultancy activity? In other words is it profound or superficial?

The truth is that corporate identity is a rapidly evolving discipline. When it is used superficially it is only cosmetic. But when it is treated with appropriate interest and respect it has serious and important implications. Its fuzzy, diffuse quality makes it rather difficult to deal with, and the prejudices that surround it – including those associated with its graphic design roots – don't make things any easier.

Nevertheless, despite these doubts and difficulties, many organizations increasingly find themselves gravitating towards the identity consultant when faced with problems that they tend to lump together and call image or identity, all of which are one way or another versions of a confusion in coherence, personality and positioning.

'The image problem', as companies call it, usually emerges from a number of different directions at the same time. Let's look at a fictitious but by no means untypical example.

BuffSanCo of Omaha, Nebraska, had unusual beginnings. It was started in 1897 by a young Englishman, Simon Fortescue, the third son of a Derbyshire vicar. He landed in New York and bought a map of the United States to find out where he was. By chance the map depicted cities, states, railroad lines and very little else.

Fortescue saw that there were a number of lines going from north to south and a few going from east to west, but there was, it seemed to him, an obvious gap. None ran from north-east to south-west diagonally across the country. So, ignorant of the physical problems involved, because the map didn't show them, Fortescue conceived the Buffalo-San Diego Railroad Corporation. He established the headquarters about half-way between the two intended extremities at Omaha, Nebraska, where it has remained ever since.

Although the railroad, for obvious reasons, never got built, the company acquired a great deal of property very cheaply in different parts of the US. In California it bought land which subsequently became massive and highly profitable fruit farms. In the middle west it got into cattle; further north, into mining, then lumber.

Fortescue, after a shaky start, proved a brillant entrepreneur. By the 1930s, BuffSanCo, as the business came to be called, was a major force in foods, mining, lumber and distribution. The various divisions, each encouraged to develop its own diversification programme, reached out into new fields of activity and geographical areas. By the late 1980s, in addition to its original businesses it was involved in aerospace and other high-tech components and systems in the US and Europe, in pharmaceuticals and biotechnology globally; it had supermarket chains in Canada and it also owned a shoe manufacturing and distribution business, as well as the world's largest shoe store in Madrid – and that was not all.

These activities were acquired by different managements at different times. Although BuffSanCo was a Fortune top 100 company, it wasn't clear what it was doing or where it was going.

When Chief Executive Officer (CEO) Steven R. Kojoski (R stood for Ruthless, executives nervously joked) joined the corporation in the early Eighties it was clear that things had to change. Kojoski worked with management consultants to develop a plan; only to be involved in those businesses where the organization was No. 1, 2 or 3 in its field; always to be at the top end for price and quality; always to give top service; and to stay in a potentially unfashionable mix of cyclical and counter-cyclical products and services in order to maintain a balanced portfolio. He began to describe BuffSanCo as a thoughtful company; a company that was to be distinguished by the way in which it thought things through, for its own employees, its customers, suppliers – for everyone. As a result of this policy, some businesses were abandoned, others acquired. The whole organization was given a clearer sense of direction.

But the image problem stubbornly remained unchanged.

Here were a few of the warning signs. Despite the facts that profits had improved since Kojoski's arrival, the share price stayed low. The financial analysts and journalists continued to write unflattering comments about the stock. It was clear from what they wrote that they didn't understand what Steve Kojoski had done or what his corporate policy was.

There were constant complaints from the internal recruitment people and from outside head-hunters that the best candidates weren't especially interested in BuffSanCo. It wasn't as glamorous or interesting as its competitors. People just didn't seem to understand what the organization actually did, or what it was all about.

The original symbol of the Buffalo-San Diego Railroad Corporation, devised by a printer in Omaha, Nebraska in June 1897. The company was from the first known by its abbreviated name, BuffSanCo.

A proposed major acquisition in aerospace components, an important growth area for BuffSanCo, failed because the shareholders in the company it intended to acquire didn't think BuffSanCo was seriously involved in the aerospace business, and so it fell into the arms of a competitor.

All the market research and tracking indicated to Kojoski that very few opinion-formers understood what the organization was doing, how large it was and what its ambitions were.

At a series of internal meetings with divisional chiefs and their marketing people it became clear that despite the reorganization, thinking internally remained as muddled and as uncoordinated as ever. The leading people within each division saw little of each other. They did not seriously consider opportunities of exchanging customer information, working out joint sales pitches to clients, exchanging R and D information or working collectively on recruitment. They took no advantage of group purchasing power and in many cases bought from the corporation's competitors without even knowing that BuffSanCo companies could supply the same goods. In other words, BuffSanCo was no more of a thinking organization than most others of its size and amorphous structure.

All this was reflected in the visual presentation of the organization, which had become a complete mish-mash.

The name BuffSanCo was associated with a symbol, which had been created at about the time the company was formed and was a typical piece of graphic design of the period. It consisted of two heads. One was meant to represent a white man, the other an Indian. It was intended primarily to symbolize the way in which railroads brought the peoples of different races together – the unity of the American people. Unfortunately, because of some less than straightforward behaviour in its early days, the company became known as the two-faced corporation, and the name stuck.

The original group name and symbol were used in the more traditional parts of the corporation, although the symbol was used in a wide variety of different colours and had been subject to a great deal of uncontrolled visual reinterpretation over the years.

Some parts of the organization used the group name and symbol together. Others used one or the other, as they thought fit.

As for the name, some parts of the business used it in its original form, with pride, or indifference, while others modified it to suit their purposes: BuffPly in timber, Buff'n'Shine in shoe polish, Buff-San in toilet tissues.

The newer, more technologically sophisticated parts of the business for the most part kept their existing names and identities on the basis that it wouldn't help them in marketing their products to get mixed up with confused, clapped-out old BuffSanCo.

All this visual chaos was, Kojoski knew, symbolic of organizational dissonance.

After much discussion Kojoski decided to act. He had a vision for the corporation, but it was clear that the vision was not becoming a reality. Eventually he called in a corporate identity consultancy. The company he chose was Thinwall and Fineline of New York, San Francisco, Paris and London. Gavin Thinwall, a founding partner – persuasive, aggressive and sophisticated – took on the assignment. We will hear more of him later.

In the meantime, let's look at a few real life examples.

At Aston University in Britain a new Vice-Chancellor, Sir Frederick Crawford, arrived in the early Eighties to find things in a poor state. He had formerly been at Stanford University where things were rather different. An article on Aston University's development that appeared in London's *Independent* newspaper (8 December 1988) began: 'In 1980 Aston University looked like a state penitentiary . . . if you could not get a place anywhere else, Aston would probably take you.' Low morale amongst academic staff, poor performance from students, cuts in grants leading to a rocky financial situation were all encapsulated in an ugly, run-down campus. The new Vice-Chancellor decided that he had to make changes quickly. So he consciously went after improved quality and reduced quantity. He cut down on student numbers and pursued academic excellence in teaching and research. He clearly and publicly stated his intention to create a technological university of the highest order.

But with a poor reputation and a main campus building that looked, as he put it, 'like something out of Kafka', it was difficult to attract talent. A place that looks run down usually has little self-esteem. It was evident to Sir Frederick that he could only improve the University's performance if he also improved its appearance and facilities, and that meant tackling its image. Without a 'good image' (a repulsive phrase but an easy one to comprehend) the University simply could not hope to make a turn around. Nevertheless, he realized that if Aston began to look good but continued to perform badly, he would have failed.

So improvement of the image went hand in hand with improvement of performance.

Corporate identity consultants were appointed. They carried out a study which culminated in a report indicating how the university was seen by all those who dealt with it on the outside: the financial grants authorities, the Department of Education, other universities, academics of various disciplines, careers teachers in schools, industry, the local community, and so on. The consultants also revealed the depths to which morale had sunk internally. They showed what the University actually looked like, how it presented itself in brochures, in signing, in the totality of its physical appearance – and they made dramatic recommendations for change.

If Aston wanted to look like a technological university it had to coordinate its activities in landscaping, building works, signing, graphic and other information materials, and in the way it behaved, so that its intentions could become clear. It had to create a new idea of itself. It needed to become a social, cultural and intellectual focus within the British West Midlands and specifically within Birmingham, the city in which it is located. It needed to look, feel, behave and talk in a different way. The proposals were accepted.

The programme began. Every development took account of the identity change. The idea behind the new Aston was expressed by new symbolism, new buildings, roads – everything. Over the last few years a new Aston has started to emerge. The *Independent* again: 'A big part of the programme was physical improvement of the campus. One thousand trees were planted, the whole area re-landscaped. Two bright new sky lifts give an image of hi-tech modernity. Thirteen buildings were pulled down . . . . A logo was created, which adorns everything from notepaper to napkins.'

'Today', says the *Independent*, 'Aston is physically unrecognizable as the same campus. It is probably the leading university in the UK in its application of information technology, and highly qualified students clamour to get in.'

Aston University in Birmingham, England has created a new identity over buildings (left), landscaping, printed material and signing, out of an unpromising urban environment. The Aston symbol is a triangle symbolizing both the shape of the site and its position as a social, cultural and intellectual focus for the City of Birmingham.

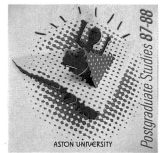

As ambition has risen, standards have steadily climbed upwards. The University's identity programme has become associated with a new sense of self-respect and higher goals. Better academic staff have attracted better students, who have produced better degrees, got better jobs and begun painfully to change the university's self-image and improve its credibility in the outside world. The Aston corporate identity programme has expressed a new vision and a new positioning. Slowly a virtuous circle is starting to turn.

These things take years to achieve. Aston will not become an M.I.T., an Imperial College or one of the French Grandes Ecoles overnight. But the crawl has evolved into a walk and is even developing into a sprint. It may take a generation – universities sometimes move slowly – but the impetus is there.

At the UK's Pilkington, profits from investing and licensing the float glass process, which revolutionized glass manufacturing worldwide, were invested in an intelligent programme of global acquisition and diversification into glass-related products for the construction transport, defence and medical industries.

Over twenty years, from the mid-Sixties to the mid-Eighties, Pilkington quietly became the biggest and strongest glass-maker in the world. Outside the industry itself, though, very few people were aware of what was going on. The new Pilkington acquisitions – Flachglas in Germany, Libbey Owens Ford in the US, and particularly a number of technologically sophisticated companies in the medical and defence business – were not overtly associated with the company; their names and their identities remained the same. So for many people Pilkington remained the technology-based, production-obsessed, family-dominated glass-maker that it had traditionally been.

Years after the investment policy had been laid down, analysts in the City of London were still asking how Pilkington was going to invest its profits from float glass. Pilkington had to develop a new identity policy which would address three crucial areas:

Pilkington is the world's largest company involved in manufacturing glass and glass-related products. The identity programme emphasizes the global nature and market dominance of the company; it also enables the diverse and decentralized parts of the organization to look and feel as though they belong to a single whole. The basic elements of the identity are the colours green and white, a tightly organized typographical system and a redesigned symbol used in various forms within the company for 150 years, derived originally from the Pilkington family crest.

Coherence – names and visual style of the acquired companies had to be associated with Pilkington.

Personality – Pilkington had to be seen to be more global in its approach, less personal, paternalistic and family-orientated.

Positioning – Pilkington had to be seen for what it was, the largest and most intelligently diverse, technologically sophisticated, worldwide manufacturer in its field, with interests in a number of high-growth, market-led businesses, all of which were in one way or another connected with glass.

That's why Pilkington started an identity programme.

Fortunately for Pilkington, its financial performance improved at about the same pace as its image changed. That is why, when it was threatened by a predator Pilkington was able to sustain support and beat off the attack. The new corporate identity programme marked the point at which a new sense of direction began to be clearly associated with the organization.

Repsol is Spain's largest single company. It comprises virtually the entire public sector activity of the Spanish oil industry. Within Repsol there were exploration companies, petro-chemical companies, distribution companies, and all the other activities that make up a major oil business. But each company had its own traditions, name and identity. As economic barriers started to break down within Europe, and BP, Shell, Esso, Elf, Mobil and the rest got ready to carve up Spain, Western Europe's last major retail petrol market, the heterogeneous Repsol group of companies began to look for a way to defend its market share.

Above all the Repsol group needed a clear identity for the products and services it was marketing at its domestic petrol stations. It could no longer present itself as a random ragbag of businesses, united only through common ownership.

The company eventually decided on a two-brand formula. It continued with a revitalized Campsa, its traditional, well-established national brand, and it created, through a new corporate identity programme, an entirely new brand under the Repsol name, intended to symbolize a vigorous Spain, outward-looking and self-confident, able to perform on equal terms with its European partners, competitors and collaborators.

So whether we are dealing with the fictitious problems of Steve R. Kojoski and BuffSanCo, or the real-life identity strategies of Aston University, Pilkington and Repsol, the problems with which corporate identity deals are similar.

Corporate identity is about corporate change. A new identity announces change, symbolizes change and is a catalyst for change. When there is a merger, a major investment or divestment, a strategic alliance,

Repsol was created to beat international oil competition within the Spanish national market. Bottom: signing system and station canopy. Far right, top: Repsol lubricating oils packaging. Centre: Repsol service station at night. Right, bottom: Repsol butane truck.

24 Horas
Servicio con Empleado
Sírvase Vd Mismo
Tarjetas de Crédito

REPSOL

a new management style, a problem with one or all of the corporate audiences, there is, inevitably, change. A corporate identity programme is one of resources which an organization uses to handle this change.

The composition of corporate identity problems varies from one organization to another. But the ingredients, deriving from mergers and acquisitions, organizational change, morale issues, pressures in the marketplace, poor internal relations, recruitment problems, lack of internal cohesion, and so on, tend to be the same.

They cannot be ignored for ever. In the longer term the Chief Executive has to grapple with such issues himself.

How does the corporate identity process begin?

Although for the most part corporate identity issues tend to become serious when they fall on the CEO's desk, it isn't always the CEO who first recognizes the problem; it may be the head of communications, or internal relations, or personnel. Sometimes corporate identity problems first emerge through line managers' problems. But nobody can really do anything about the underlying identity issues until the CEO gets concerned and decides to take action.

Once the CEO is alerted to the common factors that link a complex network of issues broadly labelled 'image', he will discuss potential action with his various advisers, on the board and elsewhere. The CEO has to resist the temptation to handle his own identity problem. As Professor Renato Tagiuri, of Harvard Business School, has pointed out, management has its own view of the corporation's identity, which is inevitably prejudiced and subjective. It would be unwise for any CEO to trust his own judgment where identity is concerned.

A thoughtful CEO will talk to his internal corporate communications people; he may turn to one of the corporation's advertising agencies (who will no doubt try to persuade him to run a corporate advertising campaign); he will talk to his public affairs advisers; and he may, after quite a lot of running around, find himself turning for counsel to a corporate identity consultancy.

The chances are that the CEO will never have been involved in a corporate identity programme before. He will know what many of the company's problems are, but he won't necessarily think that many of them are interrelated, and he may not know quite how or where to start. Nor will he necessarily take the view that some unknown outside consultant will be able to provide him with a panacea for difficulties with which he has been wrestling for years.

His communications people may well also be new to the practice of corporate identity, so for them too the learning curve will be steep. All this makes the choice of a good adviser critical.

A major problem is interface. In most organizations there is a natural point of interface between client and consultant. The financial officers of an organization deal with accountants and auditors; treasury deals with bankers; advertising and marketing departments deal with advertising agencies, and marketing consultants. But few organization have a permanently functioning corporate identity department to deal with its corporate identity consultants.

The interface problem must be dealt with before the job begins, or there will be havoc. Corporate identity is a broad-based discipline. It involves management, communication and behaviour, as well as design issues of different kinds. The emphasis between the various disciplines will change as the job progresses, so points of interface must be set up before the job begins.

The two natural points of personal interface between the client organization and its corporate identity consultants, at least in the earlier phases of the project, are (usually) the CEO himself and a senior manager. The CEO should normally be the final arbiter on the identity because in the end it is his responsibility and the corporate identity will be seen to be his creation. What's more, the organization as a whole will only take its corporate identity programme seriously if the CEO is seen to be wholly committed to it.

In addition to the CEO, another senior executive must be involved. He is usually called head of public affairs, or corporate affairs or communications – or something similar. Now and again the marketing people get their hands on the job, but that doesn't always work well.

It is essential to create a working party or committee to steer the job through the organization, as it works its way through its various stages. The nature, size and composition of the working party or steering committee will vary according to the style and size of the organization, but it always serves the same purposes, all of which are vital to the project.

First, it is the source of power.

Second, it provides the financial base.

Third, it has political sensitivity.

Fourth, it provides the forum within which the consultant and the client can jointly develop the project. The working party becomes the prime forum for debating identity options.

In order to get the project moving, the client organization has to find its consultancy – and this is not necesssarily easy.

There is no consensus amongst organizations that purport to practise corporate identity on what it is precisely that they do. The difference between what the various companies in the field offer is startling. So is the difference in their fees. Many of them prefer to emphasize their graphic design role; they offer corporate identity as part of a wide range of services. Others have a more specialized approach to the business and have non-design consultants on their pay roll or available on a part-time basis.

What they deliver also differs. The very few major consultancy companies with global corporate experience are naturally the best equipped and the most experienced. They are not always the best at providing original and bold creative solutions, though.

The process of choosing an adviser on a corporate identity programme is difficult, but it is not different in principle from making a similar choice in any other kind of professional activity. These are the kinds of things the client must look for in his proposed consultancy partner:

What sort of work do they do?

What do their clients think of them?

How are they regarded in the trade?

Who within the company will actually do the job?

How do they propose going about the work?

What will they charge?

How big are they?

What is their experience?

Where are they based?

What type of people work for them?

The most significant criteria in my judgment are:

Does the consultant have the experience and expertise to do the job?

Does he or she understand the issues?

Will we get on well together?

After the usual elimination rounds and beauty contests, a consultancy has to be picked and the job started. The methodology of creating, launching and sustaining an identity programme is now well established. Laboriously, by trial and error, consultants have developed a more or less standard format. Consultants talk of three stages of work, at one end of the spectrum, and as many as twelve at the other. It really doesn't matter too much how you break them down, but for convenience the process can usually be divided into four steps:

First, investigation, analysis and recommendations, leading to design brief.

Second, developing the design idea, and the communications and behaviour programmes.

Third, working out the final programme.

Fourth, launch and implementation.

All corporate identity programmes, however complex, involve these four stages, or something similar, as a basis for action, although the amount and nature of the work involved varies according to the job, and the rigour and experience of the consultant.

Generally speaking, it is no bad thing for the CEO to start by announcing internally that a major review of identity is under way. He will send out a memo outlining what the job is, how it will be developed, who the members of the working party are to be, and include some kind of time schedule. In the briefing note the CEO may indicate that various aspects of the organization's identity are being studied by consultants, who may be in touch with individuals for interviews. The CEO will ask that interviews be given where requested. He will confirm that the consultants will treat the interview in confidence and that answers should be given frankly and honestly. The note should indicate that further information will emerge in due course, and that the project is regarded as one of considerable significance.

The first stage of the work consists of an investigation of the organization, followed by an analysis and a recommendation, usually prepared in the form of a visual presentation backed up by a written report.

The investigation is carried out by a team of consultants who report regularly, on both a formal and an informal basis, to the working party as a whole and to various individuals within it. The team of consultants is constructed according to the nature of the job, but should incorporate business consultants, designers and specialists in communications and behaviour – or, as it is sometimes called, organizational development.

The investigation will involve an interview programme embracing individuals who represent different points of view from inside and outside the organization, and a design audit, a communications audit, and a behavioural audit.

Naturally, the number of interviews will vary according to the size and complexity of the organization, from a minimum of, say, 20-30 people up to 200-300.

The different processes that make up the first stage are likely to be carried out simultaneously, so there must be an effective project management resource.

The intention behind the interviews is to find out how the organization is perceived by the different groups of people with whom it has relationships. Normally the working party produces the basic list of interviewees. The organization's own employees at various levels of seniority, in varying geographic locations and in different divisions, are selected largely on the basis of the 'diagonal slice', topped up with a number of special cases who for one reason or another have to be on the list.

In addition, representatives of various outside groups must be interviewed: shareholders and others with a financial stake or interest in the organization, business journalists, financial institutions, customers, suppliers, competitors, collaborators, trade unions, national and local government. Consultants in public affairs, advertising, management, organization, personnel and finance are all appropriate interviewees.

The interview should be informal and confidential. It should follow a clear but unemphatic line and be designed to encourage the interviewee to speak the truth about the organization as he sees it. Inevitably, each interview is unique. Questionnaires should not be used, although clear themes should be followed.

Most skilled interviewers will confirm that when people believe there will be no breach of trust and mutual confidence is established, interviewees will be frank to a degree which is occasionally astonishing.

For the most part the themes will depend upon the nature of the organization and its problem areas. But here are some of the themes that inside interviewees are asked to deal with.

What is the size and shape of the organization?
What are its different parts?
Where do you fit?
What do you do?
What career path have you followed?
What do you feel about the way the organization performs and behaves?
What is it good at?

What is it bad at?
Who are its competitors?
What is its reputation for product quality, price, service, attitude?
Are these things consistent throughout the organization, or do they vary according to division, company, country?
Who are the dominant personalities within the organization as a whole and within divisions?
How do the different parts of the business regard each other?
What are its strengths – and weaknesses – by division and as a whole?
How independent are the different parts of the organization?
What is the opportunity for personal growth and development within the organization?
Is there mutual respect and co-operation or distrust and hostility – or a mixture of these emotions?
What is the hierarchy for the different activities?
Who comes first, who follows? To what extent does the hierarchy relate to financial achievement or trail-blazing, high-profile activity, or internal politics?
Is the organization driven by marketing, finance, technology, sales – or by nothing much at all?
Where is the organization going – up or down, or nowhere?
During the course of internal interviews with senior management, especially board members, strategic planners and the CEO himself, it's vital to get an idea of the corporate vision.

Does the organization have a clear vision? Is it based on reality, on what can actually be achieved, on keeping up with rivals, on whistling in the dark, or on personal ambition? The issues addressed in detail in Chapter 5 are relevant here.

The external interviewees have a very different attitude towards the organization. They are less involved and usually – but not always – less informed. (Sometimes they know rather more about the company than many of the people in it. Certainly they are more objective.)

For the most part themes used in internal interviews can be adapted for outside audiences, but there are a number of other issues that can with advantage be raised amongst outside interviewees.

For example:

To what extent are the organization's real size, strength and potential recognized amongst its peers, suppliers, customers and collaborators, and in the financial world?

How well known is the whole compared with its various parts?

How much does its reputation vary by country or by division?

What is the reputation of each of the divisions?

Do people think of it as it is, or as it was, or as it claims it is going to be?

What do people actually think it does?

Does it have personalities, whom some outsiders know and respect, or is it anonymous?

How profitable is it thought to be?

Do the corporation and its separate parts have a future, and if so, as what?

How do its various operational units compare with others in the field on price, on quality, on service?

Does it, as a group, have a clear personality?

If so, what is it?

The interview shows how the organization is perceived by the people who work in and deal with it. It shows what they know about it, how much or how little, and what they think of it. The interview does not seek to deal in objective truth; it deals with subjective perception.

Gradually as the interviews are analysed, a view of the organization begins to build up from different angles. When suppliers, competitors, customers, consultants and financial analysts speak about an organization and its separate parts, different perspectives inevitably emerge. The same story keeps being told, but always from a different point of view. Each version underlines and confirms the others, and gradually the reputation of the whole, and of its individual parts, emerges.

Interviews provide the basis for the first stage. But the other parts of the study, the design, communication and behavioural audits, are also significant.

Interviews show what is perceived; the audits show why these perceptions exist.

The communication audit examines how the organization talks and listens, and to whom. The design audit looks at how the different parts of the organization present themselves and how all that relates – if it does – to the presentation of the whole. The behavioural audit examines what it is like to deal with the organization, to come into contact with it in any way. Listening, looking and feeling audits, you could call them.

The purpose of the communications audit, which should be led by a consultant whose background expertise is in public affairs and external and internal communications, is to examine the ways in which the organization communicates, both with its own staff and with the various outside bodies and individuals with whom it deals.

Most large organizations are not good either at telling their own people what is going on, or at listening to what they have to say. Nor are they always very good at selecting their communications priorities.

Some organizations spend millions of dollars on communicating with customers, with whom they deal in a highly professional and sophisticated fashion, and practically nothing on any of their other audiences. Some lavish attention on investor relations, but don't regard supplier relations, government relations or employee relations as particularly significant.

Interestingly, the money spent on various kinds of communications is rarely agglomerated. Corporations are often arbitrary in their allocation of funds, spending generously on customers or dealers while being niggardly with their own staff, for instance.

The people handling the communications audit examine all these issues. In addition they look at the material that is produced: the press and TV advertising, brochures, bulletins, newsletters and videos. They examine these for content and form. They talk to the people who produce this material at group, division, company and brand level. They discuss with them the extent to which there is a communications policy, and whether there is formal or informal feedback. They look at the relationship, if any, between marketing and communications. They assess the extent to which the communication process is valued. They find out whether the people who carry out the communications task are familiar with the goals of the organization.

They determine the extent to which the communications function is satisfactory as it stands and how, if at all, it needs to change.

The design audit is in a sense both complementary to, and an integral part of the communications audit, and both are inextricably involved with the behavioural audit.

The design audit is led by one of the designers on the corporate identity consultants' team. Its task is to study and document the way in which the different parts of the organization present themselves in terms of the three traditional areas of design – factories, showrooms and so on; product and packaging, and information material; vehicle liveries, signs, brochures, advertising, instruction manuals and every other form of graphics. What does it all look like? What message is it meant to convey?

Any organization of a certain size produces frighteningly large quantities of visual material. Does this material have any consistency of visual style or quality? Is there a dominant theme?

In buildings, for example, and furnishings, is there a single concept that determines their selection? Are they expensive, cheap, international, local, grandiose, anonymous, traditional, modern? Or is there no policy? Are they all of these things in different places?

What about interiors? Do they look first rate all the way through, like IBM? Or are they glossy in the reception area, and shabby where the customers don't go? Are the flowers, if any, plastic or are they real?

Do the buildings bear the marks of the various individual personalities who have managed the business, or does there seem to be a consistency of purpose? When you move from one part of the business to another are you moving from one world to another; or are there recognizable common features? How does all this relate to the way staff and customers feel about the organization?

What about literature? Is there any consistency of style and quality in the brochures and folders? Is there a policy? Do they look cheap or expensive? Are

they written clearly and simply, or are they a hotchpotch? Do different parts of the organization explain their relationship to the whole with clarity or consistency, or does it all seem to make very little sense? Does the graphic material look as though it could have come from any company, or does it have a particular hallmark?

If the organization is a heavy spender on advertising, the advertising issue must also be examined with care. Is there consistency? Should there be? Or does each division have its own policy?

Do the products that the company makes and sells have a consistent style and quality? Or, on the contrary, is there no connection between one product range and the next? And if there is no consistency, is this intentional, because of branding – or is it an accident, a consequence of nobody caring for the whole?

The design audit concerns itself with names, as well as with style. How many names are used in different places? How do these names relate to each other? Is it easy or difficult to understand the organization? Is there an organization chart that makes sense? Does the naming and visual system clarify or confuse the structure?

In essence the behavioural audit is concerned with finding out what the different parts of the organization are actually like to deal with.

How does the organization deal with potential recruits; with employee induction programmes; with product complaints; with enquiries about service; with suppliers; with customers? What is it like at answering the 'phone, replying to correspondence? Do the people at the factory gate see their role as keeping visitors out, or welcoming them in? Are they gatekeepers, porters, or hosts?

A behavioural audit can take many forms. Michael Wolff, the eminent designer, speaks of a journey through the company starting with an exchange of letters and culminating in visits, in which the consultant monitors everything around him, including the physical state of the reception area, the date and condition of the reading matter provided and the manner in which refreshment, such as coffee or tea, is offered – and carrying on from there.

It's true that you can learn a lot about a company

by just looking and taking things in. In the 1960s I had cause to visit Bournville, in the UK, home of the respected Cadbury chocolate company. As I arrived at the porter's lodge, I saw a sign above a small shed which read: 'For directors' bicycles only'.

That sign was a prime piece of sociological information about Cadbury's at that time. For me it was information beyond price. It gave the clearest possible indication of the modest, authoritarian, paternalistic Cadbury culture with its Quaker roots. It was at the same time equally valable as material for a design audit, a communication audit and a behavioural audit.

Another dramatic way of making a behavioural point is to compare organizational reality with the 'editorializing'.

How does the impressive-seeming claim 'In order to be efficient and competitive we have to examine all aspects of our business – that's why we believe in operating the just-in-time principle with our suppliers', in an annual report for a plant equipment company, compare with the legend 'Goods received hours 7.30 a.m.-12 noon, 1 p.m.-2.30 p.m. No goods will be received outside these hours', hand-lettered on a faded sign in a depot at Rochdale, Lancashire? Or for that matter, what is the relationship between 'Our greatest asset is our people – we care deeply for every one of them', an extract from a corporate brochure of a massive financial services company, and their carefully graded hierarchy of six lunch rooms in the head offices in the City of London?

In reality, the communication, design and behavioural audits are mutually dependent, mutually reinforcing and mutually enlightening. They serve to show the client not so much what people feel about the organization, but why they feel the way they do.

Throughout the process, the weeks and months of study, the various members of the working party have met to share information about development on both a formal and an informal basis. It's all been discussed and churned over endlessly by consultant and client. If everything operates as it should, the working party – after the usual initial doubts and suspicions – forms a single entity.

After the lobbying, the informal discussion, the formal discussion, the working party agreement, the consultants start on their rounds of presentations of the Stage 1 study. First to the working party, then to the board, then maybe to other groups, too; perhaps to the heads of communication of the different divisions, to national managers, to other interested parties, non-executive directors.

The Stage 1 presentation should examine the following issues:

First: how is the organization perceived by the different groups of people with whom it deals?

Second: why is it perceived this way?

Third: what are the organization's aims and ambitions?

Fourth: how can a new identity help it to achieve its aims?

In the nature of things such a presentation is always complex and detailed – often, it is quite bruising. Few organizations emerge very well from this kind of detailed examination. It's rather like going through analysis; the patient doesn't enjoy it, but he comes out knowing himself more clearly. He understands his strengths and weaknesses. He understands why he does things. He can use what he is to make himself more effective.

But this does not mean that a presentation should become a confrontation. The real meat of a presentation should be: Do we agree with the recommendations for action? Rather than: Do we agree with the findings?

From all this a brief can be prepared for the subsequent stages of work. The brief should deal with structure. Is the organization to be monolithic, endorsed, branded – or some kind of combination? If so, what kind of visual style should the corporation adopt. The brief should be short – no more than one piece of paper – but concise.

In the next chapter we see how all this works in practice.

The painting on the wall in the BuffSanCo boardroom in Omaha, Nebraska.

Creating an Identity Programme – Managing Change

BuffSanCo

The three of them were met at the airport by a four-year-old Ford and a sixty-year-old driver carrying a pole with a hand-lettered sign saying BuffSanCo. The sign, the driver and the car all showed marks of wear and tear. 'There it is; the banner with the strange device. Excelsior,' said Thinwall. Neither of the others even smiled.

Gavin Thinwall felt that he showed signs of wear and tear too. He looked at his two companions. Liz Piper, the project director, had a suspiciously thickening figure, he thought. She was wearing a boxy kind of dark suit and looked tired. Bill Ball, on the other hand, looked fine. He was lurching along with three thick, black presentation cases, which neither Liz nor Gavin helped him with. Bill Ball was making the communications section of the presentation. All of them had spent the long hours between London and Chicago, and between Chicago and Omaha going through the work, endlessly, obsessively, fanatically.

They talked about the detail of the investigation. They checked through their findings, which indicated that the component parts of BuffSanCo were a series of separate organizations with little interest in, or knowledge of each other. They agreed that over the last four years, since Kojoski's arrival, he had been trying to introduce a powerful new corporate culture into the organization. But it was still almost entirely finance-driven. The financial reporting systems throughout the group were identical; great importance was placed on return on capital employed; divisions competed in terms of profitability; but apart from that there wasn't much to hold the whole business together.

The companies forming the group still shared no common philosophy of service or quality, although because of recent moves from the centre – in other words, because of Kojoski's various energetic changes – they all purported to show some interest in these things. Few divisions displayed any particular signs of that special thoughtfulness which was intended to be the company's hallmark.

The three consultants agreed that many of the businesses were very well managed and aggressive within their specific marketplaces. Some had excellent reputations. Others, though, especially some of the older ones, 'the cash cows', were about averagely dozy.

The three debated again and again whether or not the name and identity of BuffSanCo added anything to the individual units. On balance they felt that the investigation clearly revealed that while there were a few existing marketing situations in which it was useful, for the most part the group name and identity wasn't much help, either for most of the individual operating units or for the group as a whole.

They talked about what the various audits had revealed. The design audit showed every kind of presentation from an expensive, high-fashion image in the shoe world to low-grade commodity in lumber. The buildings in which the company's operations were housed also had no coherence. The offices in the Paseo de la Castellana in Madrid were awash with opulent leather and chrome. 'What's all this?' asked the Thinwall and Fineline man who visited it. 'Offcuts from the shoe trade?' The thick pile carpets, heavy brass door fittings and luxurious bathrooms looked like a top-class hotel in Hong Kong. What a contrast with the offices in Frankfurt: sparse, simple, almost utilitarian. In the US each operating unit had its own style. The old companies tended towards a kind of a faded grandeur; the newer ones were mostly decorated in classic office furniture, American-style. Not only was there no group coherence; there wasn't even much coherence within some of the divisions. The different companies in the aerospace division presented themselves in varying ways, from sophisticated systems organizations, who had worked out a thoughtful relationship with their clients, all the way down to low-grade component suppliers who had no real conception of their customers' requirements, and who sold only on cheapest price tenders.

The three consultants agreed that despite all this, a corporate logic was emerging and combined with the logic was an incipient corporate attitude and philosophy largely based, at this early stage of development, around the dour, rather quirky personality of the CEO, Steve (Ruthless) Kojoski. Kojoski was determined – this had emerged from interviews both with him and his closer colleagues – to give the corporation a clearer shape, to steer it into higher tech products and systems, to get rid of some of the stodgier commodity businesses but to keep a strong counter-cyclical base. So far as personality and attitude were concerned, the new BuffSanCo was to translate 'thoughtfulness' in a manner appropriate to each commercial situation. In aerospace, for instance, they always examined the possibilities of risk-sharing in finance and technology. In some parts of aerospace it worked well; in others it was a disaster. These issues naturally led the three consultants to discuss people. Every single member of the working party was analysed and dissected. Gossip kept Thinwall and his colleagues going for an hour or two.

They alternated the gossip with more serious matters. It was clear that within five years or so a new BuffSanCo would emerge. Perhaps a bit smaller in size, but much more profitable and at the higher end of the price and quality scale, and of course, global.

The BuffSanCo symbol has been modified in an uncontrolled fashion over the years. Opposite: 1925. Below: 1955.

So the issue for Thinwall and his colleagues was clear. In essence, BuffSanCo was changing, at different paces in different places. It was gradually becoming more coherent, more focused and more thoughtful. How should this affect the identity recommendation? Should they recommend a gradual change of identity in line with the corporate evolution – perhaps an endorsed identity structure of some kind, with a BuffSanCo symbol modified to look a bit more classy, and a proper policing job done on the identity? Or should they say to Kojoski that for all his tough talk and behaviour he hadn't yet got very far in creating the new BuffSanCo, and that what the whole thing needed to make it really take off was something much more radical. This meeting with the working party, the fourth major formal meeting since the job began, had been organized to discuss this issue. So the three consultants talked it through again. Somewhere over the Atlantic, they confirmed with relief that they were right in going for the radical view.

Bill Ball reminded the other two that communication between the companies and divisions was appalling, that Saxby Palmer, Head of Communications, the man who had brought them in, was relying on them to tell the working party how incoherent and uncoordinated everything was. Palmer, a former investor relations consultant with a public relations company and new to the whole business, had told them that stuck down here in Omaha, Nebraska, the company felt that it was a real power. They just didn't know how little anybody knew about them. 'Saxby is relying on us. I'm sure we're right to go for the radical view.' But would they buy it? Changing the name and identity; launching it all;

167

replacing all the communication material; upgrading and coordinating environments. It would all cost money and energy, and would take time. Culturally, the people who managed the BuffSanCo business were for the most part antipathetic to issues like PR, advertising, image and identity, which they tended to lump together as 'costs'.

The discussions between the three consultants went on and on. Through Chicago's O'Hare and onto the next aircraft. By the time they arrived at Omaha even they were sick of talking about it.

The Ford rattled up to the local Ramada Inn. All three of them piled out, checked in, mumbled to each other about meeting in the morning and disappeared to their separate rooms. It was 9.00 p.m. They had, after all, spent the whole of a very long day together, and enough was enough.

Thinwall got to his room, fiddled with the mini-bar and, as usual, failed to make it work. He ordered a whisky sour from room service. Then he considered as he lay in the bath what he ought to wear the following day.

He had the choice of three equally travel-crumpled outfits. He felt the blazer was too 'English', the suit he just didn't fancy wearing, so he decided on the Chester Barrie cashmere jacket. 'Stylish and slightly informal, almost creative, you might say.' He smiled at his own self-parody, read a bit, put the light out and went to sleep.

The following day at 7.30 a.m. the old Ford appeared with its elderly, unsmiling driver, and the three of them clambered in and drove along the grey streets to the headquarters building.

Up the granite steps – 'Two of them still chipped,' thought Thinwall – through the swing doors – 'One of them still creaking,' he noticed – into the elevator and up to the boardroom.

The boardroom had been the boardroom since old Fortescue had moved the company into the building in 1928. It was big and dark, full of mahogany and leather. It smelt of old cigar smoke and money. On the wall were two pictures. One of them was of Simon Fortescue himself, 'our founder'. It was painted in the 1930s, when he was about sixty. He had a bright red face, not much grey hair, blue eyes and a squint. 'Did that man really have a squint,' said Thinwall to his colleagues, 'or is it just an even worse painting than I thought?'

The other painting was of a post-Civil War railroad train. There was an engine, a tender and some passenger coaches. It was speeding through the richest countryside, by the side of a beautiful river, on which there was a paddle steamer. On the brown-painted carriages of the train, picked out in gold, were the words Buffalo-San Diego Railroad.

'You know,' said Steve Kojoski, who had just come into the room, 'that train never existed. This company never had a train. Fortescue, the old humbug, had the picture painted to impress the stockholders. It went out on all the brochures and share applications. You guys must have seen it on all that old stuff in the archives when you did your design audit. But Fortescue never said there actually was a train; that painting sort of implied that there might have been, though.'

Kojoski and the others laughed. Then Gavin Thinwall said quietly but emphatically: 'You know, Steve, you are going to have to get rid of that painting. It oughtn't to be in this boardroom. It stinks of what this company was once like. It goes with the two-faced symbol.' As he said that he was sure he noticed Fortescue's squinty eye winking at him.

The other members of the working party ambled in. Everybody exchanged platitudes about the trip and jet lag and how awful all the airlines were. Then they sat down. The fourth formal and umpteenth informal meeting of the corporate identity working party began.

A four-hour presentation and discussion, interrupted from time to time by thin, watery coffee in bendy paper cups and some tuna sandwiches, indicated that Steve Kojoski and the rest of the working party were taking the project seriously. By now everyone clearly understood, if they had doubted it before, that the programme was addressing fundamental problems.

They started the meeting by going through the design audit. Everyone was appropriately scandalized by the general confusion and anonymity indicated by the graphic material. The environments also came in for a hammering. After that they turned to the communications and behavioural audits. Here too, things were predictably patchy.

They then turned to the investigation. The working party laughed when Thinwall told them that research confirmed that because of the 'San' in the name a lot of people thought the company made sanitary towels. Mike Michaelis, national manager for Germany, said he thought it was funny because it was virtually the only thing BuffSanCo didn't make. As for the rest, the study indicated that many audiences thought BuffSanCo was an old, tired, directionless commodity business. All the members of the working party nodded wearily in agreement at observations they recognized from their own experience.

All the other problems of the name – its links with the past, the difficulty of spelling, confusion with Monsanto, the fact that it was only used by 25 per cent of the company (the rather older and less profitable parts) – were also recognized by the members of the team. On balance it looked as though most of the working party agreed that it was right to move towards the idea of dropping BuffSanCo as a group name.

Not everybody was enthusiastic about the implications of change, however. David Jenkinson, Vice-President and Head of Finance, was predictably tough and sensible. He asked how much it would cost to change names, how much goodwill they would lose, how much it would cost in advertising, how much it would cost to replace signs, what the legal fees would be, whether it should be done overnight, and if so what the implications would be in terms of dislocation. And he asked what would they get out of it, when they had done it all. 'Can you quantify the benefits?' he asked, looking straight at Thinwall, who was doodling more feathers on the headdress around the BuffSanCo Indian head in the corporate symbol. 'I could quantify the benefits of your recommendations to your own company; you'll be getting 4 or 5 million dollars in fees. But I'm not sure I could quantify them so readily for ours.' Gavin Thinwall looked up, straightened his tie and cleared his throat. This was just what he had been waiting for. He enjoyed 'clearing the air'.

He dropped his Lamy ballpoint on the table, raised his eyes so that he looked directly at Jenkinson and away from the squinty-eyed painting, and said: 'Look David. Look at what people both inside and outside the organization know about BuffSanCo. You've been in business for nearly a century. You are in the Fortune 100. Your financial results are improving. You are now in a whole range of good, lively, respected, growing product areas. And yet you can't recruit people; you can't make the acquisitions you want; you have a rotten price/earnings ratio. Wall Street analysts don't know what you do, and don't think you're going anywhere. And you ask me whether it's worth it? On top of all that, you are wasting one opportunity after another because your people don't talk between divisions, don't market jointly, don't even think of buying from one another.'

'No, I can't quantify exactly what it will cost you – but say we're talking about 70-80 million dollars, including fees, dislocation and changing everything. If you want to go crazy, add in another 30-40 million for some extra advertising. Honestly, it's peanuts for a company your size. Don't forget all the money you spend already painting vehicles, on brochures, on annual reports, on advertising, on videos, on packaging, on product labelling. Everything will still be done – but it will be far more effective. That won't cost you any more. You will actually be saving money.'

There was a pause. Then Thinwall said slowly and clearly: 'If your P/E goes up a few points, which it will, you will have more than paid for what it all costs in terms of the increase in the capital value of the organization. On top of that, if you can start recruiting better people, make the acquisitions you want, start sharing sales contacts internally, there

will be no end to the advantages that you'll gain. Apart from which, people will notice who you are for a change. You will be relaunching the whole corporation, a great opportunity.'

'Well,' thought Thinwall, 'that certainly shut him up.' Steve Kojoski looked pleased too.

Kojoski had managed the meeting well. He hadn't talked much; he hadn't dominated it. He let all the others have their say, but as things were drawing to a close, he simply said: 'Well now, which of you, like me, believes that the radical option is the one to go for?' After he had said that, all the other members of the working party found themselves veering towards the radical solution. Even Jenkinson, the Head of Finance, who earlier had raised so many objections, agreed that on balance he went along with his CEO.

After the meeting, Thinwall was exhausted; so were the others. It had gone well, he felt, but he wasn't sure if Saxby Palmer was big enough for the huge job that was coming up. Come to that, he wasn't sure how the consultancy would have the resources to manage it either, especially if Liz was really pregnant. No doubt if she was, he would be the last person in the office to know. He was the last person to be told anything these days.

The only real difficulty had come from that fool Theodore Donaldi, who said to him quite loudly just as the meeting was breaking up and they were walking out of the door, 'You know, you change the name of my company over my dead body. We're in a business where reputation counts for everything. Donaldi is one of the great names in the business. It

would be commercial suicide to give it up.' But Thinwall knew that they had one on Donaldi. When the presentations to each division came up, he'd release it to aerospace. Contrary to what they thought, Boeing, Lockheed, McDonnell Douglas and their other major customers didn't have the least regard for Donaldi; they felt that its reputation had slipped and they were hoping that Steve Kojoski would introduce higher standards into the Donaldi companies within the aerospace division. Paradoxically, they thought that some other parts of BuffSanCo's aerospace businesses were really doing well. One of the interviewees actually said. 'Donaldi is on the line with us.' Anyway, they had not made any name-change recommendations about the Donaldi business.

At least nobody had asked what the new name was going to be, or what the new symbol would look like. They had another three months to produce recommendations for that, always assuming that the Stage 1 recommendations got through the board.

There were more meetings in Omaha that week. Thinwall and his colleagues had further sessions, first with Saxby Palmer and then, more briefly, with Kojoski to plan their next steps.

The working party had agreed that the radical proposal should go to the board with their blessing. The board would not want a four-hour meeting; an hour-long presentation would be enough, plus some time for questions. Before the board met they would want a written paper outlining the identity recommendations and the background to them.

Thinwall and his team were well prepared. They had brought with them a storyboard with an outline of their proposed presentation to the board, and the first draft of a written background note.

The presentation storyboard started with the brief, confirming that the identity of BuffSanCo should be investigated and why. It went on to say what the consultants had done, outlined the number of interviews, broken down into internal and external, described the design audit, the communication audit and the behavioural audit. It showed how the different parts of the organization perceived each other, how they perceived the group, what various outsiders felt. The storyboard indicated that there would be quotations from various interviews and a summary of opinion. The funniest quote was from a manager at a tyre replacement depot in Strasbourg, whom one of the consultants was waiting to interview. 'Sorry to keep you waiting,' he had said when he finally turned up. 'I didn't know it was anybody important. I thought you were just a customer.' The storyboard dealt with why the organization was perceived in the way it was; its presentation, its communication, its behaviour. Here illustrations of product, packaging, environments of different kinds were to be shown.

The next section outlined the organization's ambitions; what did BuffSanCo want to become, and what was it doing in terms of reorganization, divestment, acquisition and training, to get there? Finally the storyboard turned to the recommendations concerning coherence, personality and positioning.

The characteristics that the organization wanted to project were tabulated. The storyboard outlined how a new visual identity would help the organization achieve its ambitions. It dealt with three options. First, leaving things the way they were. Second, tidying up the existing structure so that the group appeared more coherent, without looking very different. Third, going for a radical option which would involve changing the group name and visual style, keeping BuffSanCo as a traditional name in some of the divisions, and associating the new name and identity with all parts of the group. The new name and style, it was emphasized, must be able to encapsulate the ambitions, attitudes and personality of the relaunched organization.

The presentation outlined the advantages and disadvantages of each option. It indicated that the radical step had the most advantages and fewest disadvantages. The radical step was the one that could best alter perceptions of the organization and make everyone who dealt with it understand that real change was taking place. It was therefore the one the working party recommended.

The presentation emphasized, though, that this solution demanded real co-operation and commitment from senior management, that there could be no backsliding. Above all it de-

manded that a major communication operation should be mounted if the new strategy were to work effectively.

Finally the presentation dealt with what should be done next, if the decision to make a radical change was agreed.

This was the storyboard and written presentation which the consultants discussed with Saxby Palmer and briefly, later in the day, with Kojoski.

In the CEO'S office, a smaller version of the boardroom where they had sat on the previous day, Kojoski, Palmer and the three consultants tackled more of the detail. They looked at the implications in terms of time, cost and people. During the meeting Kojoski quickly nodded agreement to most of the matters that were discussed, and Palmer seemed to grow more self-confident.

That same evening Kojoski and Thinwall had dinner together. People eat early in Omaha, so by 7.00 p.m. Thinwall was munching his way through a steak and salad with blue cheese dressing. Kojoski looked a bit nervous and rather more dour than usual. 'Look, Gavin,' he said over his turkey salad, 'this had better work. I'm going to have a very hard job persuading some of these divisional heads to go along with it. You may not think much of BuffSanCo's image or, for that matter, its history, but for half of the fellows out there it's sacred. It isn't just a way of making a living. It's a way of life. They live and breathe the company. When they die they want a BuffSanCo shroud round their bodies. We are proposing to take away the things they hold most dear. Their name, their symbol, their personality . Everything. I hope you realise the implications of what you're proposing.'

Opposite: some BuffSanCo companies tried hard to bring the symbol up to date by making it more abstract.

Left: Buff'n'Shine was a shoe polish introduced in 1964 by Household Products Division. It was withdrawn from the market in 1965.

Thinwall had been through this many times, with many different clients, although he had never heard Steve Kojoski quite so eloquent before.

'Steve,' he said, 'this discussion isn't about whether we know what we are doing; it is about you, and whether you are really going to do it. You are looking into the abyss and you are saying to yourself, should I jump? Now I can't force you to jump. And you had better not jump if you don't believe in it. But I can promise you that if you jump with conviction, it will work. You want to make a new company out of an old one, with new ideas, new attitudes, a new spirit of cooperation. This is the way to signal that you really mean it.'

Kojoski looked morosely at the flickering, artificial candle which rested at an angle on the bright red tablecloth. 'Do these things ever go wrong?' he asked.

'They go wrong if the company is no good and can't stand the spotlight. If it doesn't do what it claims it can. They can certainly go wrong if you don't launch them properly and if you don't have all your people behind you. Otherwise they go right, providing you have the conviction and the organization,' said Thinwall.

The conversation droned on until the coffee came. Thinwall said to himself, 'Now he's going to ask me what the new name will be and what the symbol will be like.' But he didn't. Instead, Kojoski said: 'I'm putting a hell of a lot of faith in you. I hope you don't let me down.'

'Don't worry, Steve,' said Gavin. 'You just need to have the courage of my convictions.' Kojoski smiled. Gavin couldn't remember how many times he had made that remark. But it was true. BuffSan-Co was a sound company. Kojoski was a brilliant manager and a considerable leader, and in his way a very nice man, 'though not', thought Thinwall to himself, 'a bundle of laughs.' It would work if they did it properly. And they would, Thinwall felt it in his bones. It was going to be all right.

Although the consultants couldn't officially be briefed to work on the second stage of the job before the board had approved Stage 1, the outline proposals for Stage 2 were discussed, just before they left for London, between Palmer and the three consultants.

Each division has used the name and symbol as it thought fit. In 1972 the Timber Division introduced a new plywood product for the furniture industry – BuffPly. The logotype was adapted from the BuffSanCo symbol and typeface.
Opposite: the names Buff u matic and Buffmatic have been applied both to laundry products and timber-cutting machinery!

The tacit assumption was that they would move ahead. 'Move ahead with what, Liz?' the head of communications asked. 'I mean, do you just go away and give us a new name and a logotype. Or do we carry on with the working party and sit around looking at sketches and name proposals? I mean, what actually happens now? How do we compare your proposals with what we actually want to be? What's the process, Liz?'

There was silence. Thinwall abhorred a vacuum. He was about to leap into the breach when Liz began.

It was clear that she had only paused for breath. 'Within the overall programme of change, that is organizational and cultural change, Thinwall and Fineline are to be responsible for making recommendations for the following:

A new group name.

An endorsed identity structure, enabling divisions to retain existing names, including BuffSanCo where appropriate.

A new group visual identity appropriate to the group personality and positioning.

A communication programme which will launch the new identity internally to all employees all over the world simultaneously.

A programme of external launches to key group audiences, e.g. the financial sector, and so on.

Assisting divisions and companies on their own launch and communication programmes.

A programme for managing the new identity in relation to products, environments and communications.

Some of these matters fall into Stage 2, others into later stages. I will send you a detailed fax when we get back to London, giving you a time and cost estimate, where possible, for each item. Will that do to be getting on with?'

On the aircraft home to London Liz and Gavin sat together. 'You were on good form, Liz,' he said. 'So were you, Gavin. By the way, I think I ought to tell you that I may have a little problem over the next few months. I'm five months pregnant, and I don't know how clever it will be for me to keep flying backwards and forwards to Omaha. But I really want to do the job.'

Gavin looked at her and smiled: 'Look, Liz,' he said, 'you are, of course, entirely irreplaceable, but we'll have to limp along without you somehow. Even you can't mix babies and corporate identity programmes. Not for a bit anyway. But congratulations. We'll arrange things in London until you can come back to work. Saxby won't like it, of course, he's taken rather a shine to you.' For the next hour or so they gossiped about an appropriate replacement.

After various delays work began on the new name and design programme. A board meeting was fixed for the Stage 1 presentation. Thinwall, Liz and Bill dashed to Omaha and back again. To everyone's amazement the presentation went more or less without a hitch. Except that non-executive director, Simon J. Fortescue III, grandson of the original Simon Fortescue, was at last the one who actually asked whether the consultancy had the new name and visual proposals with them. 'It always has to be somebody,' said Bill Ball to himself, 'and it would of course have to be the grandson of the founder.'

The criteria for Stage 2 were set out and discussed both within the consultancy and with the working party.

Gavin Thinwall took the view that getting a programme through a organization was like a steeplechase. There was a whole series of hurdles. The rider could fall off at any one of them, and you only won at the very end. With BuffSanCo they'd crossed a couple. First, they'd beaten other people to the job; second, they had Stage 1 agreed. But Stage 2 was something different.

Somehow or other the criteria by which the name and identity needed to be developed had both to embrace the BuffSanCo proposition and be unique.

The problem was that there was not a great deal that was unique about the personality and positioning which BuffSanCo wanted to adopt. That phrase about being thoughtful was of course very important. But on the other hand there were at least twenty companies in the US and many others in the rest of the world that were trying to do exactly the same kind of thing as BuffSanCo – large conglomerates intent on introducing logic into a haphazard mass.

They went through it again. BuffSanCo had a counter-cyclical mix of services and products. It was global. It was, or wanted to be, 'thoughtful' in relation to all its audiences.

So how did this affect the name and symbol used? The criteria were standard: the name must be short, easy to pronounce, inoffensive in all languages; it must preferably have a positive connotation, be registerable, and so on.

The visual system must be unique, convey the characteristics of the organization, have a timeless quality, be easy to reproduce in all materials and sizes, work happily with other symbols and marks used within the group, be flexible, appropriate to all the different parts of the organization and acceptable in every social and religious culture. 'All very well,' said the team, 'but that's what they all have to be like.'

So after all the investigations and presentations the strength of the programme rested largely on the visual solution. The problem is that most clients are unsure of themselves in this area. They don't want to look silly, and are therefore inclined to play safe. Many people working in client organizations have strong views on design. Some have husbands and wives, sons and daughters who may even have attended art school for a week or two. All of these will be keen to express an opinion – after all, everyone is an expert on what things look like.

Thinwall felt, despite the constraints, that if a new BuffSanCo was to emerge with a new name and a new identity as a way of expressing Kojoski's vision, it would have to avoid the standard 'Big Company' look: 'If Steve Kojoski thinks he's been courageous so far,' he muttered to himself as he sat looking at some of the preliminary design work in front of him, 'he won't know what's hit him when he sees what we're going to give him.'

A written design and names brief was prepared by the consultancy. It covered less than one sheet of A4 paper, and it dealt with the issues that were outlined in the discussion and presentation.

Buff 'em Up

The graphic designers, who had disconsolately recorded the mixture of ostentation and banality with which BuffSanCo presented itself, now emerged as a major players.

The designers were young and trendy. Sarah Gainsborough, who disguised her tiny body in what looked to Thinwall like baggy black rags, was the star of the team. Henry Lidden, who 'rolled his own', was also a brilliant intuitive designer. He was inclined to stand on one leg, and since he had to contort his 6′4″ frame in order to hear what Sarah was saying, he was familiarly known as Heron. Despite their appearance these two were familiar with business and the corporate identity process. This was their fourth major corporate identity programme. The team leader and group director, Nigel O'Leary, was at that especially interesting stage of a designer's career when he is migrating from sweatshirt and jeans to Ralph Lauren, Hugo Boss, Giorgio Armani and Paul Smith. O'Leary was a long-serving Thinwall and Fineline designer. He had a lot of experience, a cool head and was still, even as a scarred veteran of 37, highly creative.

These formed the core of the team around whom other specialists worked.

It was to this highly intelligent, culturally open, lively trio that the visual identity programme for BuffSanCo was entrusted, under the basilisk eye of Gavin Thinwall. Thinwall, who had graduated as a designer from the Royal College of Art and the Yale School of Design at the time, as he put it, of 'the American Civil War', was still an active creative thinker. 'Too active for many of my colleagues, no doubt,' he often said.

All the work was based on three separate routes.

First, developing a logotype out of the new group name.

Second, using the name with a simple abstract mark.

Opposite: the Leather Division diversified briefly into boxing gloves and other leather-related sports products. Hence Buff 'em Up.

Right: Buff Master was a carpet sweeper imported from Taiwan and rebranded by Household Products Division.

Third, introducing a humanistic element.

It is easier, as Gavin Thinwall knew, to sell design work that looks safe and familiar than it is to sell design work that is original, thoughtful and long-lasting. Most chief executives feel like Steve Kojoski, who thought to himself, 'Are these guys going to make a fool of me? What kind of an idiot am I going to look amongst my family, friends and peers if I make the wrong decision? So let's play safe.'

This was a view with which Thinwall had every emotional, and no intellectual sympathy.

He knew graphic design is a field in which there is much expertise, a vast body of knowledge and many highly skilled practitioners. He also knew that there is clear proof that some design programmes work better than others, because they have more impact and create more sympathy amongst the people who see them.

Over the years fashions have changed in graphic design. Some design consultancies have a very strong handwriting of their own; others simply follow the current mode. Design companies, like other businesses, are strongly affected by peer-group pressure and admiration, and a lot of the work produced is intended to win approbation from others in the trade but ignores the real interests of the client.

At the other end of the spectrum, and quite as unacceptable, there is a substantial amount of work, produced especially for large, uncertain organizations, that is derivative, unmemorable and therefore ineffective.

Thinwall was clear that if a new company was to emerge out of BuffSanCo as a powerful force, truly representing a new idea, the design and naming work had to be original, forceful and longlasting. It also had to be appropriate.

Thinwall felt that Kojoski might buy a really strong solution, if it were brilliant enough and if he were persuasive enough. His job was to inspire the young team.

The naming team worked in parallel with the design team, sharing people and ideas. Thinwall and Fineline developed rough sketches and different routes towards new names and new designs. They showed all the ideas and much of the developmental work, even the most extreme and unusual, to the working party. As a result, the various members of the working party became engrossed by and absorbed in the process. They began to contribute ideas. Even David Jenkinson, perhaps the most sceptical member of the team, got enthusiastic.

The meetings with Saxby Palmer, who as Head of Communications seemed to grow both more confident and more nervous simultaneously, and the working party went on for three months. Palmer revealed an impressive political subtlety in dealing with his colleagues, and was a resolute though somewhat nervous advocate for the bold route. Some of his own contributions were respected and explored by the creative team at Thinwall and Fineline.

Work was shown, developed, rejected; new paths were opened up.

Time passed. Liz got larger; left work; went into hospital and after two days produced Daisy.

At about the same time, by a process that the participants felt was just as painful, Thinwall and Fineline produced a new name and symbol. Both were registered, checked for faults, and found to be in full working order. Both are now lusty infants.

Green-faced Osiris, Egyptian God of
death and fertility.

CHAPTER **8**

Launching and Maintaining an Identity Programme

BuffSanCo was given the full treatment: a radical change of both name and visual imagery. That is comparatively rare. It happens when, as in this case, an organization changes direction, where two companies are merging, or where an existing name has simply become inappropriate. Normally, corporations tend to change in an evolutionary fashion. For the most part they place considerable faith in their names; they believe them to be sources of goodwill, and they view the idea of a name change with reluctance. In this, their instincts are usually correct. Even companies with the most unlikely and untranslatable names can often overcome what might at first appear to be a paralyzing handicap. The French, it seems, don't think of Bosch as the enemy, or of ICI as where they happen to be, and Volkswagen is popular in Brazil even though it's virtually unpronounceable in Portuguese. No monoglot English-speaker can do better than approximate the sound of Hoechst but the company continues to thrive.

Name changes do happen, of course. The luckless British Motor Corporation became British Motor Holdings, then merged with Leyland to become British Leyland, next BL and after that the Rover Group. Now that it is part of British Aerospace, or BAe as the company sometimes perversely calls itself, Rover may be left to rest in peace. In France the union between the hotel and leisure groups Novotel and Jacques Borel begat Accor, cleverly designed to sound and look like a mixture of accord and *accueil* (welcome). It works. The merger of Dutch Naarden and British PPF, both in flavours and fragrances, produced Quest, which found enthusiastic acceptance in its world.

There has been a lot of loose talk about newly coined names being rejected because they sound like a disease or a rash, but the truth of the matter is that people do not tend to be quite so selective. The naming process usually works when the company is committed to it and fails when it isn't.

There are six different name categories. First, an individual's name, usually that of the founder – Chrysler, for example. Second, a descriptive name – Air France. Third, an abbreviated name – Pan Am. Fourth, initials – IBM. Fifth, a made-up name (these are the ones that most often come under fire) – Kodak. Sixth, an analogous name – Jaguar. Each of these categories has both advantages and disadvantages. Names may become out of date; somebody else may own them already; they may no longer relate to the main activity of the business, and so on.

Sometimes, because of merger or inappropriate association, it becomes necessary to change a corporate name. And that costs a lot of money, involves a lot of legal and logistical work, and creates massive emotional difficulties. It usually isn't worth doing unless – as in the case of BuffSanCo – you feel that you have to.

Comment accueillir 50 familles dans la région d'Alsace en ou vrant une suite pour un émir à Londres?

Accor. Une entreprise qui réunit Sofitel, Novotel, Mercure, Ibis, Formule 1 pour l'hôtellerie; Générale pour la restauration; Ticket Restaurant, Novotour, Devimco, Scapa et la Cir pour les services. Une association de Restauration, Courte-Paille, Seafood Broiler, Pizza del Arte, l'Arche de savoir-faire qui constitue un véritable capital humain dans 68 pays. ACCOR

ACCOR. L'HOTELLERIE. LA RESTAURA TION. LES SERVICES DANS LE MONDE.

...mment recevoir 200 congressistes à Singapour... faisant déjeuner 100 000 employés à Rio?

ACCOR. L'HOTELLERIE, LA RESTAURATION ET LES SERVICES DANS LE MONDE ENTIER.

Accor. Une entreprise qui réunit Sofitel, Novotel, Mercure, Ibis pour l'hôtellerie, Générale de Restauration, Courtepaille, Seafood Broiler, Pizza del Arte, l'Arche pour la restauration, le Ticket Restaurant, Novotour, Devimco et Scapa pour les services. Une association de savoir-faire qui constitue un véritable capital humain dans 60 pays. ACCOR

Far left: traditional competitors in the flavours and fragrances field, PPF of Britain and Naarden of Holland, merge under the new name and Identity, Quest – a Unilever subsidiary (1987). The new identity reduced internal wrangling, helped the former rivals to settle down together and to compete globally in this difficult marketplace.

Accor (1983) is the French hotel, catering and leisure group formed from Novotel and Jacques Borel. Existing brand names of restaurant and hotel chains, such as Novotel, Ibis, Sofitel and Ticket, are retained.

Above and left: corporate advertising announcing the new corporation.

Radical changes of visual style are, on the other hand, rather more frequent; although in this case, too, most organizations rightly cherish what they have and view dramatic changes with suspicion.

The British-based chemicals company ICI went through a major corporate identity development in 1987, but although there were modifications to the symbol, these were relatively minor and evolutionary. The main thrust of the programme was structural. Its intention was to create an identity framework that would subsume the totality of ICI's activities, including those with powerful brand and company identities of their own, into an ICI visual system. To the outside world the ICI changes seem minor and unimportant. Within ICI, however, they are of major significance.

GE of the US has been through a similar process of identity reappraisal. No doubt there have been profound and useful structural modifications to the organization's identity. Its visual style has, however, been only marginally modulated.

On the other hand, the Prudential Corporation, one of Britain's largest financial services groups, went through a major corporate identity change in 1986, in order to produce a radical solution. The organization was seen as large, bumbling, and rooted in its lower-middle-class 'Man from the Pru' origins, despite the fact that in reality it had changed dramatically: it had become a broad-based financial services organization, operating in everything from insurance and unit trusts (mutual funds), to estate agents (realtors), and it was much quicker off the mark in technology than its outward appearance gave it credit for. The new Prudential, which is based around a reinterpretation of the face of Prudence, one of the cardinal virtues and an icon of the organization since it began business, has been judged highly successful, both internally and in the outside world, in achieving a major shift of characterization.

On what basis, then, should an organization decide whether it needs to alter its visual appearance – and, if so, how and at what pace? In the end, it is a matter of judgment, but that judgment has to be based on evidence. The evidence that is developed during the investigation part of Stage 1 of the identity programme is a key factor.

The investigation carried out into both internal and external audiences, followed by analysis and recommendation, should enable the organization to see clearly how it is perceived, how well it is known, where, what for, and by whom. The analysis has to take into account other factors, too, such as the nature of the business.

Some organizations have reputations, built up over decades, that are worth millions. Their visual identities are only modulated in an evolutionary fashion over time. The deliberate intention is to give the impression that no changes have been made at all. Above and right: GE of the US, ICI of the UK.

The Prudential Corporation, one of Europe's largest financial groups (no relation to Prudential of the US), required a complete change of visual imagery. In addition to its traditional life assurance activities, upon which its fortunes were founded, it had become the largest single investor in the London Stock Exchange, one of the biggest unit trust organizations (mutual funds) and Britain's largest estate agent (realtor). The Prudential's visual imagery, which was fragmented, anonymous and largely represented by the idea of the Man from the Pru (left), was reshaped to project the real strengths and diversity of activities which exist within the organization.

A monolithic structure replaced the former fragmentation and a new visual style was launched, based on the face of Prudence – after whom the organization was originally named. Prudence, together with Justice, Temperance and Fortitude, is one of the cardinal virtues. She is traditionally depicted with a snake, the symbolic representation of wisdom; an arrow, sign of a skilled marksman; and a mirror, sign of an ability to see oneself as one really is.

The conventional view is that at one end of the spectrum a fashion business aimed at young people, like Top Shop or Benetton, Esprit or Next, should change its style radically perhaps every three years or so, while an oil company like Shell should evolve slowly over a century or more. It is generally thought appropriate to act in a less radical fashion in finance and industry and in business-to-business activities, than in the consumer world, on the basis that business is expected to be cautious, and anything radical is suspect. I find this argument specious. On the contrary, my own experience is that organizations engaged in relationships with smaller, better informed, more interested audiences can explain what they are up to more easily and economically than those with larger, less interested, mass audiences and can therefore afford to make major changes to their identity if they need to. Furthermore, blandness or lack of individuality is a handicap in any business; individuality of an appropriate sort is normally an advantage.

If the circumstances demand it, major changes should be undertaken, but background investigation must be thorough, analysis intelligent, and recommendations objective.

Suppose when all the evidence is weighed and all the discussions have taken place that the organization decides radical change is appropriate. Suppose it commissions and is presented with recommendations, involving a new name and a new visual programme intended to make an impact on the totality of the organization. How can it ensure that these will be acceptable, perhaps even welcomed, by all its employees and in all its marketplaces? How does the organization determine whether what it is proposing to do will work?

The normal solution is to carry out research. This kind of research is really about risk reduction, and risk reduction is an odd business. The word research is so often used as a form of reassurance, the whole activity is so often shrouded in pseudo-scientific gobbledygook, that with the best will in the world it is sometimes difficult to take it seriously.

The research technique most commonly used involves showing proposed names and symbols to different groups of people and asking them which they think is most suitable for a corporation operating in a given activity. Sometimes it is dressed up rather more elaborately, but that is what most name and visual research in the identity field usually boils down to. Sadly, this type of research ignores the essence of the matter, which is that what the new identity is intended to represent lies unseen and unrecognized until given a context.

Since most people being interviewed are bored, in a hurry, and want to give a good, not to say anodyne impression, their responses are normally conservative, ignorant, uninterested or guarded. This technique is therefore a recipe for licensing mediocrity. It is a pity, if understandable, that major organizations should place so much emphasis on such inadequate techniques.

Mercifully, some researchers practise their trade in a more sophisticated fashion. They take into account the complexities of the human mind and those patterns of cultural behaviour that are common to the whole of humanity, as well as those that are individual. They listen for the bias that interviewees inevitably reveal in the artificial situation of the interview. They take account of the background of the industry involved, the interviewee's knowledge of it, his or her prejudices about it, and other appropriate factors. This technique takes longer and costs more, but it produces much more helpful results. Identity needs good, thoughtful assistance from the research community. No doubt in due course researchers will be better able to provide this.

The complexities of the task are great enough when the organization is located within a single country, but today almost all major organizations operate globally. Is it possible to produce an identity

programme that will work across a wide variety of ethnic and regional patterns?

While we all know that there are considerable variations in behaviour among different peoples, it is also evident, paradoxically, that human beings throughout the world share the same basic emotions. A multiplicity of pressures is driving the peoples of the world into accepting, perhaps with resignation, an increasingly homogeneous culture. TV entertainment, pop music, young people's clothing, business school education and other universal phenomena all lead to the replacement of local brands with international, US-based equivalents, like Coke, Marlboro and McDonalds. That's why some Saudi businessmen like Country and Western music. It's also why young Japanese seem to adore Coke. At another level, tower blocks and urban motorways are making cities all over the world depressingly similar.

Top Shop is a retail brand of the UK's Burton Group, aimed at young, fashion-conscious women (aged 15-22). The design of the stores is changed regularly and often to suit the marketplace. Top row, left to right: late 1960s, late 1960s-early 1970s. Second row: early 1970s-late 1970s. Bottom: 1982.

It is clear, however, that despite the immense pressures towards homogeneity, there are equally powerful forces pulling in precisely the contrary direction. The revival of regionalism – in Catalonia, Scotland, Corsica, for instance; the resurgence of religion – especially, perhaps, Muslim fundamentalism; the re-emergence of ethnic self-confidence – all should incline us to be wary of universal cultural solutions.

This means in visual terms that what is acceptable, even welcome in some places may be abhorrent in others. Take the question of colour. White indicates purity and cleanliness in some cultures, but is the colour of mourning in others. So if we follow the path of least resistance, we get rather boxed in for choice. Putting it crudely, if red means fire, yellow means holy, and green means death, effectively we're only left with blue. If every symbol we develop has potentially disastrous political, historical or cultural implications in one market or another then perhaps we're better off just sticking to some dreary old trickery around the typeface.

That is why so many corporate identity programmes reach for the lowest common denominator. It may be boring and anonymous but at least it's safe. Risk reduction and caution, above all the need for 'scientifically'-based reassurance, all strongly prejudice management in the direction of playing it safe – of 'me-tooism'.

Like all the primary colours, green has many associations, which vary both within single cultures and from one culture to another. Far left: all over the world green represents GO – in traffic signals. In the West, green is the ecological colour. Centre left: *Rainbow Warrior* was the ship belonging to Greenpeace. Top: green is the colour of freshness in food; Dairy Crest is a dairy products company. Bottom centre: for the ancient Egyptians, green-faced Osiris was God of death and also of fertility. Centre: for the Chinese, green is associated with the Ming dynasty. Blue and green overalls were worn interchangeably under Mao. Top: green is the sacred colour of Islam and both the Saudi Arabian and Pakistan flags are largely green. Above: the Green Man has a history from pre-Christian symbolism to the English pub sign.

In the earlier decades of the twentieth century, many European artists ran away from the machine and embraced primitive art. Bottom right: painted wooden sculpture from the Ivory Coast. Right: *Woman-spoon*, bronze sculpture by Giacometti, 1926.

Nevertheless, the greatest graphic symbols are those that come straight out of the imagination, that defy logic and that appeal to the emotions. The symbol designer should, wherever possible, look for opportunities to introduce concepts that both represent the particular organization and are directly accessible to people through the visual representation of universal human values.

Jung can help us here. Carl Gustav Jung, one of the greatest figures of twentieth-century psychology, spent much of his working life studying the extent to which different cultures share common ideas and beliefs, and exploring how individuals manifest their dreams, thoughts, feelings and attitudes through visual symbolism. The development of the concept of the 'collective unconscious' and the symbolism with which it is associated were largely created by him. Jung's books and Jungian libraries in various parts of the world are a testament to the visual richness of the human imagination.

It is a source of amazement to me that graphic designers have for the most part failed to see the natural link between their work and that of Jung. Jung's ideas have a bearing on corporate identity. They are of relevance to the designer's craft. Like most professionals, graphic designers tend to live in their own world. Their enthusiasms tend to derive from their own peer group. That is perhaps why Jungian ideas, which are so rich a source, remain so far largely untapped.

Right: Van Gogh was influenced by Japanese paintings. As an exercise, he copied Hiroshige's coloured woodcut *Ohashi Bridge in the Rain* (1856/58), using oils. Below: the Habsburgs, the Medicis, the Stuarts and other royal houses patronized artists who symbolized their power and influence. Here *The Adoration of the Name of Jesus*, sometimes known as *The Dream of Philip II*, by El Greco.

The work of fine artists and sculptors could also become a major inspiration for graphic designers. Great art also transcends ethnic boundaries. Every major artistic movement inspires a response in other parts of the world. While Western art influences the Japanese today, Japan itself was a major influence on nineteenth-century Europe; African Negritude had a profound effect on French and Italian painters and sculptors of the early twentieth century, and so on. Great artists have an inner eye that re-interprets ordinary things in an original way. Designers can interpret the pioneer work of artists to make clear and original statements about organizations.

Some of the greatest works of art have been inspired by the state, and symbolize state power. It is extraordinary that relatively few companies have had the vigour, imagination and self-confidence to follow the Habsburgs, the Medicis and the Stuarts in this matter. As 3i and 'La Caixa' have shown, when this does happen the results can be startlingly effective.

Not surprisingly, though, most people like to play safe, and corporate identity consultants rarely show the courage or the vision to reach for what can be achieved. That is why some of the symbol and logotype design work carried out on behalf of organizations is so banal. When three companies in the same field adopt new corporate identity programmes, all of which look very similar, to a large extent they defeat part of the object of the exercise – which is to differentiate themselves from each other. Whichever way you look at it, simply indicating what the company does and constantly repeating it is no way to get the best value for money.

I am not suggesting that it is always best to make dramatic changes. Sometimes the power of the traditional visual style, combined with the investment that has been made in it, is so strong that evolution is the best line to pursue. ICI, Renault, GE, Shell, Pilkington and a wide variety of other organizations adopt this wholly reputable stance. I am simply underlining the view that radical change not just for its own sake, but when it seems appropriate, can frequently bring dramatic results.

The real risks involved in launching and maintaining a new identity programme lie not so much in what is created, but in how it is communicated, implemented and subsequently maintained. This is where so many organisations fall down badly; they fail to see how crucial to success the follow-on really is.

That's why communication is the key. Change must be communicated clearly and dramatically as rebirth and rededication. There are tribal analogies here, and also analogies with the 'Invention of Tradition' referred to in Chapter 1. The organization is changing its status; it is becoming something different. Changes in status are traditionally accompanied by rites of passage, which both celebrate and communicate them. Marriage, birth, confirmation exist in every society. The desire to announce the

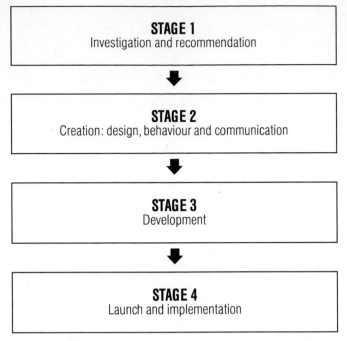

event, the ritual of the event itself – the special clothes, music, dancing, ornamentation – are common to all human experience.

For a major identity programme it is indispensable to create an event that presents the new programme to the audience as an apotheosis. Events of this kind have to be created and orchestrated with great care.

Although the techniques used today embrace lasers, holograms, multiscreen projectors and venues the size of Wembley Stadium or Madison Square Garden, the purpose is the same as it has always been. The relaunch of the Prudential Corporation wasn't very different in principle from the Imperial Durbar in 1877. There was just a bit more dry ice around the place.

The event that launches the corporate identity programme must be quite as professional as the shows that take place nightly on TV. At one level the audience is sophisticated and will be satisfied with nothing less. At another level, though, the purpose of the event must not be overwhelmed by its showbiz aspects; it must belong to the company.

Any organization that announces thorough change will meet resistance; organizations are made up of people, and people hate change. It is never possible to overestimate the extent of this problem.

The reason why people hate change is, of course, perfectly sound. It is disruptive, upsetting, uncomfortable, and usually there isn't a lot in it for those who are most affected. So change has to be handled with great skill, otherwise there will be a powerful element of 'Heads I win, tails you lose' in the process by which a corporate identity programme is introduced. If the visual aspects of the corporate identity programme are new, they may become an object of derision simply because of their novelty. On the other hand, if they are only a modification of what went before employees – and others – may ask 'What on earth is all the fuss about?'

At the launch of the new identity, management has a rare opportunity to explain what the organization is, where it has come from, where it thinks it is going, and why and how the new identity will help it to get there. The audience is captive yet captivated. It is not cynical, or half-attentive, anxious to get on with its own job. It is sitting there – having perhaps come half-way across the world – tingling with anticipation. Of course there will be plenty of cynics who will use the opportunity to deprecate what is going on around them, who will talk about how much money is being wasted, and how it could be better spent on higher salaries, but the emotion of the event will generally convert most of the uncommitted.

Although the event – or, more probably, events, since there will be many of these internal presentations to audiences at different levels in the corporate hierarchy – is the keystone of the communications programme, it is only one part of a continuing process.

There is a brief moment, when the relaunch takes place, when the organization becomes 'news' in the outside world. It's not news for long, so it has to make the most of this opportunity. For a short time it has the chance to talk to a wide variety of outside audiences as well as its own staff: investors, potential investors, financial analysts, suppliers, customers, recruits, trade unions, governments – a spectrum of different groups who will, for a relatively brief period, actually be interested in it. The organization must do everything it can to tell its story while it has its instant of glory. It must do everything it can to explain the real significance of what it is doing, and it must therefore avoid focusing on the new symbol, if there is one, for that simply invites ignorant, superficial and misleading comment. In addition to the media it normally uses to project its message – annual reports, corporate brochures, videos – it may consider using corporate advertising. Corporate advertising can be a significant part of a corporate identity programme, but it is expensive. That's why it must be integrated into the totality of the launch and implementation programme, and used with great care.

By this point in the proceedings, Stage 1, analysis and recommendation, is long behind us. Stage 2, in which the new structure of the organization and its visual identity have been created and approved for development, has also been completed. Stage 3, in which all the preparatory work for launching and implementing has taken place, has been satisfactorily negotiated and we have just launched (Stage 4) the new identity programme at a series of major events in different parts of the world. We have had events first for our own staff, then for our customers and the trade, for the media and finally for the public. Let's assume that everything has gone well. Now we've got to get on and do it – and never stop. What does this mean? What is involved? How is it done?

The board and more particularly the CEO, whose knuckles will certainly have gone white on more than one occasion during the run-up to the launch, will assume that they can now turn their attention back to the more familiar world of cash-flow, business plans, new product launches and the like.

Well, they can't. On the contrary, more vigilance is required, more effort is demanded from them, during the period that the corporate identity idea takes root. Corporate identity programmes either seed themselves into the organization and become an intrinsic part of it, or they splutter out and die. When they die, it isn't usually because something crucial has gone wrong, like an unacceptable name or a visual programme that is culturally anathema, say, in Japan or Brazil. It's because of more mundane reasons: because they are not properly managed, because nobody runs them, nobody pays for them, nobody supports them. Corporate identity is a management resource that is essentially the same as any other management resource. It needs a power base, adequate funding, proper monitoring, clear parameters of operation and all of the paraphernalia that are intrinsic to the successful operation of other classic, centrally funded management resources, such as finance, personnel management, and research and development.

Setting up a new, complex, co-ordinated management resource is not easy. It demands political sophistication, tenacity and a clear eye for the long-term objective.

So, what is the process by which corporate identity is seeded into the management infrastructure? We must start by defining the scope of the activity. Corporate identity, as I have described it in this book, deals with three areas of activity that are visible – design in information and communication, which we can call graphics, design in products and services, and design in environments, architecture and interiors, that is shops, offices and so on. In addition, identity emerges through the way the organization behaves and the way in which it communicates, both visually and otherwise.

How does all this fit into the standard organizational structure? Most organizations have nobody to look after or co-ordinate the totality of the design activity, but they do usually have one, two or even more people who are responsible for certain aspects of non-visual communication and behaviour. The way in which people behave to each other, sometimes called human relations, human resources or organizational behaviour, as well as the more traditional personnel management, is in itself a subject for major study. In any event, somewhere within the organization there will be the equivalent of a head of personnel and a head of public affairs or external relations. Somehow or other the identity management structure has to snuggle down in between these two, kicking about a bit to get more room if necessary, but respecting the realities of management life. It is generally inappropriate to drop somebody down on top of a command structure that already exists and to make the two incumbents report to a third party.

In almost all organizations the prime point of focus for the management of identity, in practice, is likely to be design. The kind of design with which identity management is concerned will, of course, depend on the nature of the business activity. In a transport system, for instance, identity management – or more properly, design management – will involve products, such as rolling stock; environments (stations, offices, shopping malls); and information material (timetables and signage). It will also embrace a range of related activities that might include anything from uniforms to advertising. In addition there will have to be a relationship with human resources and personnel management. The identity manager and his team will in effect be operating throughout the organization.

In each organization the job will vary according to the business activity. It will differ in detail in, say, banks, retail organizations, power transmission companies and universities; but in each case there will be common elements, and in each the task will be extensive.

Currently, in most companies, the concept of managing an identity is not so much alien as unknown , even though in virtually every organization the real effort involved in dealing with this issue is vast. Major organizations spend millions on design-related matters. They put up showrooms, produce packaging, design new products, mount exhibitions, launch advertising campaigns, prepare brochures, furnish new offices, purchase vehicles, commission uniforms, even replace door-knobs. If these and all the other related activities were effectively co-ordinated, they could present clear, effective messages about the organization as a whole. But as things stand, the totality of the effort is not normally perceived at all. People simply do not understand that the aggregate of all the work that they do presents the corporation to all of its audiences.

Why should someone in the purchasing department of an automobile manufacturing company involved in negotiating prices for door-handles, see any connection between his activity and that of his colleagues in the next office purchasing stationery; or, for that matter, with his colleagues in the next building commissioning an advertising campaign? Attentive readers of this book will know why: because these tasks represent differing facets of a company's activities, and should therefore embrace aspects of the same idea.

However, this harmonious thinking slashes across the vertical, water-tight internal departmental structures that companies have erected for themselves. Identity management is an uncomfortably diffuse discipline; it cuts across departments – and this makes its management difficult.

Design of product is traditionally the concern of engineers and the engineering power base; design of environments is sometimes in the hands of architects or interior designers, or – in their absence – of administrative people unskilled for the task; while design of communication material is within the orbit of advertising, marketing and public relations people.

In most organizations, each of these groups is indifferent to, and ignorant of the activities of the others. Where indifference does not prevail, hostility reigns instead. I have personally been involved in a graphic design programme for a German automobile company during the course of which we were hidden from other consultants working on product design, despite the fact that our graphics ultimately went on their product. Why? Because we, the UK corporate identity specialists, were sponsored by the communications department, while the Italian product designers were sponsored by engineering and product development people.

The job of the identity manager is to create an infrastructure and an interface between all these elements of the organization, and also to propagandize. The issue of change is the key here. Identity management brings with it the clear implication that rigid compartmentalization is no longer acceptable. It implies that each part of the organization is dependent upon every other and that mutual hostility, indifference or rivalry is counter-productive and unworkable in a new climate.

A major problem for the identity manager is to gauge where his job begins, and where it ends; where his authority actually lies and where he has only limited influence. The issue is exemplified by the use of words 'design' and 'identity'. As I try to define the role I am aware that I am inclined, perhaps unwisely, to use the words design management and identity management as if they were synonymous; but they

aren't, although they do overlap. Identity management implies a rather broader canvas of operations than design management. It implies an influence over and a participation in public affairs, investor relations, personnel management, marketing and other matters, which some people might – not unreasonably – question. But these problems of frontier responsibility are not unusual in large organizations. Even managers of more traditional resources, such as personnel and R and D, face them. Identity will inevitably leak over a whole series of activities which are not normally perceived as having a close relationship with each other. It will be necessary for the identity manager to operate at a significant level inside the organization and to create working parties and seek active co-operation from groups who may challenge his authority and seek to defend their own. Trouble could come from any quarter.

For this reason it is important that his title gives an indication of the role that he is expected to fulfil. Where the design content forms the greater part of his work, design manager or director may be appropriate. Identity manager or director sounds a bit vague, though this can, of course, be turned to advantage in some situations. The precise title given to the individual must relate to what he or she does, the position in the overall management hierarchy and the usual practice of the corporation on this kind of issue.

In any event, there must be order – a structural base. The graphic design elements provide the foundation upon which the management of the identity edifice rests. The graphic elements comprise: the name of the organization, its subsidiary names (that is, its division, company and brand names), its symbols and logotypes and its major and subsidiary alphabets of different kinds and colours. They have to be codified so that they can work effectively in every kind of application from a neon sign to a lapel badge, in every conceivable material from newsprint to textiles. The codification of all this is bound to be technically complex.

The range of items to which the visual elements are normally applied is quite daunting. Here is the Wolff Olins standard checklist.

Products and services

Products: product design; product identification; rating plates; operating instructions; calibration instructions

Packaging: inners; outer cartons; labelling; delivery instructions; installation instructions

Environments

Interiors/exteriors: buildings; reception areas; sales areas; offices; factories; shops; showrooms

Signs: main identification; general sign system

Internal/external

Exhibitions

Clothing: badges; safety hats; overalls; lab coats; smocks

Graphic information material

Stationery: letterheads; continuation sheets; memos; compliment slips; visiting cards; envelopes; parcel labels

Forms: accounting; purchasing; sales; production; personnel

Publications: corporate; personnel/training; industry packages; product

Vehicles: road transport; factory transport

Advertising: corporate; recruitment; product/services

Promotions/giveaways: flags; stickers; ties; promotional and point of sale material

These are simply general guidelines. Within each category there is a mass of additional detail.

Take road transport as an example. An organization may have thousands of vehicles consisting of a multitude of differing types. Each time the identity is applied to a vehicle it must be appropriate both to the individual truck and to the rules of the programme as a whole. Whenever a manufacturer produces a modification on a vehicle, the detailed design may have to be modified to follow suit. Consider, in an oil company, tanker fleets, storage tanks, petrol pumps of perhaps fifty different configurations, shops, lubricating oil packaging, uniforms for all seasons in countries with widely varying climates . . . and multiply all this by at least a hundred. Only now can you begin to get a feeling for the scope of the job. It becomes clear why it's all so complicated and why it needs to be codified.

Every major identity programme has a manual that documents every application of the programme, so that anyone who at any time has cause to deal with the organization and use its design programme will understand the rules. Not surprisingly, in larger organizations, these bibles run to ten, or even more volumes. I have always been somewhat suspicious of manuals, even though I am aware of their value. I suspect that more of them end up decorating the bookshelves of CEOs and communications directors than go to their proper destination – the grubby but expert hands of sign manufacturers, vehicle painters and printers.

As I write it seems that technology is at last overtaking the manual and that application material, or, as some people are beginning to call it, maintenance material, will become available in convenient, handy-to-use form on a desk-top computer. This of course means that it will become more a practical tool and less a piece of decoration.

It is not possible effectively to execute and maintain the visual part of the corporate identity programme without such documentation. There are differing points of view about whether codification should take place before the work is actually done, so that it can act as a guide, or whether it is better to carry out some applications and then enshrine the practical results a bit later. I incline to the view that it is better to do it later on the grounds that it reduces the temptation to embellish what after all should be only a simple working document.

Spreads from the design manual produced for Q8, the new international petrol brand from Kuwait Petroleum International. Since the new identity was introduced, Q8 has doubled the market share of that part of the old Gulf Oil network it replaced.

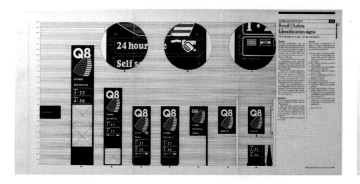

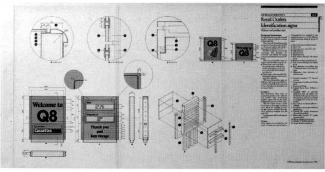

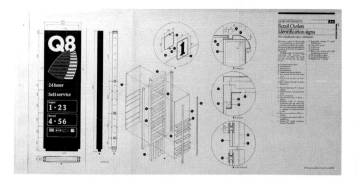

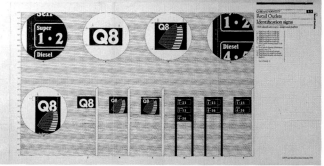

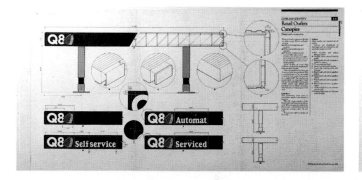

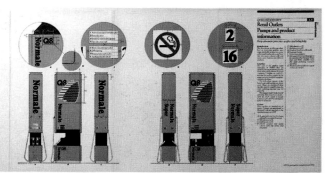

CHAPTER 8

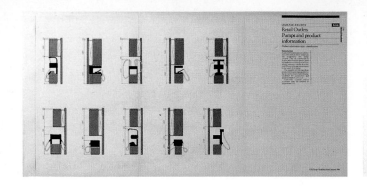

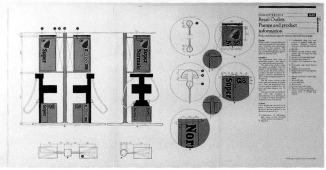

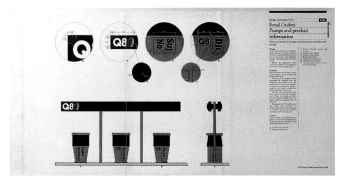

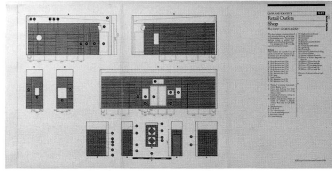

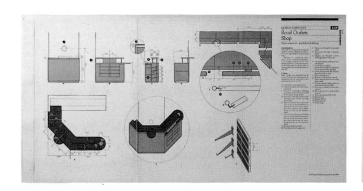

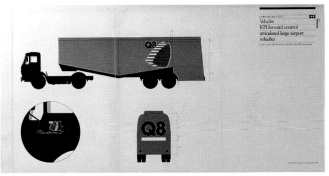

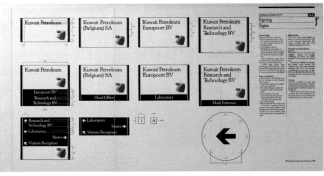

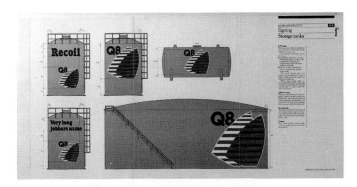

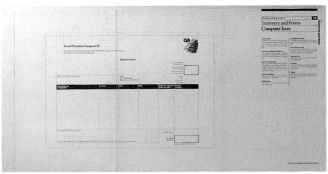

As we codify the programme, we have to consider how and when to implement it. Should the new name and identity emerge suddenly on one wonderful day? Should the transformation take place over the course of a week, a month, a year, five years? Should the launch be sudden or gradual? What costs and logistical problems are associated with each of the options? To what extent are the proposed identity changes going to be a curtain-raiser for other changes, in behaviour and structure, for example? After all, most organizations carry out a corporate identity programme in order, partially at any rate, to achieve behavioural change.

If a new identity is to act as an effective catalyst for change it needs to get going with a bang.

The issue is simple in principle but complex in detail. The higher the impact, the greater the cost both in money and dislocation. The trade-off is clear: if you want to obtain big benefits through big impact it costs more. Sometimes the organization has no choice; if it launches a new name and new identity over the totality of its operations – like, say, Alcatel, the Franco-American telecommunications company – it has to do it fast, otherwise there will be confusion. In many situations, though, changes can take place gradually in a controlled fashion on a replacement basis. Even here there are awkward issues, however: replacement of what, and when? Should the replacement cycle be by country, by division, by company? Or should there be a materials life-cycle, which would mean that letterheads, brochures and forms would be replaced quickly and regularly, while vehicles and signing might take much longer. Replacing the expendable is easy: notepaper and brochures have a short shelf-life anyway. Signs, on the other hand, especially neon signs, are much more expensive. It's not cheap to replace vehicle liveries either. And what about improvements in quality standards, such as refurbishing run-down factories, repainting and upgrading dingy reception areas? What about the whole issue of retraining staff?

Budgeting a corporate identity programme requires as much thought and skill as any other part of the process. By far the largest part of the cost of introduction relates to the cost of replacing and often of upgrading permanent or semi-permanent materials. If vehicle liveries and neon signs are allocated to the corporate identity budget they are a straight replacement cost. If, however, they become part of a publicity budget they occupy a different place in the corporate accounts. Some companies even capitalize the cost of the whole, or part of the identity programme. Each organization works out its own way of dealing with this problem.

So the launch and the subsequent implementation and maintenance of an identity programme is a major operation, involving management skills of every kind at every level. Let's look at how this might work in practice.

The identity manager will be involved initially in introducing the new programme. After the euphoria of the launch and agreement about the way in which the new identity will emerge, he and his colleagues will be immersed in the detail of application.

The identity resource will have to be represented and defended all over the corporation. This means that in every single part of the business, in every division, company or other appropriate unit, an individual will have to be appointed to introduce and monitor applications of the new identity and to champion the identity cause. Normally that person will come from within the local public affairs, advertising or marketing departments. Since whoever is appointed won't know where to start, or what is expected, he or she will need to be trained by the identity manager's team. The reporting line will be based on a matrix: at one level he will report to central identity management, at another he will have a line to his local boss, who may be a company managing director or divisional head. If his two bosses do not take the same view about the significance of the identity programme or squabble about the time, energy and money that should be devoted to the task, there may be trouble.

Curiously, although this system looks like a recipe for confusion and disaster, it usually works rather well. Provided the divisional heads have been effectively indoctrinated, have been to launch events, had meetings with the CEO, and understand what it is all for, they will co-operate. At worst, they will know that you don't win marks by fighting the system.

As the new identity programme is launched, gathers momentum and begins to bite into the fabric of the whole enterprise, its purpose as an engine for creating higher standards, achieving consistency, clarity and differentiation, will begin to emerge and this will inevitably throw up difficulties and dilemmas which the group identity manager and his or her team must tackle.

Let 's look at some items on their schedule. They will, of course, be involved with product design, perhaps working with outside consultants, inside engineers and designers. They will have to discuss countless issues: 'To what extent do the products we make present the idea of the company as a whole? How do they differentiate us from the competition? How do they present our particular personality? To what extent are they visually coherent with the rest of our activities?' These concepts may be new and challenging to the product design people.

They will be involved with graphic design, with advertising, with brochures, with signage. They will be negotiating with their own internal advertising people and, through them or with them, with the various advertising agencies used by different parts of the organization. They will also be working with design companies of various kinds. They will constantly be liaising with people within their own organization who deal with a whole range of suppliers. Much of their time will be spent discussing the minutiae of graphic design: 'To what extent do the group colour scheme, logotype and typeface affect the typography and colours used in divisional and product brochures and advertising? Do we want consistency, or do we want mere uniformity? How much opportunity is there for flexibility and originality on the part of the design and advertising agencies with whom we deal?'

They will set up a relationship with purchasing people. We can reasonably assume that unless the purchasing people have been well indoctrinated they will be unaware of and indifferent to the corporate identity resource. The philosophy in most purchasing departments is to lay down a specification and then buy the cheapest within given limits. This may not fit the spirit of the identity at all. The identity manager may have some battles here, too. He or she

1

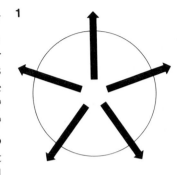

2

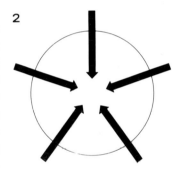

Multinationals globalize and diversify. This always leads to decentralization. Unless it is tightly monitored, decentralization creates massive centrifugal forces which will eventually have the effect of tearing the company apart.

That is why the organization sets up powerful centripetal forces in the form of co-ordinated corporate resources which act as a countervailing mechanism. Traditional co-ordinated corporate resources include Finance, Investment, Research and Development, Product Quality, Personnel and, increasingly, Identity.

will introduce concepts that may be alien: 'What kind of compromises can we make between price and quality? Do we have to buy components that we share with our competitors just because they are cheaper – or should we pay more to project our own individuality?' Gradually, the company's purchasing people will be encouraged to draw their suppliers into the network.

Every day the identity manager will sit on working parties of every kind with colleagues from various levels of the organization. One day negotiations may involve a mixture of, say, personnel people, architects and trade union representatives in discussing how rest-rooms should be furnished and who should pay to upgrade them. They may explore who should control the employee induction process, and assess whether the videos used by personnel people are of high enough quality for the purpose of introducing the corporate idea. On the following day the identity manager may be sitting on a working party with marketing people discussing how a proposed new brand will relate to the corporation as a whole: Should the new name dominate the corporate name and symbol? Should it endorse or be endorsed by them?

Inevitably, in multinational enterprises with diverse interests all over the world the identity manager will spend a lot of time on aircraft, becoming involved with local operations, negotiating how and where the group identity structure, its names, symbols, and typography, fit with current practice. Problems here will revolve around what kind of identity the group companies need to project in their various operations.

Small overseas units which have for years gone their own way, using their own colours, names and symbols in mute defiance of corporate norms, will vociferously resent what they regard as unreasonable and uninformed interference from people who merely represent 'overhead' at the centre. In cases where there is a strong minority local shareholding or a series of specific local behaviour patterns, local arguments will be sound. In other cases, though, the identity manager will find that locals are merely attempting to defend the status quo, for less worthy reasons.

The identity manager will not have the remotest hope of achieving success in these and many other matters without support from the top and unless he or she operates through a sound, secure, formal, recognized management infrastructure. When things go wrong, there must be a direct line to the top.

The Chief Executive has to declare firm commitment to the principle that the clearest way for the organization's personality to emerge is through visual coherence and differentiation, manifested through every aspect of its identity, and especially, perhaps, design. This must be done on every possible occasion, both in public and private. Eventually, though, the CEO must, paradoxically, be disengaged from the process. It is vital that the corporate identity is not identified solely with one individual's enthusiasm, otherwise it will wither when he or she goes.

That is why identity must have a secure place in the management structure. It should be placed at the heart of the organization as a major co-ordinating, centripetal resource, together with finance, investment, research and development, product quality, information technology, personnel and other, similar resources. (The precise list will vary according to the nature of the organization, of course.)

These major central co-ordinating forces are built into the corporate structure to act as countervailing pressures to the immensely powerful centrifugal forces that are endemic in most big companies. The centrifugal forces derive from the fact that in global, decentralized, diversified businesses, managers of the different parts, in different geographical and product areas, inevitably impose their own personal ideas about how their particular part should be run. This is natural; it is even, to a certain extent, desirable.

But if the managers running separate cost and profit centres were allowed a completely free rein, most businesses would spin off into separate little bits, so many managements use centripetal forces as a device to hold the business together. The juxtaposition of the two pressures, to centralize and to decentralize, is usually described by that significant but rather overworked phrase: 'creative tension'.

In any organization the prime co-ordinating resource is finance. The standard practice is that there should be a single financial monitoring and reporting system based at the centre. Linked to financial management is investment policy. Regardless of where the money is made, the centre decides where it is to be invested. In some companies, that's just about all there is in the way of central co-ordinating resources. Other organizations go further.

Research and development is usually a centrally co-ordinated activity, although increasingly it may be carried out in several places.

The same applies to product quality. Today quality has to be consistent worldwide because more and more products are sourced worldwide. Brazilian-built Mercedes trucks are sold in the US, and as they create the same kind of expectations as German-built Mercedes cars, they have to have the same kind of quality. Ford of Europe assemble cars in Spain with, say, Welsh-built engines, French-built transmission systems and Finnish-made glass. It's not good for Ford if one of their factories is not up to world standard; it affects the image of the whole. It's clear that today everywhere in the world products from a global company have to be of a single quality.

People are the scarcest commodity of all; inevitably it's increasingly the case that at a senior level the issue of people development is co-ordinated from the centre.

In principle identity is a corporate resource of equal stature with these others, so its place at the heart of the organization should be the same as theirs.

Each of the traditional corporate resources has a champion on the Board: Finance Director, R and D Director, and so on. Ideally, the champion for identity should be the Chief Executive, because he personifies the spirit of the corporation. There may, however, be situations in which this is inappropriate, either because the Chief Executive is not sufficiently interested or temperamentally suited to the role, or

because some other board member is more genuinely enthusiastic and appropriate for the task. In any event, one member of the Board should have the job.

How should the operating structure for identity work? The role model for identity management should be a combination of financial and information technology management.

Financial management must be a role model because it is the oldest and most traditional, usually the most influential, central management resource; because it is ubiquitous, pervasive, more or less unchallenged, and has a massive internal and external support structure.

Information technology is the other vital role model because it is the newest management resource and has only just succeeded in muscling its way in, to become a significant factor in corporate life. It has become immensely influential in just a couple of decades. The fight to introduce computer management was bitter and bloody. It took agonies of reorganization, false starts, mutual incomprehension between makers and users – all of which makes the current struggles of identity management look like child's play. But eventually information technology management established itself as a major corporate resource. It is now recognized that the success or failure of some organizations, such as banking, depend on the use of computers.

Using computer and financial management as role models it should be perfectly possible for identity management to establish itself.

So to sum up. We have created the new identity. We have launched it both internally and externally. We have linked the new identity firmly with other changes in organizational development. We have appointed a design or identity manager, or director – although some other title may be employed. We have looked at some of the tasks in which the hapless individual has to be engaged. We have examined the place of identity management as a corporate co-ordinating resource, and we have isolated two role models: financial management and information technology management.

Have we now done everything? Pretty much! Was it all worth it? To find out we have to turn to the next chapter.

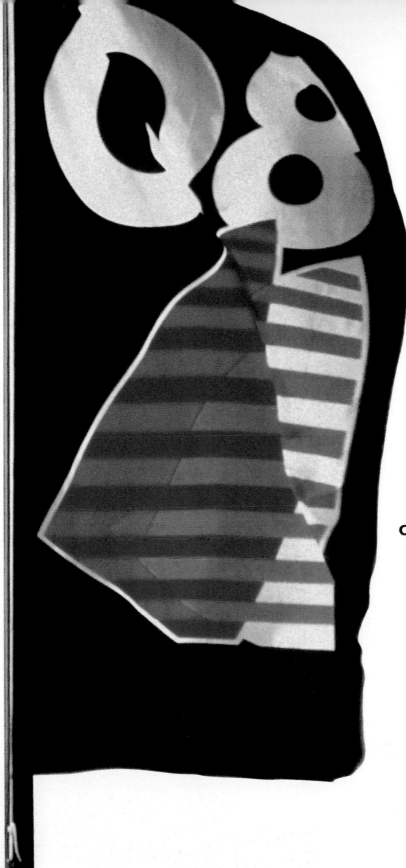

To join the big league in the international oil business you have to be rich and brave. Kuwait Petroleum is both. In 1984 the company decided to go into the retail petrol business worldwide, which made it the first OPEC country to move in that direction.

The basis for development was for Kuwait Petroleum's international arm to acquire the greater part of Gulf Oil's European network. By agreement KPI had to get rid of the old Gulf Oil name and symbol. The company opted for an entirely new name and identity, intended for possible eventual worldwide application, linked – and this was another brave decision – to a pricing policy aimed at the same level as the competition. Working with corporate identity consultants, they created a new name, Q8 (based on the English pronunciation of Kuwait), and a new symbol, based around the idea of sails, like traditional Kuwaiti trading vessels.

The programme was introduced in the orthodox fashion: first to staff and then to dealers, through seminars, teach-ins and so on. The staff and dealer network, who had become apathetic after years of uncertainty under Gulf Oil, responded enthusiastically to the programme.

The changeover from Gulf Oil to Q8 took place in 1986. Over 3000 petrol stations were involved in six countries: Sweden, Denmark, Belgium, the Netherlands, Luxembourg and Italy. Just before the change took place the Gulf Oil share in the six countries was a shade under 4 per cent. After the change to Q8 the market share rose to 5.5 per cent. Retail volume sales

Right: Q8 flags, signs, balloons.

Far right: when Swiss Nestlé took over UK's Rowntree (1988), its main purpose was to bring well-known, well-established brands, which it considered were underutilized, into world markets.

Rowntree brands – and therefore the whole company – were valued for potential to develop. In other words brand name and image were given a financial value. Opposite: Kit Kat and After Eight – major Rowntree brands.

were 2.1 billion litres in 1984. They rose to 3.0 billion litres in 1987, which was the first full year of operation in the new style. This represents a volume increase of nearly 50 per cent in a static market. More significantly, it also means that the increase was gained at the expense of competitors. In succeeding years Q8 has sustained its position.

Although there has, of course, been some advertising, the company attributes the success of its programme largely to the impact of the new corporate identity programme. On the face of it, the whole story is a marketing man's dream come true and seems a powerful argument for corporate identity.

Even in a relatively uncomplicated programme like this, however, it is not easy to work out exactly why sales have increased. A whole series of closely interlinked factors is probably involved. Is it, for instance, because the stations look better; because, that is, they are better designed and have better lighting? Is it because they are better maintained; because staff and dealers are better motivated, have higher self-esteem, look after the facilities better and are, in an overall sense, more effective? Because of the varied nature of their impact, it isn't always possible to find out exactly which aspects of a corporate identity programme have been the most successful and why.

On the other hand, it is possible through various research techniques to monitor how or, indeed, whether awareness of a corporation increases as the corporate identity programme begins to see the light of day.

Thoughtful organizations that have made a major commitment in time, money and emotion to creating, launching and implementing corporate identity programmes want to know, quite naturally, whether what they have done actually works. A great deal of research is carried out in this field, much of it good. What the research generally shows is that, other things being more or less equal, we as individuals prefer to deal with organizations that we know than with those that we don't. Again and again, in company after company, research tells us that the good organization that is well known is also more admired and better liked than an equally good company that is not so well known. It can therefore

attract more and better people to work for it, can more readily make acquisitions, more effectively launch new products and generally perform better.

So, comfortingly, research confirms that the enlightened and virtuous are rewarded not necessarily in Heaven, but quite often here on earth. Those who do not follow the righteous path of corporate identity don't get such rewards.

If a new corporate identity programme can, amongst its other benefits, have an effect in raising Stock Market prices, does this mean that it might conceivably have a long-term impact on the financial worth of the corporation?

In 1988 it became clear, with the Nestlé purchase of the UK's Rowntree confectionery and chocolate group, that brands had a value related to their potential as well as their actual performance. *The Economist*, along with other publications, has speculated that if brand reputations can have value of this kind, so might corporate reputations.

Put into real-life terms, this means that if a corporate identity programme has the effect of revaluing a corporation's overall capitalization upwards, then there may be a few instances where a corporation gets its new corporate identity programme free – so to speak. It's a nice thought, isn't it?

There is, however, a catch – as there always is. It is much easier to gauge a reputation for a brand than it is for a corporation, because a brand only deals in a carefully monitored, straightforward relationship with one group of people – customers – while a corporation lives a complex life involving a tangled web of relationships.

Today the corporation is no longer assessed exclusively on its commercial achievements. It is already assessed informally by many overlapping groups of people, on a mass of other criteria as well: on its social attitudes, its behaviour to its workforce, and on the minutiae that lie behind these and related issues. These factors are rapidly increasing in significance, which will make the job of assessing the corporate reputation in the round increasingly complex for the future.

What all this means is that, from the vantage point of, say, 2050, twentieth-century businesses will look naive and simple-minded. We take the view today that we live in a complicated and difficult world, one in which corporate behaviour can no longer be isolated from its social impact. We already know that strict regulations about polluting the environment make some products more expensive and less performance-efficient. We are also conscious that the complex of existing management-employee consultative arrangements also affect output efficiency. But these are only faint rumblings of what the future may bring.

If current trends are perpetuated – and there is every reason to assume that they will be – today's corporations will seem as free and unfettered to businessmen of the late twenty-first century as John D. Rockefeller the First, Jay Gould and the US robber barons of the nineteenth century do to us today.

It is already the case that a number of major international corporations have been driven by assaults from various directions to shed their investments in politically unpopular countries. Barclays, the major British-owned bank, left South

Manufacturers are becoming increasingly aware of environmental factors – and are attempting to pass on the additional costs of manufacture to consumers.

Right: group of 'ozone friendly' consumer products.

Africa partially, at least, because of its unpopularity with students, who were customers, potential customers and vociferous, although minute shareholders.

It is interesting to compare this situation with the 1930s, when nobody, not even the most radical anti-Nazi, even hinted that the major multinationals should withdraw from Hitler's Germany. The thought simply never occurred to anybody. In the event, Shell, Colgate–Palmolive (Palmolive was a popular soap in pre-war Germany), Ford, Unilever, GM and others traded right through the Third Reich, working with even-handed willingness for both Allies and Nazis. Today such a situation would be unacceptable. Society does not reject the corporation; on the contrary, increasingly it welcomes it into its bosom. But it demands from it what it regards as socially acceptable behaviour. And this means high and sometimes contradictory standards. If this induces new strains and pressures into the corporation, well, too bad.

Take environmentalism. Greens are no longer an eccentric fringe group. Especially in the richer countries of Northern Europe, they are becoming a powerful political force. Greens espouse a series of causes grouped around the environmental idea; seals, whales, lead-free petrol and rain forests are all grist to their mill. This, inevitably, makes headlines out of apparently unrelated issues, or – more complicated still – out of contradictory or at least paradoxical ones. Nuclear power stations are anathema, but so are acid-rain clouds, which are partially caused by coal-fired power stations. Who can say which form of power generation is more environmentally damaging, or what the energy sector should do about it? In trying to please one section of the community it may find itself alienating another.

Some multinationals operated for both sides in the Second World War. Ford, a manufacturer of vehicles for American, Canadian and British armies, also made trucks for the German Wehrmacht. Such a situation would be inconceivable today.

Opposite: an advertisement for German-built Ford trucks in 1942. Below: catalogue for Ford trucks in the US at about the same time.

While environmentalism has had an active few years, consumerism has been relatively quiet. It seems as though the militant consumer movements of the 1970s have, at least temporarily, shifted their focus. But consumerism in the form of increased agitation, leading to legislation, about product content – the E-number syndrome, as it is called – rumbles on. It cannot be long before it is back with us in a big way.

Meanwhile, individuals who want to invest in industry without getting their hands (or their consciences) dirty can now do so. The newish breed of so-called ethical unit trusts (mutual funds), which eschew corporations involved with defence, gambling, drink, tobacco and repressive regimes, is already here. In the US the hippies of the 1960s have become the socially aware investors of the 1990s, according to a spokesman of the US-based Social Investment Forum, quoted in the London *Times* of 31 December 1988. The same anonymous spokesman claimed that 8 per cent of US investment is socially screened.

These and other parallel developments mean that corporations of all kinds are going to have to watch their step if they want to survive and grow in the longer term. The pressures on corporations are not just social; technological factors also have intense and widespread impact, and work patterns are changing rapidly. In some industries the conventional office and factory system is already obsolescent. It is being replaced by a computer-age network version of the primitive outworker system in which people carry out their tasks in a dispersed fashion. Even in organizations where radical change of this kind is not predicted, important cultural and physical changes are taking place in the workplace in order to attract and retain the educated graduate sector of the workforce, which – because of changing demographic patterns – is increasingly able to pick and choose what work it wants to do and what kind of company it wants to be associated with.

The introduction of flexible working hours, the elimination, or at least reduction, of overt manifestations of hierarchy and traditionalist authoritarian behaviour, together with physical interior design changes, such as common spaces, more informal relaxation areas, single-status eating arrangements, are all ways in which managements demonstrate that they know which way the world is moving and that they feel the corporation to be an integral part of society.

These attitudes are not unique to any single country or part of the world. Although the level of interest, the sense of urgency and the need for action varies, sophisticated corporations everywhere share these concerns. In Britain alone, not a country generally admired for advanced management practice, a number of high-profile individuals have dwelt on these themes. Sir John Harvey-Jones, one of the country's outstanding managers and former Chairman of ICI, deals with both the greater and lesser implications of such issues in his book *Making it Happen* (1988). For example, he makes the point that it has been customary for large companies to move an executive around from place to place without troubling too much. Now, however, the executive's wife's career may be as important as her husband's (indeed, the executive may be a wife and mother), so the corporation must learn to be more accommodating.

In the Anglo-Swedish book *Managing Knowhow* (1987), Karl-Erik Sveiby and Tom Lloyd predict the tumultuous growth of what they call 'know-how' companies. These are usually organizations that think up ideas for other companies to use. Sveiby and Lloyd say that these newish, freewheeling, loosely structured, highly motivated and incentivized know-how companies may well cream off the best talent from the major corporations.

All this tumult has had some effect even on companies like GM, which appear at last to have noticed that when they treat people like human beings they get better results. A few of the GM plants where things have changed have been turned into showpieces. They are now obligatory stopping points on the standard journalists GM facilities tour. *Car* magazine went to visit the Vanguard plant in Saginaw. This is a quotation from the January 1989 issue: 'Here we have a factory of the future that produces front-drive half-shafts by courtesy of robots. There is an eerie absence of humanity, and everything seems to work without a hitch. How happy the erstwhile workforce feel about such developments, I do not know, but those who are left smile contentedly.' On the other hand, GM as a whole still reveals, according to *Car*, 'A picture of a cumbersome but well-meaning giant trying to come to terms with a world of industrial uncertainties.'

In some countries and in some industries the old rust-belt attitudes still dominate, but even in these, as is clear from the changing attitudes within GM, it's only a matter of time before movement begins to take place.

While all this ferment is going on, the corporation still has to make a living. Economic and commercial life is moving on, too, and fast. Massive economic changes are taking place that will also bring both huge opportunities and problems for corporations.

In his impressive book *The Rise and Fall of the Great Powers* (1988), Paul Kennedy talks of the revival of multi-polarity in the modern world. The world is no longer dominated by one or two economic and military power blocs; instead a number of separate and more or less equally significant power blocs are emerging.

As all of us in the West know well, the dominant military and economic power in our part of the world since 1945 has been the United States. And it was clear during the heyday of US influence, and is equally clear in retrospect, that American military and political supremacy was accompanied by psychological supremacy. This was symbolized by a whole range of dominating and archetypical American companies, products and services, from those in the high-tech world, like Boeing and IBM, through to consumer goods, like Wrigley's chewing gum, Marlboro cigarettes, Levi's jeans and the Big Mac. The emotional dominance of the American company, product and service was reinforced by the formidable Dream Machine of Hollywood and its TV successors, which remorselessly cranked out films, and then TV series, celebrating various aspects of the American Way of Life. Its current examples are *Dallas* and *Dynasty*. Inside the United States itself, none of these phenomena was seen as particularly American; they only derived their 'American-ness' from outsiders. Much of the rest of the world envied, admired and aspired to this American Way. Natural-

ly, the US has always produced highly sophisticated, fashionable and well-made products too, as the Herman Miller company – for example – shows, but these do not figure in the non-American mind as 'truly American'. They don't fit the archetype.

As the United States begins to meet economic competition from other parts of the world, it will inevitably come across ideological competition too.

The two new significant competing power blocs are Japan and Europe. Japanese and European corporate ideas, their ways of doing things and the products and services that represent them are different, both from each other and from those in America.

The European idea is just beginning to take shape. Almost inevitably, it is clearer in the minds of outsiders than of Europeans themselves. Some non-Europeans already perceive common characteristics that Europeans cannot see in, for example, Perrier, BMW, Laura Ashley and Philips. It has something to do with small physical size and perceived high-level quality of design, manufacture and technology – and therefore exclusivity.

In time, this concept will relate not just to products, but to services and to the corporations that produce them. The European Way of Life will emerge over the next few years as powerfully and tangibly as the American Way of Life has done over the second half of the twentieth century.

This presents an astonishing opportunity to those European companies that are able and willing to grasp it.

Multi-polarity implies that there will be a Japanese option, too – in corporation, product and lifestyle. We can see its first stirrings not just in Nissan and Hitachi, but also in Yohji Yamamoto and Issey Miyake and in the fashionable Japanese restaurants that have popped up in the world's major cities.

In one sense we are simply experiencing the old marketing challenge writ large and a little differently; but at another level there is a formidable new opportunity for the intelligent and sensitive corporation to present what it is and what it does and get a large slice of world markets.

Each major power bloc is symbolized visually through a range of products that seem to represent aspects of its culture. Each perception is inaccurate and distorted, but their impact is seen in the marketplace.

Opposite: for non-Americans, the idea of America is symbolized through a series of big, brash, cheap, popular products.

Left: increasingly, non-Europeans are beginning to characterize European products as small, high-quality, expensive and rather elitest.

Two products that epitomize these attitudes are both fizzy drinks – Coke and Perrier.

Such changes hit different industries in different countries at differing times and at different speeds. While a number of corporations are already alert to these issues, and probably to a few more besides, it's clear that in the majority of organizations, traditionalist views and attitudes still apply.

No corporation can afford to ignore the noises that are being made by the various groups of people with whom it has relationships. The consumer has always been greedy for attention, and the whole process of marketing has always been about giving consumers what they want, preferably before they even know they want it. But today it is not only the customer who has to be satisfied. Employees, shareholders, financial analysts, journalists, environmentalists and several other interested parties all have different, often contradictory, issues to raise. But one way or another all these needs must be satisfied – or at least acknowledged.

All this in turn means that the corporation of any size, anywhere, is going to have to adjust so that it can market itself not only to one of its audiences, its customers – which many have found difficult enough – but to all the different groups of people with whom it deals. And this is going to be a new, complicated and unsettling experience. The reality is that the corporation's most important audience is in the future going to be its own staff.

The spirit of the times is so strong that no organization will be able to ignore its wider role in society for very long. In fact, some corporations are already beginning to compete with each other as much on the basis of what they are like to work for and deal with, as of what they do. In his fascinating book *The Global Market Place* (1988), Milton Moskowitz describes some of the world's largest corporations outside the US not just in terms of what their businesses do, and who owns them, but more significantly, and often hilariously, in terms of how they behave and what kind of personalities they have. He shows, for example, that while Nissan and Toyota are both Japanese vehicle-builders, the former is rather rough and the latter rather nice. The stuff of which corporate identity is made is coming more and more to the forefront of managements' activities throughout the world.

The groups of people with whom every corporation deals are called target audiences. Broadly speaking, they can be divided into two categories: those who work for the company – the internal audience – and those who deal with it as outsiders. Everything that the corporation is, everything that it does, communicates – to everybody with whom it deals. But everybody perceives all these communications individually.

Everyone who works for an organization, sees it through his or her own eyes. Individuals are affected by their age, seniority, closeness to the corporate headquarters, nationality, the nature of their job – everything. A student, a member of the academic staff and a cleaner employed on campus are all part of Stanford University, say, but each has his perspective on the institution. A computer technician in a bank is unlikely to see himself as a career banker. He remains a computer man with a temporary home in a banking environment. European employees of Honda cannot feel the same way about the company as Japanese in similar positions.

The corporation, while recognizing that different groups of employees have varying relationships with it, must adopt a consistent attitude to them all. Its underlying message, behaviour and identity in the broadest sense must be constant in this as in all other matters.

Not all internal audiences actually work inside the corporation. There are some semi-internal audiences, half-in, half-out. Many trade unionists fall into this category. So do the families of staff, pensioners and shareholders. None of these groups have the same interest in, or expectation of the corporation as any of the others, but they must be dealt with by the corporation both on their own terms and in relation to each other, using the standard that the corporation applies to all its affairs.

External audiences represent an even broader franchise. There are customers, both direct – that is, the trade, dealers and so on – and indirect – the final consumer. The corporation will have had a long-term relationship with these groups. Then there is a tangled network of suppliers, competitors and collaborators. Sometimes a supplier may be a competitor and a collaborator. The mass of interlocking alliances that exist between the various members of the European aerospace industry exemplifies this.

Here, consistency of attitude and performance is paramount for any kind of lasting success. A company that is an unsatisfactory supplier must not expect to be favourably regarded as a potential partner. Mud sticks.

There are also the opinion-formers. Groups who may not have day-to-day contact with the organization but who see it in comparison with its peers from some distance: journalists, financial analysts, bankers, and so on.

Nobody lives in a vacuum. It is a mistake to believe that each of these audiences lives tidily in its own little box. People buy things, so a financial analyst may also be a customer. People hold opinions that affect their judgment. A journalist might also be an environmentalist. Individuals are influenced – often unfairly – by personal experience. I know a powerful journalist on a responsible newspaper who persists in abusing London Regional Transport whenever he sees an opportunity, simply because his family constantly complain about the inadequacy of public transport in the metropolis. He personally uses a car.

Schools, universities and other educational institutions, trade bodies of various kinds: all represent different external audiences. These may well have conflicting attitudes towards an organization. A university may like a local chemical company as an employer but dislike it as a polluter. The attitudes of the university can be ameliorated in the long term if the company engages itself in a proper dialogue over a wide range of issues, but this isn't simply a matter of patronage, of giving money away; it's a matter of showing where mutual interest lies and of projecting a consistent idea.

Then there is central and local government, whose attitudes may at crucial moments become critical even for the survival of the enterprise. The natural relationship between government and industry is for the most part characterized by mutual indifference, punctuated by bouts of ambivalence and hostility. This is unsatisfactory for all parties. The thoughtful corporation cultivates its political contacts over years.

The British government of the 1980s did a deal to sell most of its nationalized ailing truck industry to GM – a course that would have been sensible for both parties. British public opinion, however, rejected it as a sell-out to foreign interests. The government caved in, and both sides suffered. Of course, the weakness of the government was to blame, but so was GM, who had operated in Britain for three-quarters of a century, whose trucks had powered the British army for generations and who had brought considerable prosperity to a number of Britain's communities. Too late, it recently ran an intelligent corporate advertising campaign in the British media, focusing on the benefits – economic, technical and social – that it has certainly brought to the country. But the major opportunity in the truck business has gone. The lesson from this cautionary tale is not just that you have to be consistent in communications over the long term; it is that audiences overlap. For instance, legislators sit in parliament as representatives of local communities and as members of a political party. The sad fact is that most people are often ignorant and misinformed, which means that they can sometimes be misled. And in turn this means that unless the corporation is really consistent in projecting its identity it will probably become a victim of rumour, gossip and unsubstantiated myth.

There is only so much that each of us as individuals is able, or prepared to absorb. Most people are only vitally interested in and knowledgeable about the few things that directly concern them. Our prime concerns are a jumble of social, business and personal matters. Some of us have immense knowledge about matters of special interest to us – football, popular music, model railways, Napoleon. But although there is a plethora of information available from every conceivable source, although the information technology by which we are surrounded grows more sophisticated daily, our poor old brains stay much the same.

We only take in the very few things that we have to, or that really absorb us. This inevitably means that we sometimes express opinions or advance arguments about serious and complex matters based on the flimsiest knowledge. The fact that most of us don't know what we are talking about most of the time doesn't seem to inhibit us from expressing powerful prejudices.

As the corporation is absorbed into the mainstream of society, it will inevitably become a major topic for discussion. Unless the corporation takes active steps to change things, the discussion surrounding it will for the most part be ill-informed, partial and distorted. It will be based on half-digested, inaccurate, third-hand information mixed up with comment, gossip and myth – taxi-driver talk. We all do it. We all listen to, are influenced by and spread unreliable gossip. We extravagantly praise or blame organizations often on the basis of a single encounter or even on hearsay. 'TWA is dreadful', 'The police are thugs', 'Bloomingdales has awful service': these are typical of the kind of ill-considered remarks that influence us, and that we make ourselves.

As society becomes more aware of corporate behaviour, the corporation will have more cause to maintain and project its corporate identity. Everything that the corporation does in every way communicates. It will have to demonstrate what it is and what it stands for through consistency of behaviour and performance to its own staff, its customers and all its other audiences – the very sources from whom we, the general public, derive our opinions. If the corporation does this successfully, it means that rumour, myth, gossip and hearsay will for the most part be consistent and favourable – and that, in an imperfect world, is as much as anyone can expect.

Inevitably, corporate identity and its management have a crucial role in all this. It is only the most powerful, ubiquitous, well-organized, heavily backed, visually appealing, effectively communicated corporate identity programmes that will break through into people's consciousness.

Where a corporate identity programme is truly integrated, where it involves every element, where it is communicated with consistency and commitment, it has a chance. Where there is hesitation, lack of coordination, disagreement, there will be perpetual confusion in the minds of the audiences, and myths of a destructive kind will reign unbridled.

So the corporation has problems of both identity and communication. The realization that these prob-

lems exist is growing, although it is still partial and uneven. Nevertheless, the corporation is looking for help. It will not be able fully to diagnose its own ailments. It may believe that it has a whole series of problems in the field of identity, behaviour and communication, only some of which are linked. In any event, although it may, and increasingly it does, turn to corporate identity consultants for help, it may also turn to more traditional and long-standing advisers for assistance.

If you didn't know what corporate identity was, but you vaguely felt, as a CEO, that you had a problem with communication, you might turn to your traditional communications adviser – the advertising agency. Advertising agencies are the biggest, richest, most prominent players in the communications trade. They have been around for a long time; some of them have world-famous names and they are deemed to have practically legendary powers to communicate and persuade practically anybody about practically anything. That's why some corporations assume that their natural partner in any activity involving image and communication is the advertising agency.

Anybody who has had intimate dealings with an advertising agency knows that this portrait of the advertising company as ubiquitous and expert communicator is nonsense. Advertising agencies make their money out of creating advertising for mass-market products and services. They have therefore developed considerable expertise around one of the corporation's target audiences – the final consumer. But they have never needed to learn much about other target groups, let alone matters to do with design or behaviour. They are inflexible, inappropriate and expensive when used outside their normal area of activity. If you push them a little it's possible to persuade advertising agencies to direct their activities at the trade, the financial community and other opinion-formers, and even recruits. But they have no interest or experience in dealing with internal audiences, and have only a superficial understanding of the corporate identity process.

Some people who work in the advertising world are, of course, gifted communications consultants. These individuals have the ability to counsel their

clients on matters way beyond the consumer advertising area. Such people can often advise on the
creation and development of corporate identity
programmes and they can help with the internal and
external communications programmes that the corporation will need to project its identity to its target
audiences.

All this activity with new target audiences, increasingly described as 'corporate communications',
is making some advertising agencies rather uneasy.
The conventional branded goods advertising activity
is mature; there isn't much growth in it. Corporate
communications – in which advertising plays a part,
sometimes a dominant one – is growing quickly. So
a number of advertising agencies are plunging into
this business, buying recruitment, business-to-
business, and financial advertising agencies and
expanding into other areas of communication activity, such as public relations and design, which they
see as subsuming corporate identity. These new
businesses will enable the advertising agency to deal
with the much wider range of target audiences that
the corporation now considers important.

A few advertising agencies are even going beyond
this into boardroom consultancy. They recognize
that they need to deal with the top level of their
clients and that advertising isn't always the best route
in. Boardroom consultancy, which deals with both
hard and soft issues, will naturally lead them directly
into the whole corporate identity process which this
book describes.

With their financial strength, their excellent client
contacts, their intelligence and their reputations,
there is little doubt that a number of major advertising agencies will successfully mutate into corporate
communications consultants, and some of these may
move further into the handling of major corporate
identity programmes in all its aspects, including
design and behaviour. But they won't all make it.

Quite a few advertising agencies will find it difficult to make the necessary adjustment required to
assess the corporation's identity and communication
needs from a strategic rather than a tactical point of
view.

Some corporations, wary, perhaps, of the bias that
advertising agencies display towards paid advertising, have tended to use public relations companies to
advise them on what are often called 'image issues'.

The base from which public relations companies
operate is wider and more flexible than that of
advertising agencies. They deal with a broad spectrum of external and internal audiences using
different media, although their knowledge and
understanding of the power of design seems limited.

Despite this, they have a real chance to develop
into credible advisers on a wide range of issues relat-
ing to identity, image and communications. Within
the public relations business worldwide, there are a
number of highly sophisticated and thoughtful practitioners. These individuals are quite capable of
advising major corporations on long-term identity
programmes and on the communications programmes that derive from them.

For one reason or another, public relations people
have been relatively slow, generally speaking, to see
the power of design in industry. It is possible that, as
a result, they will fail to grasp all the opportunities
presented. The PR business may not, therefore, get
the share of the new business that its strategic position warrants.

Nevertheless, some of the most lively and farsighted, independently owned PR consultancies are
mutating into corporate communications businesses
as fast as they can. They are buying into or starting
up advertising agencies and design companies, especially those that specialize in corporate identity, and
they are tailoring their existing lines of activity in
investor relations, internal communications, trade
relations, so that they can fit the corporate communications needs of their clients.

In addition to public relations consultancies and
advertising agencies, the corporation often has a
relationship with strategic or boardroom consultants. Many of these companies are like some advertising agencies: clever, rich and famous – in a quiet
sort of way, of course. Sometimes the work of these
management consultants on hard issues brings them
directly into contact with corporate identity issues.
From time to time they work in tandem with other
consultants who may be working on corporate
identity problems. So far they have had the will-
power to stick to what they know. But a number of

managing partners in strategic consultancy businesses see the opportunities and may not be able to resist the temptation to become involved.

Some forms of consultancy are closer in spirit to corporate identity than others; some, though starting from a different base, embrace much of its content. A number of individuals and small companies engaged in various kinds of behavioural – or, as it is currently called, 'organizational development' – consultancy have spotted the links that exist between their activities and those of graphic design-based corporate identity consultancies. But for the most part their businesses are too small and too inexperienced to present themselves as significant competitors to corporate clients. Instead, sensibly, a few are starting to forge commercial links between themselves and corporate identity consultancies.

Then there are the corporate identity consultancies themselves. Despite the fact that most graphic design consultancies are small and that they are generally equipped to execute only the graphic design aspects of corporate identity work, there seems to be some recognition among major corporations that of all the contenders who seek to work on corporate identity programmes, consultants stemming from graphic design roots are the most appropriate.

A small number of corporate identity consultancies have now clearly emerged from the graphic design discipline and devote themselves to the identity business exclusively. There are a few corporate identity consultancies that are big, financially stable and well connected, and who enjoy good reputations. None are yet as famous or as rich as the major advertising agencies, although they are moving in this direction.

A few of the best-known corporate identity consultancies have been bought by advertising agencies as part of their corporate communications activities. Others have been bought or developed by large design consultancies, who deploy them as part of their overall design activity in product, interiors and graphics. Just a very few of the major corporate identity consultancies are, with stubborn independence, developing the extensive range of services that they believe their corporate clients will be demanding over the next few years. So there is a lot going on.

Reliable statistical information in this area is sparse. However, the indications are that in some countries corporate identity consultancy – and this presumably includes some aspects of graphic design – has grown at about 40 per cent annually since the early 1980s.

Awareness among corporations of corporate identity as a discipline also seems to be growing very quickly, although it varies greatly by country and industrial sector.

The power of suggestion and desire for emulation are very strong. In one industry after another – airlines, chemicals, oil, financial services – corporate identity programmes instituted by one major player are followed by others. In some cases they are carried out superficially and badly, in others, thoroughly and well. But it's clear that the corporation is beginning, tentatively, to see the potential for this newest manifestation of an ancient resource.

The corporation is struggling, just as it did with information technology, to understand and gear itself up to handle this resource in an effective way. Strictly demarcated functions like marketing, product design and advertising are beginning to look increasingly inadequate. The organization is experimenting with new management concepts in which some kind of matrix is established between conflicting and overlapping areas. As it gropes away internally to find an appropriate structure, the corporation experiments with some of its traditional outside suppliers and some new ones as well, in order to work out an effective way of handling the power of the new discovered identity and corporate communications resource.

As major corporations become more experienced and demanding and as they create more opportunities, their suppliers will continue to jostle for their patronage. Advertising agencies will compete with design consultancies, who will compete with PR companies to carry out work that will be broadly similar, although it may be shaped by each sector in a fashion appropriate to its own particular skills.

These structural changes that are taking place, both inside corporations and amongst their suppliers, are going to change the shape of existing suppliers, and over time will create companies based on rather more complex and interrelated skills than those that we know today.

The century-old domination of the communications business by advertising agencies, with their impressive, sophisticated, but highly specialized skill base, is coming to an end.

The whole business of researching, creating, developing, launching and then communicating an identity programme is going to become so complex that it may lead to the appearance of a business structure familiar in the defence, construction and aerospace industries but so far virtually unknown in the communications field: the consortium.

A consortium will come together to work on a specific operation. It will be formed from, say, corporate identity consultants, PR companies, advertising agencies, organizational development consultants, strategic consultants, product design consultants, marketing service people, researchers and so on. It will be a coalition formed for a particular assignment, which may be quite long term. Within the consortium there may be companies that, as well as possessing complementary skills, are, in other situations, suppliers to and competitors of each other. Each consortium will be led by a main contractor. This contractor might well be authorized by the client to handle the whole project, in which case he will both appoint and be responsible for the performance of each sub-contractor.

Naturally, in this situation the main contractor will as far as possible appoint companies from within his own communications group for such tasks as are appropriate to them. Alternatively, though, the client may decide to appoint the sub-contractors jointly with the main contractor, in which case the main contractor's role will be somewhat more restricted. In either case the plum job in any consortium will be that of the main contractor, and that's what each communictions supplier will be fighting for.

In the long term, over the next thirty or forty years, who knows how things may develop? I am inclined to the view that the consortium, which is after all a temporary association of collective skills, is likely to give way to a more permanent association of such skills. There is a probability that massive communications groups will grow out of today's advertising agencies and from some of today's PR, design and corporate identity consultancies. These vast groups will embrace a wide range of design, organization development, communications and research disciplines. They will be deeply involved in top-level strategic consultancy, operating in every city around the globe, wherever they have clients.

There will be only a few of these massive global consultancies, and snapping at their heels will be hundreds of hopeful ambitious companies on their way up. And because the laws of entropy are immutable, there will also be quite a few depressed, decaying companies on their way down.

Then there will be thousands of aspiring, lively young people with no money or influence, but a lot of initiative, who make the world go round – and they will have plenty of new ideas for development.

There will be dramatic growth and great change. It's going to be an exciting time.

In the end, of course, it is economic power that wins the day. But economic power derives increasingly from moral, aesthetic and cultural power. The organizations that can marshal the totality of these strengths will lead the world in the twenty-first century.

Select Bibliography

Curiously, although it is a very rich subject, there hasn't been a great deal published about corporate identity as such. There has, of course been a lot written about design, art, architecture, art history, anthropology, business, psychology and all the other subjects from which it derives its origins.

I have tried in this select bibliography to give a flavour of some of the books that have influenced me or from which I have drawn useful material. I have divided the material arbitrarily into four sections – on business; on design and architecture; on history; on psychology, anthropology and philosophy – and into a fifth called 'miscellaneous', which deals with subjects that don't seem to fit elsewhere. The list is both partial and personal. I am sure that there are many very good and useful books that I have failed to include.

These, however, should make a basis for beginning to get to know the subject.

A) On Business

Barman, Christian	*The Man who Built London Transport*	1979
Bernstein, David	*Company Image & Reality*	1984
Green, Edwin; Holmes, A.R.	*Midland – 150 years of banking business*	1986
Handy, Charles	*Understanding Organisations*	1976
Handy, Charles	*Gods of Management*	1979
Handy, Charles	*The Future of Work*	1984
Harvey-Jones, John	*Making it Happen*	1988
Heller, Robert	*The Naked Manager*	1985
Heller, Robert	*The Supermarketers*	1987
Heller, Robert	*The Supermanagers*	1985
Katz, Michael; Levering, Robert; Moskowitz, Milton	*Everybody's Business*	1980
Levitt, Theodore	*The Marketing Imagination*	1983
Lloyd, Tom; Sveiby, Karl-Erik	*Managing Knowhow*	1987
Moskowitz, Milton	*The Global Marketplace*	1988
Ohmae, Kenichi	*Triad Power*	1985
Payne, P.L.	*British Entrepreneurship in the Nineteenth Century*	1974
Porter, Michael C.	*Competitive Advantage*	1985
Rodgers, Buck; Shook, Robert L.	*The IBM Way*	1986
Sloan, Alfred P.	*My Years with General Motors*	1986
Sloan Allen, Jane	*The Romance of Commerce and Culture*	1983
Wilson, Charles	*The History of Unilever*	1954

B) On Design and Architecture

Arikist, M.	*Soviet Commercial Design of the Twenties*	1987
Banham, Reyner	*Theory and Design in the First Machine Age*	1960
Bayley, S.; Garner, P.; Sudjic, D.	*Twentieth-Century Style & Design*	1986
Boilerhouse Museum	*Coke*	1986
Brooklyn Museum	*The Machine Age*	1986
Buddensieg, Tilmann; Rogge, Henning	*Industrial Culture: Peter Behrens and the AEG*	1979
Butler, A.G.	*The Architecture of Sir Edwin Lutyens*	1950
Caplan, R.	*By Design*	n.d.
Coleman, Terry	*The Liners*	1976
Costa, Joan	*Imagen Global*	Spain, 1988
Davis, Alec	*Package & Print*	1967
Forty, Adrian	*Objects of Desire*	1986
Foucart, Bruno; Offrey, Charles; Robichon, François; Villers, Claude	*Normandie*	1986
Grant, John	*Encyclopaedia of Walt Disney's Animated Characters*	1987

Heskett, John	*Design in Germany 1870-1918*	1986
Loewy, R.	*Industrial Design*	1979
Lorenz, C.	*The Design Dimension*	1986
Mironey, Phil; Rees, Helen	*Coca-Cola 1886-1986: Designing a Megabrand*	1986
Mollerup, Per	*Coca Kodak – The Corporate Design Progression*	1980
Morgan, Hal	*Symbols of America*	n.d.
Museum of Modern Art, Oxford	*Art into Production: Soviet Textiles, Fashion, and Ceramics 1917-1935*	1984
Neret, Gilles	*The Arts of the Twenties*	1986
Opie, Robert	*Rule Britannia – Trading on the British Image*	1985
Opie, Robert	*The Art of the Label*	1987
Papanek, Victor	*Design for the Real World*	1985
Pevsner, Nikolaus	*Studies in Art, Architecture and Design, Vol. II: Victorian & After*	1982
Pevsner, Nikolaus	*The Sources of Modern Architecture and Design*	1968
Pevsner, Nikolaus	*A History of Building Types*	1979
Pilditch, James	*Using Design Effectively*	1988
Selle, Gert	*Design – Geschichte im Deutschland*	1987

C) On History

Barnett, Corelli	*Bonaparte*	1978
Braudel, Fernand	*Civilization and Capitalism, 15th-18th Century*	
	Vol. 1 The Structures of Everyday Life	1981
	Vol. 2 Wheels of Commerce	1982
	Vol. 3 Perspective of the World	1985
Brogan, Hugh	*The Longman History of the United States of America*	1985

Catton, Bruce	*Penguin Book of the American Civil War*	1966
Commager, H.S.; Morison, S.E.	*The Growth of the American Republic*	1930
Davies, Major George B.; Kirkley, Joseph W.; Perry, Leslie J.	*The Official Military Atlas of the Civil War*	1983
Hibbert, Christopher	*The Great Mutiny*	1978
Hobsbawm, E.J.	*Industry & Empire*	1968
Hobsbawm, E.J.	*Age of Capital 1848-1875*	1976
Hobsbawm, E.J.	*Age of Empire 1875-1914*	1987
Hobsbawm, E.J.; Ranger, T.	*The Invention of Tradition*	1983
Kennedy, Paul	*The Rise and Fall of the Great Powers*	1988
Schama, Simon	*The Embarrassment of Riches*	1987
Seton-Watson, Hugh	*Nations & States*	1977
Stern, Fritz	*Gold & Iron*	1977
Trevor-Roper, H.	*Princes and Artists*	1985
Weiner, M.J.	*English Culture and the Decline of the Industrial Spirit*	1981

D) On Psychology, Anthropology and Philosophy

Barthes, R.	*Elements of Semiology*	1984
Bennet, E.A.	*What Jung Really Said*	1966
Campbell, Joseph	*The Hero With a 1000 Faces*	1949
Campbell, Joseph	*Myths To Live By*	1985
Jung, C.G.	*Man and His Symbols*	1964
Jung, C.G. (Ed. Jaffe, Aniela)	*Memories, Dreams, Reflections*	1983
Kiernan, V.G.	*Lords of Human Kind*	1969

E) Miscellaneous

Harvey, Chris	*Great Marques: MG*	1983
Kimes, Beverly R.	*The Star and the Laurel*	1986
Rosellen, Hans Peter	*BMW*	1973
Rosignoli, Guido	*Army Badges & Insignia of World War II*	1974

Author's Acknowledgments

Writing a book brings out one's obsessive characteristics – endlessly talking, thinking, scribbling and tinkering. Such behaviour cannot be pleasant to put up with. My very real thanks therefore to my colleagues at work to whom I was probably more of a trial than usual and to my family at home.

Thanks to all the people who helped me, who gave me insight and read the whole or parts – Peter Gorb, Hans Günther Zempelin, Renato Tagiuri, Weldon Miller, Edwina Olins, Rufus Olins and particularly Dornie Watts.

Alison Woodhouse typed the manuscript – she must have been very grateful that God invented the word processor. Jane Constantinis-Bunn and Katie Harvey managed the process and put up with all the difficulties that this involved; Julia Engelhardt dug out the most arcane and obscure pictures; everyone at Wolff Olins/Hall helped throughout; and Neil Svensen was almost as obsessive as I was as he handled the design of the book – I hope he is pleased with the result.

Illustration Acknowledgments

9	Wolff Olins/Hall
10	Bibliothèque nationale, Paris
12-13	Wolff Olins/Hall
14-15	From *The Official Military Atlas of the Civil War*, Washington 1891-95
16	British Library – India Office Library
17	(top) British Library – India Office Library (bottom) Collection Wally Olins
18-19	(top) Reproduced by gracious permission of Her Majesty the Queen (bottom) British Library – India Office Library
20	(top) Lauros Giraudon, Paris (bottom) British Library
21	Malmaison, Musée national du châteaux. Photo Réunion des musées nationaux, Paris
22	(left) Interfoto MTI, Budapest (right) Musée d'Orsay, Fonds Eiffel. Photo Réunion des musées nationaux, Paris
23	Bibliothèque nationale, Paris
24-25	Imagination Ltd, London
26-27	Wolff Olins Ltd
28	(top right) Courtesy of Parker Pen (UK) Ltd; Sheaffer Pen (UK) Ltd; Lamy Ltd, Photo Wolff Olins/Hall. (left and bottom) Wolff Olins/Hall
29	Sony (UK) Ltd
30	Harrods Ltd. Photo Wolff Olins/Hall
31	Wolff Olins/Hall
32	Coca-Cola Northern Europe
33	(top) Coca-Cola Northern Europe (bottom) Wolff Olins/Hall
34	(top) Robert Harding Picture Library, London (main picture) Daily Telegraph Colour Library, London
35	(top) Tony Stone Photo Library, London (bottom) Topham Picture Library, London
36	Wolff Olins Ltd
37	Wolff Olins Ltd
38	Wolff Olins Ltd
40-41	Wolff Olins Ltd
42-43	Wolff Olins Ltd
44-45	Wolff Olins/Hall
47	Michelin

124   (top) Hulton Picture Co, London
        (bottom) Wolff Olins/Hall
125   Wolff Olins/Hall
126   (top) Popperfoto, London
        (bottom) Fiat UK Ltd
128   John Calmann & King Ltd, London
129   Collection Robert Opie, London
130-131 Daimler-Benz AG, Stuttgart
136   KHBB, London
137   Wolff Olins/Hall
138   (top) Dornier GmbH, Friedrichshafen
        (centre) Daimler-Benz AG, Stuttgart
        (bottom) AEG (UK) Ltd
139   (top) Jeremy Flack Aviation Photographs
        International, Swindon
140-141 Wolff Olins/Hall
143   (clockwise from bottom left) Dornier GmbH,
        Friedrichshafen; AEG Frankfurt; Daimler-Benz
        AG, Stuttgart (3 photographs); Ullstein, Berlin;
        Ullstein-Charlotte Wunsch, Berlin
144   Wolff Olins/Hall
146   Wolff Olins Ltd
150   Wolff Olins Ltd
152-153 Wolff Olins Ltd
154-155 Wolff Olins Ltd
156-157 Wolff Olins Ltd
164-165 Western Americana Picture Library, Bath
166-167 Wolff Olins Ltd
170-171 Wolff Olins Ltd
172-173 Wolff Olins Ltd
174-175 Wolff Olins Ltd
176-177 Robert Harding Picture Library, London
178   Wolff Olins Ltd
179   Wolff Olins Ltd
180   (top) Wolff Olins Ltd
        (centre and bottom) Landor Associates, London
181   Wolff Olins Ltd
182-183 Fitch and Co, London
184   (left) Wolff Olins/Hall; Rex Features, London
        (right, top and bottom) Wolff Olins Ltd;
        Greenpeace, London. Photo Gleizes; Robert
        Harding Picture Library, London

185   (main picture) Tony Stone Photo Library,
        London
        (top and right) Wolff Olins/Hall
186   (left) Musée national d'art moderne, Centre
        Georges Pompidou, Paris
        (right) Fondation Maeght, Saint Paul © Dacs
187   (top left) Österreichisches Museum für
        angewandte Kunst, Vienna
        (top right) Vincent van Gogh Foundation,
        National Museum Vincent van Gogh,
        Amsterdam
        (bottom) Arxiu Mas, Barcelona
        © Patrimonio Nacional, Madrid
188   Wolff Olins Ltd
193   Wolff Olins Ltd
194-195 Wolff Olins Ltd
197   Wolff Olins Ltd
201   Wolff Olins Ltd
202   Wolff Olins Ltd
203   Wolff Olins Ltd
204   (top) British Newspaper Library
        (bottom) Wolff Olins/Hall
205   National Motor Museum, Beaulieu
208-209 Wolff Olins/Hall; Tony Stone Worldwide,
        London; The Image Bank, London; Ace Photo
        Agency, London; National Motor Museum,
        Beaulieu

Thanks also to Jaguar, Apple Computers,
Lacoste, Nike, Rolex, Burberrys, Austin Rover
Group, Airbus Industrie, Caffins of Dorchester
(Mercedes), J. Dege and Sons Ltd (military
buttons), Mitsubishi Colt, Motoren und
Turbinen Union, National Westminster Bank

The three-pointed star in the ring and the three-
pointed star with the wreath of Mercedes-Benz
are registered trademarks of Daimler-Benz AG.

Index

Italic numerals refer to illustrations

ABB 145
AEG 48-53, *49*, 50, 67, 75, 136, 137, *138*, 139, *141*, 142
AEG dishwasher *141*
absorption of corporate acquisitions 9, 124, 133, 139, 144
Accor 178, *179*
acquisitions by corporations 38, 102, 104, 106, 137-8
advertising 31, 33, 86, 110, 162, 189, 192
advertising agencies 212-14, 215
aerospace mergers with motor industry 135-7, 142
Aerospatiale 127, 137
After Eight *202*
Agip 82
Air France 86, 178
Airbus 126-7, *126*, 136, 137
aircraft manufacture 126-7, 135-7
airlines 34, 78, 86
Akzo 36-42, *37*, *40*, *42*, 74
Alcatel 196
Allied Lyons 78
American Civil War 13, 15
Anderson, Sir Colin 50
annual reports 132-3, 134
Apple *68*, 69, 71
Apricot 69
Arco 82
Armani, Giorgio 174
Armstrong Siddeley 135
Asea 145
Aston University 152-3, *153*
Austin 135

BAe 135, 136, 137, 178
BASF 37, 74
BL 178
BMC 104
BMW 78, 90, *90*, 92, *93*, 96
BP 82, 156
badges 20
Bank of America 64, *65*
Bank of China *65*
Bank of England 56, 61
banks, banking 56-67, *56*, *58*, *59*, 78, 134
Barclays Bank *56*, 204
Bastille Day *22*, 23
Bauhaus 48
Bayer 37, 75
Bayerische Motoren Werke *90*, *93*; *and see* BMW
Beetle 104
behavioural audit 162-3
behavioural consultancy 214
Belgium *see* Airbus
Benedetti, Carlo de 134
Benetton 54, *55*, 182
Benz 144, *145*

Benz, Carl 142, *142*
Berliet 142
Berliet, Marius 142
Betty Crocker 116, *116*
Bibendum, Mr *46*, 73
Big Bertha 126
Big Mac 207
Billiton 79
Black Knight *126*
Bloomingdales *30*, 31, 212
Blue and the Gray, the 14, 15
Boeing 126, 170, 207
Bonaparte (Corelli Barnett) 20
Bonio 120, *121*
Bosch 178
Boss, Hugo 92, 174
Bourbons 74
Bournville 163
Braganzas 74
brand development 9
brand reputation 203
branded identity structure 78, 79, 108, *108*, 110-28
branding 115-28, *128*
brands 39; for animals 120; neglected 124-5
Bremen 50
Bristol Aeroplane Company 135
British Aerospace 135, 136, 137, 178
British Airways 86
British army 100, *101*
British Leyland 178
British Motor Corporation 124, 178; *and see* BMC
British Motor Holdings 178
brochures 42, 196
Brooks Brothers 88, *89*, 133
Brown Boveri 145, *145*
Brumat, Professor Carlo 35
'Brummagem' 19
Brut 120, *121*
budgeting 196
BuffSanCo 149-51, *150*, *164*, 166-75, *167*, *171*, *175*, 178
Buick 104, *105*
buildings as expression of identity 7, 29, 42, 56, 58, 64, 162
Burberry *119*
Burton Group 183
business plan 132
Butler, A.G. 56

CSA *see* Confederate States of America
Cadbury 115, 163
Cadillac 104, *105*
Caja de Pensiones ('La Caixa') 62, *62*
Cambridge, University of 102, *103*
Campsa 156
Car 206, 207
Cassandre *51*
Castlemaine lager 78
chemical companies 35, 74-5

Chevrolet 104, *105*
China 128, 185
Christian church 7
Christianity *72*, 73
Chrysler 104, 124, 178
Chrysler, Walter 104
Coca-Cola 33-4, *33*; *and see* Coke
Cohn, Bernard S. 17
Coke 183, *209*
Colbert, Jean-Baptiste 102
Colgate-Palmolive 204
colours as expression of identity 9; *and see* green
commercial positioning, effect of corporate culture on 35-6
communication departments 25
communication material as manifestation of identity 7, 29
communication problems 212
communication-led identities 31, 33-4
communications audit 161-2
Communist symbolism *22*
Compagnie Générale Transatlantique 50
computers 67, 69; *and see* information technology
Confederate States of America *12*, 13-15, *14*, *15*
Conoco 36
consumer products and branding 115, 122
consumerism 206
Container Corporation of America 50, 67
co-ordination of group acquisitions 144; *and see* endorsed identity structure
coronation 20
corporate behaviour 7, 9, 29, 34, 204, 206-7, 210
corporate communications 213
corporate culture represented by products 209
corporate identity *see* branded identity structure, endorsed identity structure, monolithic identity structure
corporate identity consortium 215
corporate identity consultants 9, 38, 106, 148-9, 152, 158-9, 188, 213-15; choice of 159
corporate image working party 158
corporate infighting 133-4
corporate strategy 132-45
corporate structure 9, 42, 78-128, 198, 214-15
Crawford, Sir Frederick 152
Cross, the *72*
Crusader 126
Cunard White Star 50
customers 82, 171

Daimler 144, *144*
Daimler, Gottlieb 74, 142, *142*

Daimler-Benz 74, 102, 136-9, 141, 142, 144-5
Dairy Crest *185*
Dali, Salvador 62
Dallas 207
David, Jacques-Louis 20, *21*
Davidoff 94, *95*
de Soto 104
decentralized structure 38, 39, 197, 198
design: audit 162; management 191; as a commercial tool 53; of communication material 191; of corporate identity 48, 50, 56, 174-5, 190; of product *49*, 191
Deutsche Aerospace 144
Deutsche Bank 59
Deutsche Werkbund 48, 75
Din Associates 55
Dior 94
District Bank 59, *59*
'Dixie' 15
Dodge 104
Dornier 136, 137, *138*, 139, 142, *142*
Dornier, Claude 142
DoX flying boat *138*
Du Pont 36, 74
du Pont, Pierre and Irenee 36
Dunhill, Alfred 94, *94*, 96
Durbars 17, 18, 19, 42
Dynasty 207

EDS 104, 136, 144
Economist, The 203
Egypt 177
Eiffel, Gustave *22*
Eiffel Tower *22*, 23
El Greco, *The Dream of Philip II* 187
electrical products 48, *138*, *141*
electro-engineering 138, 145
Elf 82, 156
endorsed identity structure 78, 79, 99, *99*, 100-6, 144
Enka 37, *37*
environmentalism *185*, 204, 205-6
environments, corporate 29, 31, 191, 192
Escher, Max 59
Esprit 54, *55*, 182
Esso 82, 156
ethical unit trusts 206
Europa 50
European power bloc 207
European products 207, *209*
exhibitions 23, 42, 192
Expert, Roger-Henri *51*
expression of identity 9
external audience of corporations 210-11
Exxon 82
Eyston, Captain George *125*

Fascist symbol 59
fashion business *55*, 182

Fiat *25, 85,* 126, 136
Finance for Industry (FFI) 61
financial institutions 56-67, *65,* 122, 123
financial management 199
Financial Times 137
Flachglas 154
Focke-Wulf 137
food packaging 120, 128
Ford *25,* 96, 104, *138,* 199, *205*
Ford, Henry 137
Fortune 100 149, 169
Foster, Norman 64, *65*
Foulds, Jon 61
France:
    Empire 20; First Republic 20;
    Revolution 22; Third Republic
    23; Paris, Arc de Triomphe 20,
    22; Eiffel Tower *22,* 23;
    Pompidou Centre 64; *see also*
    Accor, Aerospatiale, Air France,
    Airbus, Alcatel, Berliet,
    Compagnie Générale
    Transatlantique, Dior, Iveco,
    Lacoste, Lamy, Michelin,
    Novotel, Perrier, Renault,
    Snecma, Sofitel, Ticket, Unic,
    Yves Saint-Laurent

GE 48, 136, 180, *180,* 188
GM *see* General Motors
Gaudí y Cornet, Antoni 62
General Mills 116
General Motors 36, 78, 103, 104,
    136, 137, 144, 204, 206, 207, 211
generic style 64, 67, 69
German army 100
Germany 204-5; *and see* AEG,
    Airbus, BASF, Bayer,
    Bayerische Motoren Werke,
    Benz, Bosch, Daimler,
    Daimler-Benz, Deutsche
    Aerospace, Deutsche Bank,
    Dornier, Flachglas, Focke-
    Wulf, Hamburg-Amerika,
    Hanomag-Henschel, Henkel,
    Hoechst, Iveco, Krupp, Lamy,
    MBB, MTU, Magirus,
    Mercedes, Mercedes-Benz,
    Messerschmitt, Motoren und
    Turbinen Union,
    Norddeutscher Lloyd,
    Telefunken, Volkswagen
Giacometti, Alberto *186*
Glaser, Milton 121
glass-making 154
global culture 183
Global Market Place, The (Milton
    Moskowitz, 1988) 210
'Go' represented by green *185*
Goldsmith, Sir James 121, 135
Gould, Jay 204
Grand Union 121
graphic design 191, 197
graphic designers 186

graphic elements of corporate
    identity 191
graphic symbolism 39, 58-9, *105,*
    184
Gray, Harry 106, *107*
Great Britain: Birmingham 19, 25,
    153; Bradford 71; *and see* Airbus,
    Allied Lyons, Armstrong
    Siddeley, Austin, BAe, BL,
    BMC, BP, Barclays Bank,
    Billiton, Bristol Aeroplane
    Company, British Airways,
    British Leyland, British Motor
    Corporation, British Motor
    Holdings, Burberry, Burton
    Group, Cadbury, Cunard White
    Star, District Bank, Dunhill,
    Harrods, ICI, Iveco, Jaguar,
    Jowett, Laura Ashley, Lever,
    Leyland, Lloyds Bank, Lloyd's
    of London, London Regional
    Transport, MG, Marks &
    Spencer, Midland Bank,
    Morris, Murray, National
    Provincial Bank, National
    Westminster Bank, Next,
    Orient Line, P. & O., PPF,
    Pears, Peninsular & Oriental
    Steam Navigation Company,
    Pilkington, Players, Prudential
    Corporation, Quest, Rolls-
    Royce, Rover, Rowntree, Royal
    Bank of Scotland, SS Cars,
    Sainsbury, Savoy Hotel, Tesco,
    Top Shop, Unilever, Vauxhall,
    Vickers, Vidal Sassoon,
    Westminster Bank, Yorkshire
    Bank
green *185*
Green Man, the *185*
Greenpeace 185
Greens (environmentalists) *185,*
    205-6
Griffin, Terence 59
Gropius, Walter 48, 49
Gross, Sydney 112
growth strategy of companies
    102, 133, 145
Gulf Oil *193, 202*

hairdressing 53-4, *53*
Hamburg-Amerika 50
Hanomag-Henschel 144
Hanson, Lord 134, 135
Harrods *30,* 31, 134
Harvard Business School 157
Harvey-Jones, Sir John 206
Hawkeye 126
Heinkel, Ernst 142, *142*
Henkel 118, 137
heraldry 9, 58, *59;* coats of arms 18
Herman Miller Company 207
Hershey 115
Hiroshige, *Ohashi Bridge in the
    Rain* 187

Hitachi 207
Hoechst 178
Holiday Inns 31
Honda 136, 210
Honeywell 67
Hong Kong *see* Bank of China,
    Hongkong and Shanghai Bank
Hongkong and Shanghai Bank 64,
    65
house flags 74, *75, 202*
Hughes 104, 136, 144
Hughes, Howard *138*
Hungary: national symbols *22*

IBM 48, 50, *66,* 67, 68, 69, 78, 88,
    92, 96, 162, 178, 207
ICFC 61
ICI 178, 180, *180,* 188, 206
ICL 67
Ibis *179*
identity: as an instrument of
    management 106; crisis 145;
    definition of corporate 7, 9, 78;
    launch 42, 189; management 7,
    9, 190-2, 196-9; problems 212;
    revision 85
image improvement 152; benefits
    169-70; costs 169
Independent 125, 152
India 17-19, *16, 17, 18;* New Delhi
    18, 19, 56; Order of the Star of
    India *16,* 17; *and see* Durbars
Industrial and Commercial
    Finance Corporation 61
Industrial Culture (Tilmann
    Buddensieg and Henning
    Rogge, 1979) 48
information techniques 31, 33
information technology 199; *and
    see* computers
information technology industry
    66, 88
internal audience of corporations
    210
interview themes for corporate
    investigation 159-61
Invention of Tradition, The (Eric
    Hobsbawm and Terence
    Ranger, 1983) 13, 17
Investors in Industry 61, *61, 62,*
    67, 187
Ira cigarettes *128*
Islam, sacred colour of *185*
Italy *see* Agip, Benetton, Fiat,
    Iveco, Lancia, Missoni, O.M.,
    Olivetti
Iveco *25, 126*
Ivory Coast *186*

Jacques Borel 178, *179*
Jaguar company 29, 178
Japan 207; *and see* Hitachi, Honda,
    Mitsubishi, Nissan, Sony,
    Toyota, Yamaha
Jeep 124
Jefferson, Thomas 36

Jobs, Steve 69
Jordan, Paul 48, 49
Jowett brothers *70,* 71
Jung, Carl Gustav 185

KHBB 136
KPI 202
Kellogg, W. K. 115
Kellogg's Toasted Corn Flakes
    Company 115
Kipling, Lockwood 18
Kipling, Rudyard 18
Kit Kat *202*
Kodak 178
Krupp 144
Kuwait *see* Kuwait Petroleum, Q8
Kuwait Petroleum (KPI) *193, 202*

La Caixa 62, *62,* 67, 69, 71, 187
Lacoste *119*
Lamy *28,* 29
Lancia 25
Landor Associates 33, 62, 86
Laura Ashley 207
Lauren, Ralph 174
Lever 108, 111, 112, 118
Lever, William Hesketh 110, 112,
    118
Levis 69, 207
Leyland 125, 178
Libbey Owens Ford 154
liberty, symbol of *22*
Lidden, Henry 174
Lifebuoy 112
Lincoln 104
Lippincott & Margulies 106, *107*
Lloyds Bank *56*
Lloyd's of London 64, *65*
Lockheed 170
logos 9
London Motor Show *70*
London Transport 50, 211
Louis-Napoleon 20
Louis-Philippe 20
loyalty, creation of 25, 82
loyalty, symbols of 25
Lutyens, Sir Edwin 19, 56, *56, 58,*
    64
Lux flakes 112

MBB 136, 137, 139, 142
MG 124-5, *125*
MTU 136, 137, 139, *139, 142*
McCann Erickson 33, 75
McDonalds 183
McDonnell Douglas 170
Macintosh 69
Magic Magnette *125*
Magirus *25*
Maharajah of Indore *16*
Man, Isle of 59, *59*
Management and Machiavelli
    (Anthony Jay, 1967) 134
Managing knowhow (Karl Erik
    Sveiby and Tom Lloyd, 1987)
    206

Marks & Spencer 88, *89,* 92, 133
Marlboro 183, 207
Marseillaise, the 20
Maybach, Wilhelm 142, *142*
Mercedes 139, 144, 199
Mercedes-Benz 90, 137, 139, 142, 144
Mercury 104
Messerschmitt *see* MBB
Messerschmitt, Willi 142, *142*
Meyer, Adolf 48
Michelin Man (Mr Bibendum), *46, 73*
Mickey Mouse 73
Midland Bank 56, *56,* 58, 64
Midland Group 122, *123*
Mies van der Rohe 48, 49
military equipment, branding of 126, *126*
military identity structures 100
military uniforms *14, 17,* 100, *101*
Ming dynasty *185*
Miró, Joan 62, *62*
mission statements 28, 39
Missoni 119
Mitsubishi 96, *97,* 144
Miyake, Issey 207
Mobil 82, 156
Model T Ford 104
Monkey Brand *108,* 112
monolithic identity structure 78, 81-96, *81,* 139, 144
Monsanto 169
Morita, Akio 29
Morris 135
motor industry 90, 104, *105, 124-5, 125,* 135-7
Motoren und Turbinen Union *see* MTU
Mountbatten, Lord 19
Mugabe, Robert 23
multinationals, decentralization by 197, 198
multinationals supplying both sides in wartime 204, 205
multi-sector businesses 102
My Years with General Motors (Alfred Sloan, 1963) 104

Naarden 178, *179*
names, change of 139, 142, 144, 173-5, 178
names as expression of identity 9, 20, 39, 178
Napoleon, Emperor 20, *21*
national anthems 20
national flags 9, *15,* 20, *185*
national monuments 23
National Provincial Bank 56, 59, *59*
national symbols 13, 20
National Westminster Bank 59, *59*
Nazi symbol 73
Nestlé 115, *202,* 203
Netherlands *see* Airbus, Akzo, Enka, Naarden, Organon,

Philips, Quest, Shell, Sikkens, Unilever
Next 54, *55,* 182, *182*
Nike 69, *119*
Nissan *207, 210*
Norddeutscher Lloyd *50*
Normandie 50, *51*
Novotel 178, *179*
Noyes, Eliot 50, 67

Oakland 104
Ogilvy, David 112
oil companies 28, 82-3, 85-6, 156, 192, 202-3
Oldsmobile 104, *105*
O'Leary, Nigel 174
Olivetti 50, 74
O.M. *25*
Orders of Chivalry 16
Organon 37, *37*
Orient Line 50
Osiris *177, 185*
Otis Elevators 79
Our Mutual Friend (Charles Dickens) 58
overseas units, reaction to corporate identity 198
Oxford, University of 102, *103*

P. & O. 74, *75,* 78, 102
PPF 178, *179*
packaging 33, 42, 192
Pakistan, flag of *185*
Palmolive 204
Pan Am 178
Panther tank 126
Parker *28,* 29
patronage by royal houses *187*
Peach Tree 69
Pears soap 124
Pentagram *145*
Perrier 207, *209*
Pershing 126
Persil 118
Philips 37, 207
Piano, Renzo 64
Pick 50
Pilkington 154-5, *154,* 188
Plantol 112
Players cigarettes *101*
Plymouth 104
Poison 120, *121*
police forces 34, *34, 35,* 212
Pontiac 104, *105*
positioning 148
Pratt and Whitney 79, *107,* 136
primitive art *186*
Prinsep, Val *19*
Procter & Gamble 73, *73,* 78
product design 49, 191
product quality 199
products as manifestation of identity 7, 29, 162
programmes for establishing and reforming corporate identity 39, 48, 50, 61, 106, 148-99;

developing the design, communication and behaviour programmes 173-5, 180; failure of programme 189; investigation, analysis and recommendations 159-63, 166-73, 180, 182; launch and implementation 180, 188-9; managing change (fictitious case study) 166-75; manual 192; replacement cycle 196
propaganda 20, 21, 48, 128
Prudential Corporation 180, 181, *181,* 188
public relations companies 213
public speeches 23
purchasing departments 197-8

Q8 *193,* 202-3, *202*
Quaker 115
Queen Elizabeth 50
Queen Mary 50
Quest 178, *179*

Rainbow Warrior 185
Rathenau, Emil 48, 50, 142, *142*
Rathenau, Walter 48, 50
Raymond (Mr Teazy-Weazy) 53
Red Army Star *128*
Red Star *22*
Regina toilet soap *128*
regional roots of corporations 62, 69, 71
regionalism, revival of 184
religious resurgence 184; ritual 20; symbolism 9
Renault 74, 136, 142, 188
Repsol 156, *156*
research and development (R & D) 38, 39, 199
retailing 88, 120, *121*
Reuter, Edzard 138
revising or changing corporate identity 178, 180, 182, 196, 202-3
Riley, Bridget 59
Rise and Fall of the Great Powers, The (Paul Kennedy, 1988) 207
rites of passage in corporate life 9, 39
road transport 192
Roberts of Kandahar, Frederick Sleigh, Field Marshal, First Earl 18
Rockefeller, John D. 204
Rogers, Richard 64, *65*
Rolex *119*
Rolls-Royce 135, 136
Rosatelli, Celestino 136
Rothmans 94
Rover 124, *125,* 136, 178
Rowntree *202,* 203
Royal Armoured Corps 100
Royal Bank of Scotland 59
Royal Green Jackets 100

SAS 86, *86*
SS Cars *see* Jaguar
Saab 136, *136*
Sainsbury 121
Saint Gobain 102
Saint-Laurent, Yves 94
St Michael 88, *89*
Samuel, Marcus *84*
Sassoon, Vidal 53-4, *53*
Saudi Arabia, flag of *185*
Savoy Hotel 134
service-based organizations 34
Shapiro, Irving 36
Sheaffer *28,* 29
Shell 79, *80,* 82, *83-5,* 85, 96, 156, 182, 188, 204
Shepherd & Woodward 103
shipping companies 50, *50, 51*
signs 192, 196
Sikkens 37, *37*
Sikorsky *107*
Skidmore, Owings & Merrill *65*
Sloan, Alfred 104, 106, 135
Smith, Paul 174
Snecma 136
soap-making *108,* 110-12, *111-12*
Social Investment Forum 206
socio-economic groups 56, 118
Sofitel *179*
Sohio 82
Sony 29, *29,* 48
Spain *see* Airbus, Caja de Pensiones, Campsa, La Caixa, Repsol
Spruce Goose *138*
Stanford University 152, 210
stars and bars 15, *15*
stars and stripes 14, *14*
strategies for corporate identity 38, 42
Sunlight soap 110, *111*
Sutton, Phil 61, *61*
Sweden *see* Asea, Saab, SAS, Unisys
Switzerland *see* ABB, Nestlé, Rolex
symbolic monuments 23
symbolism of a corporation 148
symbols: as expression of identity 9, 71, 73-5; at heart of creative process 73; of power 82

3i *see* Investors in Industry
TA *125*
TWA 212
Tagiuri, Professor Renato 157
target audiences 118
Telefunken 139
Tesco 78, 121
Thomas, Christopher 110
Thompson, W.S. 110, 112
Thornley, John 124
Ticket *179*
Tiger tank 126
Times, The 206
Tin Goose *137*

titles 20
Top Shop 182, *183*
Tornado *139*
Toyota 210
trade mark protection 75, 110
tradition, invention of 9, 13-25, 39
Trident 126

USA *see* United States of America
USSR 128
Unic *25*
Unilever 78, 110, 112, 118, 124, 204
Unisys 17
United States of America: consumption of Coca-Cola 33; military and economic supremacy 207; national symbolism of 13; for non-Americans 207, *209; see also* Alcatel, Apple, Apricot, Arco, Bank of America,

Bloomingdales, Boeing, Brooks Brothers, Buick, Cadillac, Chevrolet, Chrysler, Coca-Cola, Colgate-Palmolive, Conoco, Container Corporation of America, Davidoff, de Soto, Dodge, Du Pont, EDS, Esprit, Esso, Exxon, Ford, GE, General Mills, General Motors, Gulf Oil, Herman Miller Company, Hershey, Holiday Inns, Honeywell, Howard Hughes, Hughes, IBM, Kellogg's, Kodak, Levi, Lincoln, Lockheed, Macintosh, McDonalds, McDonnell Douglas, Mercury, Mobil, Monsanto, Nike, Oakland, Oldsmobile, Otis, Palmolive, Pan Am, Parker, Plymouth, Pontiac, Pratt and Whitney,

Procter & Gamble, Quaker, Rothmans, Sheaffer, Sikorsky, Sohio, TWA, United Technologies, Vanguard, Wrigley, Xerox
United Technologies 78, 79, 106, *107*

VW Beetle 104
Van Gogh, Vincent *187*
Vanguard 206
Vasarély, Victor 59, 74
'Varsity' mixture *128*
Vauxhall 135
Vickers 135
Victoria, Queen-Empress of India, 'Kaiser-i-Hind' 18, 19
Vim 112
visual elements checklist 191-2
visual style of corporations 174, 180

visual symbolism 185-7; in products *209*
Volkswagen 102, 178

Walkman 29, *29*
Washington Crosby Inc 116
Watson, Thomas, Jr 50, 67
Westminster Bank *56, 59*
Wilson, Charles 110
Wolff, Michael 61, *61,* 162
Wolff Olins 61, *75,* 191
woolmark 73
work patterns, changing 206
Wrigley 207

Xerox 69

Yamaha 96, *97*
Yamamoto, Yohji 207
Yorkshire Bank *56*

Zimbabwe 23